D

Including the Dartmoor & Exmoor National Parks

William Fricker

Appledore

LOCATOR MAP

26

40

Ilfracombe
Mortehoe
Woolacombe
Combe Martin · Martinhoe
Berrynarbor
Kentisbury
Bittadon
Arlington
Shirwell
Bratton Fleming
Croyde · Georgeham
Braunton
Chivenor · Ashford
Goodleigh
Fremington · Barnstaple
Landkey
Bishop's Tawton · Swimbridge
West Buckland
Newton Tracey · Chittlehampton
Alverdiscott
Atherington · George Nympton
High Bickington
Roborough · Burrington
Beaford
Ashreigney

58

68

76

Hartland · Clovelly
Abbotsham
Bideford
Landcross
Weare Giffard
Littleham
Welcombe · Woolfardisworthy
Buckland Brewer
West Putford · East Putford
Frithelstock
Great Torrington
Morwenstow
Bradworthy
Newton St Petrock
Little Torrington
Peters Marland
Dolton

90

94

Sutcombe
Milton Damerel
Thornbury
Bradford
Petrockstow
Dowland
Winkleigh
Wembworthy
Poughill
Pancrasweek
Cookbury
Monkokehampton
Broadwoodkelly
Stratton
Marhamchurch · Bridgerule
Holsworthy
Highampton
Hatherleigh
Exbourne
Bude
Widemouth Bay
Clawton
Halwill
Beaworthy
Inwardleigh
Jacobstowe
Sampford Courtenay
Whitstone
North Tamerton
Tetcott
Ashwater
Okehampton
Sticklepath
Jacobstow
Luffincott
Virginstow
Germansweek
Belstone
South Tawton
Canworthy Water
Bratton Clovelly

110

130

Broadwoodwidger
Sourton
Throwleigh
Bridestowe
Gidleigh
Stowford
Lewtrenchard
Lydford
Lifton
Launceston
Marystow
Dartmoor
Lawhitton
Brentor
Milton Abbot
Mary Tavy
Dunterton
Lamerton
Peter Tavy
Widecombe in the
Sydenham Damerel
Stoke Climsland
Tavistock

150

Horrabridge
Gunnislake

116

Calstock
Yelverton
Bere Alston
Bere Ferrers
Bickleigh
Landulph · Tamerton Foliot
Cornwood
South Brent
Saltash
Ivybridge
Torpoint
Plymouth
Plympton
Ermington

200

Plymstock
Yealmpton
Holbeton
Wembury
Newton Ferrers
Kingston
Bigbury
Bigbury-on-Sea
Thurlestone
Malborough

2

50

ndon · Oare · Porlock · Selworthy **Minehead**
Luccombe · Dunster
Wootton Courtney · Timberscombe · Withycombe
E x m o o r · Exford · Cutcombe · Treborough
B3223 · B3224
Withypool · Winsford · Exton

82
· Twitchen · Hawkridge · Brompton Regis
Molland · West Anstey · Duverton · Morebath · Clayhanger
Bishop's Nympton · Knowstone · Brushford · Bampton · Huntsham
Meshaw · Oakford · Holcombe Rogus
Rackenford · Stoodleigh · Uplowman
elbridge · Witheridge · Loxbeare · Templeton **Tiverton** · Sampford Peverell
Washford Pyne · Cruwys Morchard · Butterleigh · Willand · Uffculme
Orchard · Bickleigh · Cullompton · Willand
Bishop · Cheriton Fitzpaine · Bradninch · Dunkeswell
Copplestone · Stockleigh Pomeroy · Silverton · Payhembury · Broadhembury
Crediton · Shobrooke · Clyst St Lawrence · Feniton
Newton St Cyres · Broadclyst · Whimple
Tedburn St Mary · Whitestone · Clyst Honiton · Broad Oak
eriton · Alphington · Exeter · Clyst St. Mary · Newton Poppleford
Dunsford · Dunchideock · Topsham · Clyst St.George · Colaton Raleigh
retonhampstead · Christow · Ashton · Exminster · Woodbury · East Budleigh
Hennock · Kenn · Exton **Budleigh Salterton**
tleigh · Chudleigh · Powderham · Lympstone
Bovey Tracey · Starcross · **Exmouth**
Ilsington · Ideford · Ashcombe
Kingsteignton · Dawlish
96 Newton Abbot · Bishopsteignton
hburton · Abbotskerswell · **Teignmouth** · Shaldon
dscove · Kingskerswell · Ipplepen
oadhempston · Marldon · **Torquay**
artington · Collaton St. Mary · Torbay **Paignton**
Totnes · Stoke Gabriel · **Brixham**
Dittisham
dge · Dartmouth
Blackawton · Kingswear
Stoke Fleming
Strete
dge · Slapton
Stokenham
South Poole
ortlemouth

86
Brompton Ralph · Clatworthy
Upton · Wiveliscombe
Skilgate · Chipstable

164
Wellington · West Buckland · Hatch Beauchamp
Sampford Arundel · Staple Fitzpaine · Ashill
Culmstock · Churchstanton · Buckland St Mary · Horton
Otterford · Combe St Nicholas
Hemyock · Whitestaunton
Upottery · **Chard**
Dunkeswell · Stockland
Broadhembury · Monkton · Dalwood
176 · Hawkchurch
Honiton · Kilmington · **Axminster**
Gittisham · Northleigh · Musbury · Charmouth
Ottery St. Mary · Colyton · Uplyme
Sidbury · Colyford · Lyme Regis
Branscombe · Axmouth
Sidmouth · Beer **Seaton**

156

168

140

186

■ **NORTH DEVON & EXMOOR**

■ **MID-DEVON**

■ **WEST DEVON**

■ **DARTMOOR & SOUTH EAST**

■ **EAST DEVON**

■ **TORBAY**

■ **SOUTH HAMS**

3

To Mike Cheyne, who gave me my first job and introduced me to the world of publishing.

Research and Text: William Fricker

Photography: William Fricker (unless credited with an initial - see Acknowledgments)

Second Edition, 2017

First published in the United Kingdom, in 2007.

Goldeneye, Broad Street, Penryn, Cornwall TR10 8JL

www.goldeneyeguides.co.uk

Text copyright © 2017, William Fricker

Photographs copyright © 2017, William Fricker

Image Selection: William Fricker

Maps copyright © Goldeneye, 2017

Maps taken from Goldeneye's Digital Database

Book design and layout: Camouka

A CIP catalogue record for this book is available from the British Library. EAN Number: 9 78185965 203 9

Printed in the EEC

With special thanks to my son Harry and the guys at Atlantic Longboards, and Surf South West, for checking our surfing details.

Correct Information

The contents of this publication were believed to be correct and accurate at the time of printing. However, Goldeneye accepts no responsibility for any errors, omissions or changes in the details given, or for the consequences arising thereto, from the use of this book. However, the publishers would greatly appreciate your time in notifying us of any changes or new attractions (or places to eat, drink and stay) that you consider merit inclusion in the next edition. Your comments are most welcome, for we valu the views and suggestions of our readers. Please write to: The Editor, Goldeneye, Broad Street, Penryn, Cornwall TR10 8JL

Abbreviations in Text

C14   14th Century

Mar-Oct   1 March to 31 October (inclusiv

NT   National Trust property

EH   English Heritage property

BHs   Bank Holidays

W/Es Weekends

East   Easter

E/C   Early Closing

TIC   Tourist Information Centre

M   Monday

Tu   Tuesday

W   Wednesday

Th   Thursday

F   Friday

Sa   Saturday

Su   Sunday

SS   Supplied by Subject (reference illustrations)

WL   Wolsey Lodges

Beach & Surfing Abbreviations

HT   High Tide

HZ   Hazardous/Dangerous

Ls   Lefts (left turns)

LG   Lifeguard

LT   Low Tide

N   North

P   Parking

Rs   Rights (right turns)

S   South

S-B   Surfboard

SW   Southwest

WC   Toilets

"Hail thou, my native soil! Thou blessed plot,

Whose equal all the world affordeth not!

Show me who can so many crystal rills,

Such sweet clothed valleys, or aspiring hills;

Such woods, grand pastures, quarries, wealthy mines,

Such rocks in which the diamond fairly shines;

And, if the earth can show the like again,

Yet, will she fail in her sea-ruling men.

Time never can produce men to o'ertake

The fames of Grenville, Davies, Gilbert, Drake,

Or worthy Hawkins, or of thousands more,

That by their power made the Devonian shore

Mock the proud Tagus; for whose richest spoil

The boasting Spaniard left the Indian soil

Bankrupt of store, knowing it would quit cost

By winning this, though all the rest were lost."

William Brown of Tavistock 1590-1645

5

Devon is an awesome County! I have always known this, from having produced Map-Guides, cycling and walking maps to North and South Devon, and from working on the previous edition of this book. But, having completely revised this book which was, in itself, a massive project. I have (again) under estimated the scale of my ambition. From the planning of the photography which rarely goes to plan given the precarious weather patterns, and then the research which reveals more than one can physically place in a book of 224 pages. Is a frustration one can live with because one can plan a further 32 pages, or more, in the next edition. This book, along with the others in the series, will be (so long as I am producing them) always a work in progress. How can I be ever satisfied with the final outcome? These guidebooks will be refined, year on year, and this allows you, the reader, to add your pennyworth of input, if you would be so kind.

The old adage reveals that "An army runs on its stomach" may be an obvious truism. But the habits of today reveals our interest and obsession with food and its producers. Nowhere in England is there such a rich vein of seafood, livestock and dairy produce, and this has been tapped into by the many environmentally conscious hotels,

cafes, inns and restaurants thereby (hopefully) supporting low food miles.

The images in the following pages reveal my abiding interest in domestic farm animals and the fishes and crustacea of our rivers and sea, and I make no apologies for my love of pigs. They are such lovely warm and temperate animals with a friendliness akin to dogs. Though the fact that I still love a good sausage may seem a contradictiion given that I would never consider eating my adorable Salar (English Springer Spaniel) so you may well ask why a sausage? Devon is not Devon without its country characters and rambling farmsteads often to be found isolated at the end of pot-holed lanes. So get off the beaten track and wander along the country lanes. The best bits are to be found on the edges of Dartmoor and Exmoor, and on the peripheral borders of the county in East and West Devon.

More variance in budget options – As one doesn't always want a formal meal, or an expensive bed for the night. I have included more options, more variance such as Light Bites (cafés, fish and chips, burger bars, vegan eateries and fish mongers for self-caterers), and

alternative places to stay, from a country house hotel (Hotel Endsleigh) to a Celtic Roundhouse (Upton Roundhouse), to country inn (Lamb Inn, Sandford), to glamping in yurts and gypsy caravans (Vintage Vardos). One can not ignore airbnb either. A brilliant idea, but sometimes one worries about the fire risks involved, and you can not always be sure that breakfast is available.

Navigation & Clarity – For ease of use, Devon is split into seven regions. At the start of each is an area map followed by the respective guide text and illustrations. Each section is colour-coded and the area maps either overlap, or are juxtaposed, to allow easy navigation.

As always, the places included in this book are chosen on merit, and merit alone, and do not pay any kind of advertising fee. This allows me the freedom to choose only those places that I think are special enough to be part of this Guidebook, and I always pay my way. I would also like to point out that I rely on information provided by my team of friends and acquaintances. That I provide 85% of the images for the book has meant that I have visited the places of interest on more than one occasion; usually 6 times, or more. That I have holidayed, played cricket and cycled across the county, and lived in Devon for 14-years has given me a perspective, I believe, rarely matched.

My designer, Phil Butcher, was born in Devon and lives in Great Torrington. He tells me he has been preparing his skills for this project for many years. Thanks Phil.

I believe Devon (and Exmoor) to be a truly magical destination. Whether you are alone, or with friends and family. Whether you have a particular interest in beach combing, gardens and historic churches, or simple, hedonism. Take a deep breath of air, shrug off your working persona and live the life fantastic.

William Fricker, Penryn May 2017

River Teign, Fingle Bridge

Holne Bridge

CONTENTS

Devon is a big county, England's third largest after Yorkshire and Lincolnshire. It has been described as the most beautiful county in England. A land of rich pastures; green fields, rivers and woodland encompassing two National Parks, and a coastline diverse in its ruggedness and endless charm. A landscape so achingly beautiful with beaches, coastal views, hedgerows, meadows and rivers unmatched elsewhere in England.

It is a county with a long and chequered history, producing men with big ideas; Drake, Hawkins, Raleigh who sailed the seas in tiny craft, in the name of Elizabeth 1, and England. These men were Soldiers, Privateers, Men of Letters, Scientists, Navigators, brave beyond measure. They brought great pride to Devon, and wealth to the merchants of Dartmouth, Plymouth and London, and power, to England.

It is a sobering thought to digest, that as we watch the divisions of race and class in the US, that arguably started with the Slave Trade, that Devon and England's wealth originated from this dastardly business. Although most of the commercial underwriting came from Bristol and London, it was to the Devon Privateers that these merchants looked to do their horrific deeds.

Devon was on the Front Line against the Spanish, Dutch and the Portugese. It was indeed the Wild West of its day, and it was to Devon Men that England sought to defend our trade routes and protect us from marauding Spaniards.

Life in the countryside was spare and unforgiving. The peasant's lot was not to be envied. The land was owned by a small number of families who came over from Normandy with William the Conqueror. Town life saw the upheavals of plague and fires. One-half of the clergy were wiped out in the plague of 1348.

It was not until the Railway Age that tourism took a foothold in the economy of the region. Shipbuilding has been a constant provider of work, precarious at times, for the yards of Devonport and Appledore.

Devon is now England's greenest county. The County Council is championing Sustainable Tourism to combat global warning. There are more green businesses and organic food producers here than anywhere in the UK. We have included many of the best farm shops, restaurants, hotels and gastro-pubs. Our selection has been severe. We expect them to use local produce, for Devon's larder is so abundant, there should be no excuses for providing less than excellent fare. We expect top quality. So look to feast on this green and pleasant land. Bon Appetit.

Devon has long been a favourite family holiday destination, and many who come, year on year, have second homes. South and East Devon has long been a last port-of-call for the genteel retired. North Devon has a growing reputation as Devon's surfing centre. The M5 stops at Exeter, and this creates two westbound routes that strike to the north, and south, of Dartmoor. Those Cornwall-bound press their foot down and leave behind a Devon foolishly unexplored and ignored. But before you, too, head off on a fast-flowing A-road, consider branching off onto an unbeaten track. Put your sat-nav aside and take time to wander aimlessly across the back reaches of Exmoor and Dartmoor, into the hidden depths of mid-Devon, and beyond. You may well find your paradise.

These recommendations are in no order of preference.

1. Exmoor pony trip – there are many riding schools which organize daily or weekend rides. See the Exmoor Visitor newspaper.

2. Take a surf lesson in Croyde, Saunton or Woolacombe – two hour, or half-day lessons.

3. Hire a yawl (small boat with motor) from Salcombe and explore the estuary, or fish for bass and mackerel (tackle provided).

4. Evensong at Exeter Cathedral.

5. Dartmoor Tors Walk – bag five tors in a morning or afternoon.

6. Tour the Blue Plaque buildings in Sidmouth.

7. Cycle a section of the Tarka Trail, the Granite Way or the Drake's Trail.

8. Take an Exmoor Safari in a Land Rover Defender and spy the wild deer.

9. Take a trip to Lundy, and swim with the seals.

10. Treat yourself to a Dry Martini (007's Cocktail) in the Art Deco setting of the Burgh Island Hotel.

11. Catch the Dart Valley Railway from Paignton to Kingswear.

12. Take a boat trip up the River Dart from Dartmouth to Totnes, or vice versa.

13. Descend to the Teign Gorge from Castle Drogo.

14. Drive the coastal road from Porlock to Lynmouth.

15. Treat yourself to a Devon Cream Tea.

16. Lunch at an English Country House hotel; Gidleigh Park, Hotel Endsleigh or The Pig at Combe.

17. Fish n Chips at Babbacombe.

18. See the fan vaulting, St Mary's, Ottery St Mary.

19. Visit the Devon Guild of Craftsmen, Bovey Tracey and then see the Rood Screen in the Parish church. An opportunity to compare old and new craftsmanship.

20. Take a trip to Widecombe in the Moor. To reach it you will have had to cross the Moor. You must decide whether to go North, South, East or West to it or from it..

21. Aimlessly follow a South Hams country lane in Late May/Early June and marvel at the wild hedgerows.

22. Family bucket and spade beaches; Putsborough (North Devon), Hope Cove (South Hams), Blackpool Sands (South Hams).

23. Retail Therapy: Dart Farm Village, Topsham.

24. Festival Fever: Literary or Music Festivals at Dartington.

25. Surf Festival (Ocean Fest) Croyde.

26. Food Festivals at Dartmouth and Exeter.

27. Visit a Castle, Country House or Garden.

Lympstone Manor ss

Glazebrook House ss

Red Lion, Clovelly

This is a selection to make choosing your place to stay an easy and quick process. We suggest you view their websites to find one that suits your tastes, expectations and budget. It is often the unexpected that will surprise you with a luxurious bathroom, an exquisite view or a quirky atmosphere that will draw you back again, and again.

BOUTIQUE HOTELS

Browns Hotel, 27-29 Victoria Road, Dartmouth. 01803 832572
brownshoteldartmouth.co.uk

Burgh Island Hotel. 01548 810514
burghisland.com

Glazebrook House, South Brent.
01364 73322 glazebrookhouse.com

Hotel Du Vin Exeter, Magdalen Street, Exeter. 01392 790120
hotelduvin.com/locations/exeter

Orestone Manor, Rockhouse Lane,, Torquay. 01803 897511 orestonemanor.com

South Sands Boutique Hotel, Salcombe.
01548 845900 southsands.com

Southernhay House Hotel, 36 Southernhay East, Exeter. 01392 439000
southernhayhouse.com

CAFÉ/RESTAURANT WITH ROOMS

Anzac Street Bistro, Dartmouth.
01803 835515 anzacstreetbistro.co.uk

Bayards Cove Inn, Dartmouth. 01803
839278 bayardscoveinn.co.uk

Café Alf Resco, Dartmouth. 01803 835880
cafealfresco.co.uk

Café, Porlock Weir. 01643 863300
thecafeporlockweir.co.uk

Dartmoor Inn, Lydford. 01822 820221
dartmoorinn.com

Kentisbury Grange, Nr Barnstaple. 01271
882 295 kentisburygrange.co.uk

Plantation House Hotel, Ermington. 01548
831100. plantationhousehotel.co.uk

Salty Monk, Church Street, Sidford. 01395
513174 saltymonk.co.uk

Boringdon Hall Hotel & Spa ss

Woody Bay Hotel. 01598 763264
woodybayhotel.com

CAMPING

Bridge Farm Camping, The Orchard, Croyde 07779 371195

Mitchum's Campsites, Moor Lane, Croyde 07875 406473.

Incledon Farm, Georgeham. 01271 890200.
incledonfarm.co.u

COUNTRY HOUSE B & B

Basket Factory, Weir Quay. 01822 841455
weir-quay.com

Dartmoor House B&B, Belstone. 01837 840337dartmoorhouse.co.uk

Larkbeare Grange. 01404 822069 larkbeare.net

South Hooe Captain's House, Nr Bere Alston. 01822 840329.

COUNTRY HOUSE HOTELS

Arundell Arms, Lifton. 01566 784666
arundellarms.com

Bovey Castle, Nr Moretonhampstead. 01647 445016 boveycastle.com

Buckland-Touts-Saints. 01548 853055
tout-saints.co.uk

Gidleigh Park, Chagford. 01647 432367
gidleigh.co.uk

Hotel Endsleigh, Nr Milton Abbot. 01822 870000 hotelendsleigh.com

Lympstone Manor, Nr Exmouth. 01395 202040 lympstonemanor.co.uk

Mill End, Chagford. 01647 432282
millendhotel.com

Northcote Manor, Nr Burrington. 01769 560501 northcotemanor.co.uk

Percy's Country House Hotel. 01409 211236
percys.co.uk

The Old Rectory Hotel, Martinhoe. 01598 763368 oldrectoryhotel.co.uk

The Pig at Combe, Gittisham, Nr Honiton. 01404 540400 thepighotel.com

FAMILY B & B

April Cottage, Tavistock. 01822 613280

Castle Hill Guest House, Lynton. 01598 752291 castlehillguesthousedevon.co.uk

Docton Mill Gardens & Tea Room, Nr Hartland. 01237 441369 doctonmill.co.uk

Mount Tavy Cottage. 01822 614253
mounttavy.co.uk

Rosemary Cottage B&B, Knowstone. 01398 341510 rosemary-cottage.co.uk

2 Harton Manor B & B, Hartland. 01237 441670 twohartonmanor.co.uk

Silver Cottage B&B, Braunton. 01271 814165
bedandbreakfast-braunton.co.uk

FAMILY HOTELS

Thurlestone Hotel. 01548 560382
thurlestone.co.uk

Woolacombe Bay Hotel. 01271 870388
woolacombe-bay-hotel.co.uk

TOWN HOTELS

Bedford Hotel, Tavistock. 01822 613221
bedford-hotel.co.uk

Hotel Riviera, The Esplanade, Sidmouth.
01395 515201 hotelriviera.co.uk

Royal Castle Hotel, The Quay, Dartmouth.
01803 833033 royalcastle.co.uk

St Olaves Hotel & Treasury Restaurant, Mary Arches Street, Exeter.
01392 217736. olaves.co.uk

FARM HOUSE B & B

Combas Farm, Pusborough 01271 890398 combasfarm.co.uk

Hele Farm, Nr Gulworthy. 01822 833084 dartmoorbb.co.uk

Higher Biddacott Farm, Chittlehampton. 01769 540222 heavy-horses.net

Hindon Organic Farm, Nr Minehead. 01643 705244 hindonfarm.co.uk

West Titchberry Farm, Nr Hartland. 01237 441287 westtitchberryfarm.co.uk

GLAMPING

Big Sky Retreat, Hookhill Plantation. 01363 866146 big-grass.com

Bulworthy Project, Rackenford. 0759 4569441 bulworthyproject.org.uk

Faithful, Brixham Marina. 07939 850680

Grey Willow Yurts, Knowle Farm, Nr Hemyock. 079666 17488 greywillowyurts.co.uk

Owl Valley Glamping, Bideford. 01237 239204 owl-valley.co.uk

Treetops Treehouse, Fox & Hounds Hotel, Eggesford. 01769 580345 foxandhoundshotel.co.uk

Upcott Roundhouse, Upcott Barton. 01363 866182 upcottroundhouse.co.uk

Vintage Vardos, Fisherton Farm, Atherington. 07977 535233 fishertonfarm.com

Wagon With Faraway Views, Serstone Farm. 01363 82366 wego.here.com

Weirmarsh Farm, Nr Umberleigh. 01769 560338 weirmarshfarmrestaurant.co.uk

HOLIDAY COTTAGES/SELF-CATERING

Church House Inn, Village Road, Marldon. 01803 558279 churchhousemarldon.com

Emmetts Grange, Simonsbath. 01271 377432 emmettsgrange.co.uk

Beara Farmhouse. 01237 451666 bearafarmhouse.co.uk

Fursdon House. 01392 860860 fursdon.co.uk

Grey Cottage, Lee. 01271 864360 greycottage.co.uk

Pickwell Manor, Georgeham. 01271890110 pickwellmanor.co.uk

Hollies Trout Farm, Slade Lane, Ottery St Mary. 01404 841428 holliestroutfarm.co.uk

Holne Chase Holiday Cottages. 01364 631471 holne-chase.co.uk

Lundy Island: Landmark Trust, 01628 825925, or call Lundy on: 01237 431831

Ruggelstone Inn, Widecombe-In-The-Moor. 01364 621327 rugglestoneinn.co.uk

Upcott Farm, Upcott. 01271 816009 upcottfarm.com

HOSTELS/ON A BUDGET/ADVENTURES

Adventure Okehampton (YHA), Klondyke Road, Okehampton. 01837 53916 adventureokehampton.com

Ocean Backpackers, Ilfracombe. 01271 867835 oceanbackpackers.co.uk

Skern Lodge, Nr Appledore. 01237 475992 skernlodge.co.uk

INNS WITH ROOMS

Blue Ball Inn, Countisbury. 01598 741263 blueballinn.com

Bush Inn, Morwenstow. 01288 331242 thebushinn-morwenstow.com

Castle Inn, Ledford. 01822 820242 castleinnlydford.com

Chagford Inn. 01647 433109 thechagfordinn.com

Cott Inn, Dartington. 01803 863777 cottinn.co.uk

Cricket Inn, Beesands. 01548 580215 thecricketinn.com

Culm Valley Inn, Nr Wellington. 01884 840354 theculmvalleyinn.co.uk

Drewe Arms, Drewsteignton. 01647 281409. thedrewearmsinn.co.uk

Duke of York, Iddesleigh. 01837 810253 dukeofyorkdevon.co.uk

Elephant's Nest, Horndon. 01822 810273 theelephantsnest.co.uk

Exmoor Forest Inn, Simonsbath. 01643 831341 exmoorforestinn.co.uk

Fortescue Inn, Salcombe. 01548 842868 thefortsalcombe.com

George Hotel, Hatherleigh. 01837 811755 thegeorgeinnhatherleigh.com

Hoops Inn & Country Hotel, Nr Clovelly. 01237 451222 hoopsinn.co.uk

Hunters Inn, Heddon Valley. 01598 763230 thehuntersinnexmoor.co.uk

Kings Arm, Tedburn St Mary. 01647 61224 kingsarmsinn.co.uk

Lamb Inn, Sandford. 01363 773676 lambinnsandford.co.uk

Maltsters' Arms, Bow Creek, Tuckenhay.
01803 732350 tuckenhay.com

Masons Arms, Branscombe. 01297 680300
masonsarms.co.uk

Millbrook Inn, South Pool. 01548 531581
millbrookinnsouthpool.co.uk

New Inn, Coleford. 01363 84242
thenewinncoleford.co.uk

Nobody Inn, Doddiscombsleigh.
01647 252394 nobodyinn.co.uk

Old Inn, Widecombe-In-The-Moor.
01647 281276

Rams Head Inn, Dolton. 01805 804255
theramsheadinn.co.uk

Ring of Bells, Cheriton Fitzpaine.
01363 860111 theringofbells.com

Rock Inn, Haytor Vale. 01364 661305.
rock-inn.co.uk

Royal Oak Inn at Luxborough.
01984 641498
theroyaloakinnluxborough.co.uk

Sea Trout Inn, Nr Dartington. 01803 762274
seatroutinn.co.uk

Sloop Inn, Bantham. 01548 560489.
thesloop.co.uk

**The Salutation Inn, 68 Fore Street,
Topsham.** 01392 873060
salutationtopsham.co.uk

Tally Ho! Country Inn, Hatherleigh.
01837 810306

Tarr Farm Inn, Tarr Steps. 01643 851507
tarrfarm.co.uk

The Thatch, Croyde. 01271 890349
thethatchcroyde.com

Three Crowns, Chagford. 01647 433444
threecrowns-chagford.co.uk

Tower Inn, Slapton. 01548 580216
thetowerinn.com

LUXURIOUS B & B

**Agaric Rooms B&B, 30 North Street,
Ashburton.** 01364 654478
agaricrestaurant.co.uk

Bickleigh Castle. 01884 855796.
bickleighcastle.com

Burnville House, Nr Brentor. 01822 820443
burnville.co.uk

Catsheys, Nr Romansleigh. 01769 550580
catsheys.co.uk

Frogmill B&B, Tedburn St Mary.
01647 272727 frogmillbandb.co.uk

Highcliffe House, Sinai Hill, Lynton.
01598 752235 highcliffehouse.co.uk

Old Manse B&B, Sandford.
01363 899423/07713 976578.

Spears Cross Hotel, Dunster. 01643 821439
spearscross.co.uk

Tor Cottage, Chillaton. 01822 860248
torcottage.co.uk

Westwood, Torrs Park, Ilfracombe.
01271 867443 west-wood.co.uk

White House, Chillington. 01548 580505
whitehousedevon.com

ROOM WITH A VIEW

Hartland Quay Hotel. 01237 441218
hartlandquayhotel.com

Henley Hotel, Folly Hill, Salcombe.
01548 810240 thehenleyhotel.co.uk

Red Lion Hotel, Clovelly. 01237 431237
stayatclovelly.co.uk

Soar Mill Cove Hotel. 01548 561566
soarmillcove.co.uk

SMALL HOTELS

Crown Hotel, Exford. 01643 831554
crownhotelexmoor.co.uk

Edgemoor Country House Hotel.
01626 832466 edgemoor.co.uk

Fox & Hounds Hotel, Eggesford.
01769 580345 foxandhoundshotel.co.uk

Habit Boutique Rooms, Ilfracombe. 01271
863272 habitboutiquerooms.com

Lydgate House, Postbridge. 01822 880209
lydgatehouse.co.uk

The Luttrell Arms Hotel, Dunster.
01643 821555 luttrellarms.co.uk

Prince Hall Hotel, Two Bridges.
01822 890403 princehall.co.uk

SPA STYLE

Boringdon Hall Hotel & Spa, Plympton.
01752 344455 boringdonhall.co.uk

**Dart Marina Hotel & Spa, Sandquay Road,
Dartmouth.** 01803 832580 dartmarina.com

Salcombe Harbour Hotel & Spa.
01548 844444 salcombe-harbour-hotel.co.uk

North Morte Camp Site **17**

DEVON OFFERS LUXURY...AND ADVENTURE...

The Pig at Combe ss

Lympstone Manor ss

Wild Camping, North Devon

Culm Valley Inn ss

Home Farm Cafe, Parke ss

Lamb Inn, Sandford

Thomas Carr, Ilfracombe ss

Devon has some of the most amazingly located places to eat and drink in the UK. Either by overlooking a golden beach or tucked away in a village overlooking a medieval church and village green. It also has a fast-growing café culture where you can buy some amazing bread and cakes. If you arte worried about your waistline, why not get out onto the Coast Path, or bag a few Dartmoor Tors before Dinner.

Many will choose a pub, or café, at the beginning, or end of a circular, or cliff top walk. I hope our selection below will make your life a little easier to plan. All entries are described in the following pages. Not all entries are listed below.

CAFÉ CULTURE/DELIS

Bayards Cove Inn, Dartmouth.
01803 839278 bayardscoveinn.co.uk

**Beatsworkin, Queens House, 6 Queen St,
Barnstaple.** 01271 321111 bwskateshop.com

Brick House, 26 East St. Ashburton.
01364 653939 thebrickhouseashburton.co.uk

Café du Parc, Burton Art Gallery, Bideford.
01237 429317

Café Alf Resco, Lower Street, Dartmouth.
01803 835880 cafealfresco.co.uk

Central Café, Moretonhampstead.

**Charlie Friday's Coffee Shop, Church
Steps, Lynton.** 07544 123324.

Coffee Rush Café, Shaldon. 01626 873922
thecoffeerush.co.uk

Corn Dolly, 115a East Street, South Molton.

Courtyard Café & Shop, Chagford.
01647 432571

**Curator Café & Kitchen, The Plains,
Totnes.** 01803 865570 italianfoodheroes.com

Earls Coffee House, Burleigh Salterton.
01395 445445

**Espresso Café Bar & Grill, 1 St James
Place, Ilfracombe.** 01271 855485
seafoodrestaurantilfracombe.co.uk

Exploding Bakery, Queen Sreet, Exeter.

Fish Deli, 7 East Street. Ashburton.
01364 654833 thefishdeli.co.uk

Hotel Endsleigh ss

Flying Pickle, 40 Gold Street, Tiverton.
01884 242661 flyingpickle.co.uk

Griffin's Yard, North Street, South Molton.
griffinsyard.co.uk

Home Farm Café at Parke. 01626 830016
homefarmcafe.co.uk

John's Deli & Café, Appledore & Instow.

Joshua's Harvest Store, Gosford Road,
Ottery St Mary. 01404 815473 joshuasltd.co.uk

More Café Restaurant, Cider Press Centre,
Darlington. 01803 847524
dartingtonciderpress.co.uk

Old Forge, Chagford. 01647 433226
theoldforgechagford.co.uk

Otterton Mill. 01395 568521
ottertonmill.com

Plant Café, 1 Cathedral Yard, Exeter.
01392 428144

Rockets & Rascals, 7 The Parade,Barbican,
Plymouth. 01752 221295 rocketsandrascals.
com

Sandleigh Tea Rooms, Moor Lane, Croyde.
01271 890930

The Café, Porlock Weir.

The Stables, Croyde.

Toast Café & Patisserie, 155 High Street,
Honiton. 01404 598067 cafetoast.co.uk

Vanilla Sky, 44 High Street, Budleigh
Salterton.

Vineyard Café, Sharpham Vineyard.
01803 732203 sharpham.com

Wild Fig Deli & Café, 53 Fore Street,
Totnes. 01803 864829 thewildfig.co.uk

FOODIE HOSTELRIES (DINING PUBS)

Chagford Inn, Chagford. 01647 433109
thechagfordinn.com

Church House Inn, Marldon. 01803 558279
churchhousemarldon.com

Cornish Arms, West Street, Tavistock.

Culm Valley Inn, Culmstock. 01884 840354
theculmvalleyinn.co.uk

Fortescue Inn, Union Street, Salcombe.
01548 842868 thefortsalcombe.com

Fox & Goose, Parracombe.
01598 7633239 foxandgooseinnexmoor.co.uk

King's Arms, Georgeham.

Lamb Inn, Sandford. 01363 773676
lambinnsandford.co.uk

Horse Pub & Nosebag, Moretonhampstead.
01647 440242 thehorsedartmoor.co.uk

Hour Glass, 21 Melbourne Street, Exeter.
01392 258722 hourglassexeter.co.uk

London Inn, Molland. 01769 550269
londoninnmolland.co.uk

Masons Arms Inn, Knowstone.
01398 341231 masonsarmsdevon.co.uk

Millbrook Inn, South Pool. 01548 531581
millbrookinnsouthpool.co.uk

Nobody Inn, Doddiscombsleigh.

Rams Head Inn, Dolton. 01805 804255
theramsheadinn.co.uk

Rock Inn, Haytor Vale. 01364 661305.
rock-inn.co.uk

Royal Oak Inn at Luxborough. 01984 641498
theroyaloakinnluxborough.co.uk

Noel Corston, Woolacombe ss

Ruggelstone Inn. Widecombe-In-The-Moor. 01364 621327
rugglestoneinn.co.uk

Salutation Inn, 68 Fore Street, Topsham. 01392 873060 salutationtopsham.co.uk

Ship Inn, Noss Mayo. 01752 872387 nossmayo.com

LUNCH IN FORMAL SURROUNDINGS

Arundell Arms, Lifton. 01566 784666
arundellarms.com

Gidleigh Park, Chagford. 01647 432367
gidleigh.co.uk

Hotel Endsleigh, Nr Milton Abbot. 01822 870000 hotelendsleigh.com

Lympstone Manor, Exmouth. 01395 202040
lympstonemanor.co.uk

Pig at Combe, Gittisham, Nr Honiton. 01404 540400 thepighotel.com

Taylor's Restaurant, 8 The Quay, Dartmouth. 01803 832748
taylorsrestaurant.co.uk

RESTAURANT WITH ROOMS

Dartmoor Inn, Lydford. 01822 820221
dartmoorinn.com

The Café, Porlock Weir. 01643 863300
thecafeporlockweir.co.uk

Percy's Country House Hotel & Restaurant. 01409 211236 percys.co.uk

CAFES/RESTAURANTS/PUBS WITH A VIEW

Beach House, Bigbury Bay. 01548 561144
beachhousedevon.com

Beachcomber Café, The Esplanade, Woolacombe. beachcombercafe.co.uk

Blue Ball Inn, Countisbury, Lynmouth. 01598 741263 blueballinn.com

Boardwalk Restaurant & Cafe Bar, The Esplanade, Woolacombe. 01271 871351
theboardwalkwoolacombe.co.uk

Cricket Inn, Beesands. 01548 580215 thecricketinn.com

Dick and Wills, 42 Fore Street, Salcombe. 01548 843408 dickandwills.co.uk

Fremington Quay Café. 01271 268720 fremingtonquaycafe.co.uk

No 11, The Quay, Ilfracombe. 01271 868090 11thequay.com

Pavilion Café, NationalPark Centre, Lynmouth.

Smugglers Cottage Beach Cafe, Lee.

South Sands Boutique Hotel, Salcombe. 01548 845900 southsands.com

SEAFOOD RESTAURANTS

Browse Seafood, The Quay, Brigham.

Crab Shed Seafood Restaurant, Fish Quay, Salcombe. 01548 844280 crabshed.com

Fatbelly Fred's, 16 Maiden Street, Barnstaple. 01271 345700 fatbellyfreds.co.uk

Mor-shellfish-t-eat, 2 Rockleigh House, Mortehoe. 01271 870633
mor--shellfish-t-eat.co.uk

Oyster Shack, Milburn Orchard Farm, Aveton Gifford. 01548 810876
oystershack.co.uk

Salcombe Harbour Hotel & Spa, Salcombe.
01548 844444 salcombe-harbour-hotel.co.uk

Seafood Restaurant, 33 Southside Street, Plymouth. 01752 229345
piermastersrestaurant.com

Start Bay Inn, Torcross. 01548 580553
startbayinn.co.uk

TOWN RESTAURANTS

Hathaways, Dunster. 01643 821725
hathawaysofdunster.com

Kupp, The Guildhall, Queen Street, Exeter.
01392 531777 kupp.co

NC@EX34 Noel Corston), South Street, Woolacombe. 01271 871187 noelcorston.com

Olive Room, 56 Fore Street, Ilfracombe.
01271 867831 thomascarrchef.co.uk

Rendezvous Wine Bar & Restaurant, 38 Southernhay East, Exeter. 01392 270222
rendezvous-winebar.co.uk

River Cottage Canteen & Deli, Trinity Square, Axminster. 01297 631715
rivercottage.net

Rusty Pig, Yonder Street, Ottery St Mary.
01404 815580 rustypig.co.uk

Woods Bar & Restaurant, 4 Bank Square, Dulverton. 01398 324007 woodsdulverton.co.uk

Yukisan, 51 Notte Street, Plymouth.
01752 250240 yukisan.co.uk

The Pig at Combe ss

Gidleigh Park ss

Salutation Inn, Topsham ss 23

North Devon is a rural landscape of small villages, rich pastures, secluded coves and long sandy beaches. The two ancient ports of Barnstaple and Bideford have grown up beside the wide estuary of the Taw and Torridge rivers.

Stretching southwards from these ports is the gentle pastoral countryside known as 'The Land of the Two Rivers' so vividly brought to life in the works of Henry Williamson. The warm equable climate, together with the nature of the countryside provides excellent recreational opportunities, particularly for the walker, fisherman and surfer, and remains a favourite destination for family beach holidays.

The Hartland Peninsula on the western tip is Devon's Land's End, and a place tempered by the punishing seas and dramatic coastline. Often overlooked because of its isolation, a visit should be planned in with its neighbour, Clovelly. The coast is in sharp contrast to the pastoral, inland country that runs in an Easterly direction from Great Torrington to Tiverton.

The Exmoor National Park is largely in Somerset, with a small portion lying in Devon. At times the climate is harsh with mist, cloud and rain, and is reminiscent of Scotland. When the skies clear, the wild, wide beauty is unsurpassed. The landscape is undulating, full of rolling hills, marshland, bracken, heather and gorse, and divided by swift flowing streams which cut through the steep-sided valleys, known as combes.

The rolling moorland provides splendid views seawards across the Bristol Channel to Wales. In places the coast is crowned with high cliffs that fall precipitously to the sea.

The Exmoor sheep and wild ponies are seen everywhere, as are buzzard and raven. The roaming red deer are rarely seen and if startled (although unlikely, for they will hear and smell you coming) they can be a dangerous animal.

Of a somewhat gentler aspect than Dartmoor, and formerly a royal hunting forest. Exmoor is the only highland area of England to overlook the sea. Like Dartmoor, it provides contrasting landscapes of remote moorland and snug villages, but also a fine rugged coastline. It is noted for its ponies, somewhat smaller than the Dartmoor variety, and is the only place in England where red deer can still be seen. Less than half the National Park lies within the Devon boundary, but this includes the towns of Lynton and Lynmouth, the Doone Valley with its romantic associations, the beautiful Heddon Valley and over 20 miles of truly magnificent coastline.

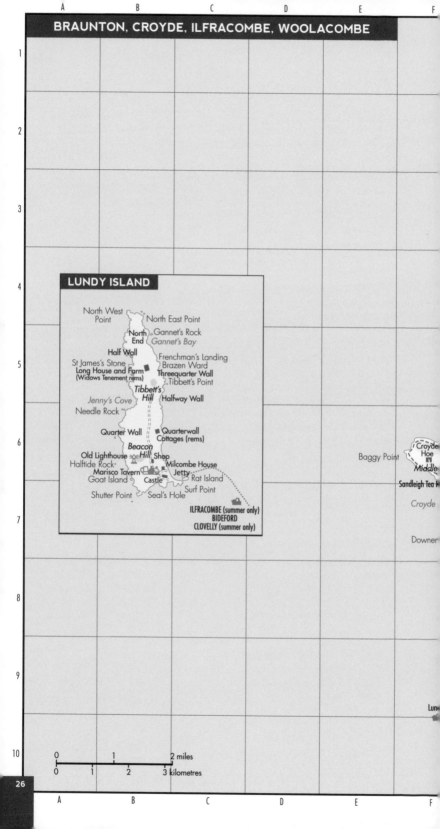

LUNDY ISLAND

North West Point
North East Point
North End
Gannet's Rock
Gannet's Bay
Half Wall
St James's Stone
Long House and Farm
(Widows Tenement rems)
Frenchman's Landing
Brazen Ward
Threequarter Wall
Tibbett's Point
Tibbett's Hill
Jenny's Cove
Halfway Wall
Needle Rock
Quarter Wall
Quarterwall Cottages (rems)
Beacon Hill
Old Lighthouse
Shop
Halftide Rock
Milcombe House
Marisco Tavern
Jetty
Goat Island
Castle
Rat Island
Shutter Point
Seal's Hole
Surf Point

ILFRACOMBE (summer only)
BIDEFORD
CLOVELLY (summer only)

Baggy Point

Croyde Hoe
Middle
Sandleigh Tea H
Croyde
Downer

Lund

0   1   2 miles
0   1   2   3 kilometres

26

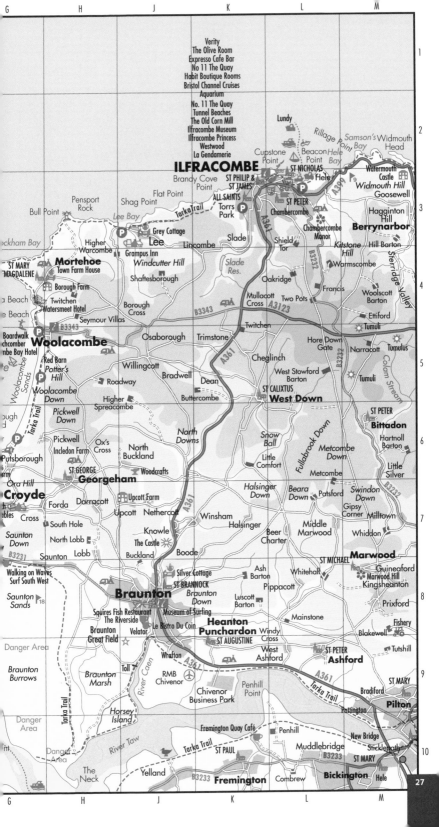

Verity
The Olive Room
Expresso Cafe Bar
No 11 The Quay
Habit Boutique Rooms
Bristol Channel Cruises
Aquarium
No. 11 The Quay
Tunnel Beaches
The Old Corn Mill
Ilfracombe Museum
Ilfracombe Princess
Westwood
La Gendamerie

ILFRACOMBE

Lundy

Rillage Point
Samson's Bay
Widmouth Head

Cupstone Point
Beacon Point
Hele Bay
ST NICHOLAS
Hele

Watermouth Castle
Widmouth Hill
Goosewell

Brandy Cove Point
ST PHILIP & ST JAMES
ST PETER
Chambercombe

A399

Flat Point
Shag Point
Tarka Trail
ALL SAINTS
Torrs Park
Slade
Chambercombe Manor

Shield Tor
Kitstone Hill
Hill Barton

Berrynarbor

Pensport Rock
Lee Bay
Lincombe

Bull Point
Grey Cottage
Lee
Grampus Inn
Windcutter Hill

Higher Warcombe
Shaftesborough

Slade Res.
Oakridge

Warmscombe

Francis
Woolscott Barton

Stenridge Valley

Ettiford

ST MARY MAGDALENE
Mortehoe
Town Farm House

Borough Farm
Twitchen
Watersmeet Hotel
Seymour Villas
Borough Cross

B3343

Mullacott Cross
A3123
Two Pots

Twitchen

Tumuli

Colam Stream

Tumulus

Woolacombe
Red Barn
Potter's Hill
Osaborough
Trimstone

A361

Hore Down Gate
Narracott

Tumuli

Boardwalk
Combe Bay Hotel

Willingcott
Bradwell
Roadway
Dean
Buttercombe

Cheglinch
West Stowford Barton
ST CALIXTUS
West Down

Tumuli

Woolacombe Sands
Woolacombe Down
Higher Spreacombe

North Downs

Snow Ball

Fullabrook Down
Metcombe Down

ST PETER
Bittadon

Hartnoll Barton

Tarka Trail
Pickwell Down
Pickwell
Incledon Farm
Ox's Cross
North Buckland
Woodcrafts

Little Comfort
Metcombe

Little Silver

Putsborough
ST GEORGE
Georgeham
Upcott Farm

Halsinger Down
Beara Down
Patsford

Swindon Down
Gipsy Corner
Milltown

B3232

Ora Hill
Croyde
Forda
Darracott
Upcott
Nethercott
Winsham
Halsinger
Beer Charter
Middle Marwood
Whiddon

Cross
South Hole
North Lobb
Knowle
The Castle
Boode

ST MICHAEL
Marwood

Saunton Down
B3231
Saunton
Lobb
Buckland

Ash Barton
Pippacott
Whitehall

Guineaford
Marwood Hill
Kingsheanton

Walking on Waves
Surf South West
Silver Cottage
ST BRANNOCK
Braunton Down

Luscott Barton
Mainstone

Prixford

Saunton Sands
18
Squires Fish Restaurant
The Riverside
Braunton
Museum of Surfing
Velator
Le Bistro Du Coin

Heanton Punchardon
ST AUGUSTINE
Windy Cross

Blakewell
Fishery

Braunton Great Field
Wrafton
West Ashford
ST PETER
Ashford
Tutshill

Danger Area
Braunton Marsh
Toll
RMB Chivenor
Chivenor Business Park
Penhill Point

A361
Tarka Trail
Bradiford
ST MARY

Braunton Burrows
Horsey Island
River Caen

Pottington
Pilton

Danger Area
River Taw
Fremington Quay Café
Penhill
New Bridge
Sticklepath

Tarka Trail
Muddlebridge
ST MARY

Danger Area
The Neck
Yelland
Tarka Trail
ST PAUL
B3233
Fremington
Combrew
Bickington
Hele

27

BRAUNTON

Bustling village, and one of the oldest in Devon. An early Celtic settlement developed by the legendary St Brannock who arrived by sail in a stone coffin from Brittany! In Devon, considered to be the West Country's centre for the surf and board industry. At the last count there were twelve surf (and factory) shops in the village. Not to be missed, the charming church of St Brannock. Velator is the former shipping centre and harbour for the village. The village has a number of pubs and coffee shops serving light meals.

Velator Creek, Braunton

LIGHT BITES...

Visitors to the beaches of North Devon often refer to **Braunton** as the place with the traffic lights. The architecture is uninspiring apart from the **Norman Church of St Brannock** and the cottages on **Church Street**. There are a number of eateries that cater for families. On your left is Squires the fish and chip emporium, and a little further on **Stoned**. A stunning space producing wood fired pizzas, rump steaks and other delicacies. Open M-Sa from 9 for coffee/ cakes, Pizzas M-F 5-8.45pm, Sa 12-9.15pm. At the traffic-lights, **Le Bistro Du Coin** trying hard to impress you with their French credentials. Posters and artworks galore. Breakfast Th-Sa 10-12, Dinner 7 til late. 01271 813897. Straight over the Lights, and on your left **The Siam Bistro**. A Thai restaurant and takeaway that is causing quite a stir. Breakfast from 10. Takeaways from 6-9.30. 01271 816567 thesiambistro.co.uk

On the **Croyde/ Woolacombe** road is The Riverside. Opens for breakfast at 8.45. A pleasant cafe/restaurant serves popular burgers and steaks, salads and pancakes. Al fresco dining overlooking the River Caen.

There are no gastro-foodie pubs to encounter; the London Inn is for hard drinkers and TV sports, the Mariners for sailors and seafarers, and the Black Horse behind the church is small, and the local's Local, serving Doom Bar. For a family style pub, the Braunton Inn at Chivenor serves average fare, and on a clear day has a spectacular view across the Estuary. (J8)

SPECIAL PLACES TO VISIT...

Braunton & District Museum, Caen Street Car Park. Super little museum illustrating local life, village crafts, strip-farming and coastal sailing ships. TIC. Open M-F 10-5, Sa 10-1. (J8) 01271 816688

Braunton Burrows. 2,400 acre National Nature Reserve extending three miles along the estuary and coast. Important for the study of evolution of sand dunes and associated plant ecology (400 species). Abounds in wildlife; foxes, rabbits, hedgehogs, moles, weasels, mink, shrews, lizards and voles. Also butterflies, birds and rare plants. Free public access except for an area sometimes closed for military training. Recently categorised by UNESCO as a Biosphere Reserve to accord it international protection. Nearby is Braunton Great Field (best seen from the hill above), a rare survival of the ancient strip tenure system of farming. Originally divided into one acre strips (on Edward 1's ruling) -

the Chief (Lord of the Manor) would have at least 500 acres, the Freeman 100 acres and the peasants rented strips from their Chief. Families would share their ploughs and oxen. Today, five farmers work this land. (G9)

Braunton Countryside Centre, Caen St Car Park. Their mission is to increase the understanding, awareness and enjoyment of coastal and farmed landscapes in and around Braunton, and to appreciate the North Devon Biosphere. Open Apr-Oct M-Sa 10-4. (J8) 01271 817171

Braunton Marsh. Former wild, tidal salt marsh now tamed into lush pastureland inhabited by cattle, wild flowers and bountiful birdlife. Protected by the Great Sea Bank stretching from Velator to Broadsands (White House) built in 1808. (G9)

Crow Point. Naturally formed in 1809 and sticks out like a hook. It's 30 feet high in places topped with (protected) Marram grass. Not as accessible as it used to be due to the placement of some hideous lumps of rock. Apparently, to stop overnight campers. (H10)

Museum of Surfing, The Yard, Caen St. The heritage and history of British surfing. The first stop for all experienced, and would-be surfers, where you will get a perspective of this tricky sport, and obsessive life-style. Open Tu-Sa 10-3. (J8) 01271 815155 museumofbritishsurfing.org.uk

400,000 bce
Acheulean hand axes deposited in Kent's Cavern.

250,000 bce
Hand axes deposited in Axe Valley.

NORTH DEVON

Saunton Sands. Extensive 4-mile stretch of compact sands cleansed by the rolling Atlantic waves. Overlooked by the giant rabbit warren, Braunton Burrows. Immortalised in the 1920s works of Henry Williamson: "The Dream of Fair Women", "The Pathway", "Tarka the Otter" and "Salar the Salmon". Film location in WW11 for Vivien Leigh's Cleopatra, then subsequently mined (Chivenor was an anti U-Boat base), to be later used as a practice venue for the US Normandy Landings of June 1944. Superb situation for water sports; sand-yachting, beach casting, surfing and windsurfing. Lifeguards in summer. Surf and sea survival school and shops at north end. Beach huts (bungalows) for rent: 01271 892002. Sands Café Bar open for food (and drink) only; breakfast, light lunches and dinner. In superb position overlooking the car park (!), and at an excruciating angle for one's neck, the beach. Apparently the local residents blocked the architect's original plans to provide a view. Open

Heavy Seas, Saunton

from 10 in season. For a really superb view, and a light lunch on the balcony on comfortable sofas, the **Saunton Sands Hotel** is recommended. (G8)

St Brannock's Church. Norman tower and recently restored lead spire. Noted for its superb medieval bench ends. (J8)

VELATOR

Former shipping centre and port to Braunton that traded with South Wales and the Bristol Channel ports in coal, salt, manure and flour. The trade was dictated by tide and weather, and eventually proved too difficult after the channels silted up. (J8)

WHERE TO STAY...

Silver Cottage B&B, 14 Silver Street. Two modern double-bedrooms in a quiet backwater close to the fleshpots of North Devon. 01271 814165 (J8) bedandbreakfast-braunton.co.uk

Upcott Farm, Upcott. Two luxurious self-catering cottages beside an old farmhouse in an idyllic valley close to the beaches of North Devon. Blissful comfort with all the mod cons. 01271 816009 (J7) upcottfarm.com

Walk To Baggy Point, Croyde

THE TARKA TRAIL

Braunton

A 180-mile trail (280km) follows the route taken by Tarka the Otter on his travels through "The Land of the Two Rivers", the Taw and Torridge, as depicted in Henry Williamson's classic novel "Tarka the Otter" written in the 1920s. The trail can be walked but also offers on and off-road cycling. The trail becomes a dual purpose walkway-cycleway allowing for relatively easy and safe cycling starting at Braunton. The route runs on tarmac beside the Taw Estuary to Barnstaple and can be enjoyed depending on the wind direction. Just hope it follows you. There is however abundant birdlife to hold your interest. From Barnstaple along the south side of the Taw Estuary to Instow with refreshments to be had at Fremington Quay, or John's Deli in Instow. The route now becomes more interesting beside the Torridge to the Puffing Billy pub below Great Torrington, or across the river to Watergate Bridge, the trail joins a bridle path and what follows is arguably the most interesting section of this trail. It is cyclable on a hybrid, touring or folding bike all the way to Meeth. Look out for the excellent little cafe at Yarde, the Railway summit. So you have 32 miles (51km) of traffic-free cycling. There is bike hire at Braunton, Fremington Quay (also bike shop), Bideford and the Puffing Billy, Gt Torrington.

CROYDE

A popular holiday and surfing centre with pretty thatched cottages, camp-sites and (too few) pubs and restaurants. The village can become unduly hectic and rowdy. Croyde sets the Bar. They say "If you can surf Croyde, you can surf anywhere". The rips and currents are like no other. The Oyster Fall (just off Downend Point) sets the Bar (see Surfing details). Bracing walks to Baggy Point. A number of fields open for the 2-months of July-August, and become camp sites: Freshwater, Mitchum's and Ocean Pitch and are placed overlooking the sea on the Baggy Point road. (G7)

PLACES TO VISIT...

Baggy Point. Given to the National Trust in 1939 by Constance and Florence Hyde. A bracing circular 40-minute walk can be had up to the Point where you may see rock climbers traversing the wall, and fisherman aspiring for bass and conger. Inspired Henry Williamson to write many of his nature stories. Note the unusual plaque at entrance. Access possible for wheelchairs but be prepared for a steep push. NT car park. (F6)

WHERE TO STAY...

Bridge Farm Camping, The Orchard. This is for tents and small campers. It's basic, convenient and on an incline, and central to Croyde's action. 2-Showers and loos on hand. 07779 371195 (G6)

Combas Farm, Putsborough. Isolated at the end of a long bridle path but within easy walking distance of Croyde and Putsborough. A quaint old-fashioned C17 farmhouse that offers homespun comforts. Large kitchen garden and farm produce delivers fab breakfasts. (G6) 01271 890398 combasfarm.co.uk

Mitchum's Campsites, Moor Lane. Tents and small vans only. Open in summer months. 07875 406473. (G7)

Braunton Marsh, Crow Point

LIGHT BITES...

Sandleigh Tea Rooms, Moor Lane. Overlooks the north side of the beach, and the entrance to Baggy Point. A great find and an oasis after a long walk, or surf. Recommended. Opens daily Feb to November for breakfast. The Oyster Catcher gift shop. (F6) 01271 890930

The Stables. A welcome addition to Croyde. It's a deli/coffee shop full of West Country delights; Jams, beers, cheeses, croissants, home-made cakes. Open M-Th 8.45-4, F-Su 9-4.30. (G7)

The Thatch. A pub patronised by surfers (and hangers-on) and their surf chicks. It can be busy in summer. Real Ales. Variety of lagers. Excellent salads, thick-cut sandwiches and solid fare. 6-rooms for B & B. Next door, **Billy Budds**, more surfy, same ownership. (G7) 01271 890349
thethatchcroyde.com

Pickwell Manor. There are 8 luxurious apartments to rent from The Chapel (sleeps 2) to Bliss (sleeps 8), within 6-acres of gardens and grounds a mere 5-minutes' drive, or 10-minutes walk to Putsborough Sands. Great for children and weddings. (G6) 01271 890110
pickwellmanor.co.uk

Ruda. This is a camp site housing mobile homes and space for large tents. Shop, indoor pool, and fish and chips. It hustles and bustles. (G7)

GEORGEHAM

Largely unspoilt village with thatched cottages. Henry Williamson, author of Tarka the Otter, lived much of his life here, settling in Skir Cottage on his return from the First World War. In 1928 he was awarded the Hawthornden Prize for writing Tarka, and with the money he bought some land at Ox's Cross and built his Writing Hut. He's buried in the churchyard. Much expansion and building of new homes. Village store and two Inns; The Rock (traditional pub) and The King's Arms (surfy crowd), both are worthy of your patronage for they were once my locals. (H7)

WHERE TO CAMP...

Incledon Farm. A basic and laid-back site on a slight slope ideal for tents and campers. Basic shower block. Dogs (and children) on lead at all times. Walking distance to pubs. 01271 890200.
incledonfarm.co.uk

1,600-1,200 bce
Middle Bronze Age cultures in Devon.

600 bce
Iron Age cultures arrive in Devon.

CROYDE VW FESTIVAL

55
Roman occupation of Exeter area.

80
Exeter becomes capital of the Dumnonian tribe as Isca Dumnoniorum.

ILFRACOMBE

A popular holiday centre developed by the Victorians in the Railway Age. A place of high cliffs and rocky beaches bordered by the sweeping Exmoor hills. Well situated for fine coastal walks and excursions to Exmoor. The ancient harbour is a great attraction and has been refurbished. The loan of Damien Hirst's 66 ft bronze sculpture, Verity (a modern allegory of truth and justice), to the town has brought controversy, publicity and the catalyst for much-needed business to the coffee houses and galleries. The town may have seen better days, but it's on the up and is a popular place to live, and property is good value. New restaurants and galleries are opening, as are contemporary places to stay. It is also close to the beaches of Woolacombe and Croyde and must be considered a place to stay. St Nicholas Chapel and Lighthouse surmount Lantern Hill. Hillsborough Iron Age Fort (a fine walk). Torrs walks. Trips from the quay on Paddle Steamer Waverley and Queen of Cornwall. Landmark Theatre. Cinema. Victorian Fair in July. Lundy Island office. E/C Th.(K3)

SPECIAL PLACES OF INTEREST...

Aquarium, The Pier. Award-winning, all-weather, family attraction provides a fascinating journey into the aquatic life of North Devon. Follow a unique-zoned journey from an Exmoor stream to Lundy and its marine reserve. Shop and café with outside seating. Open daily Feb-Oct 10-4. (L3) 01271 864533 ilfracombeaquarium.co.uk

Bristol Channel Cruises. On board the paddle steamer Waverley (the last ocean-going paddle steamer in the world) and motor cruiser M.V. Balmoral from Minehead and Ilfracombe July-Oct 1/2 term, timetable from website. (K3) 01446 721221 waverleyexcursions.co.uk

Chambercombe Manor, Chambercombe Lane. An attractive small manor house with C16-C17 additions. Period furnished rooms, armour and porcelain. Haunted chamber. 4-acres of Herb and water garden. Cream teas. Paranormal Events. Holiday Cottages. Guided tours. Open East-Oct Su-F. (L3) 01271 862624 chambercombemanor.org.uk

Damien Hirst's Verity, The Harbour. Damien Hirst, the mega-rich artist has a farm near Combe Martin. He has invested heavily in a local art gallery, restaurant and an eco-property development. I believe he realized that Ilfracombe needed energizing, or a heavy kick up the backside. Indeed, the Burghers who manage the town were quite happy with the Status Quo. How to change things? He has loaned this controversial sculpture to the town until 2032. It shows a heavily pregnant young woman. Her stomach is exposed on one side. Hirst describes its meaning to be "Truth", a modern allegory on truth and justice. It is 66 feet tall and is made of stainless steel and bronze. Some like it, others don't. It invites debate, and has placed Ilfracombe firmly on the map. Hence, the new restaurants and boutique B&Bs. (L2)

Keypits Quads. naturally a speciality, as is local DevoQuad bikes, Karting, paint Ball Battles, Thunderball and 4x4 Off Road Drives. Open East to Oct 10-5. Winter opening by appointment. (M3) 01271 862247 keypitts.com

Ilfracombe Harbour

200
Exeter enclosed within city walls.

300
St Brannoc the missionary preacher arrives in Braunton from Ireland.

Ilfracombe Museum, Wilder Rd. Fascinating collections of natural history, minerals, Victoriana, maritime and local history. Open daily Apr-Oct 10-5, Nov-Mar Tu-F 10-1. (L3) 01271 863541

Ilfracombe Princess, The Harbour. Wildlife and coastal cruises to view seals, porpoises and dolphins, and sea birds. Take binoculars. (L2) 01271 879727 ilfracombeprincess.co.uk

Hele Corn Mill & Tea Room, Watermouth Road. Restored C16 watermill with 18ft overshot wheel produces stone ground flour. Cream teas and homemade cakes. Open Easter, W/Es and 1/2 term weeks, daily July-Aug 11-5. (L3) 01271 863185 helecornmill.com

Osprey Charters, The Quay. You can charter Skipper Paul Barbeary's boat (a Pro-charter 40) for deep sea fishing, wildlife trips, film work and surveys. 07970 101407. (L2)

S & P Fish Shop, The Quay. A hut overlooking the harbour where you can buy fresh fish direct off the local trawlers. Open daily. 01271 865923/07896 909091. (K3)

Tunnels Beaches. Established in 1823; four unique tunnels were handcarved through the rocks to create a stunning, sheltered beach with tidal seawater pool. It's ideal family bathing with swimming and paddling pool. Café Blue Bar. Open daily Feb 1/2 term, Apr-Sept 10-5, July-Aug 10-7. Small fee. (K3) 01271 879882 tunnelbeaches.co.uk

PLACES TO STAY...

Habit Boutique Rooms, 46 Fore Street. A new venture in Ilfracombe, and very welcome, too. Clare will look after your every need, and teach you Pilates if asked. It's an 11-bedroom boutique guest house with bar and lounge, and terrace for al fresco dining. (K3) 01271 863272 habitboutiquerooms.com

Ocean Backpackers. An established independent youth hostel that caters for singles, families and groups. Good value and close to the coastpath and beaches of North Devon. 01271 867835 oceanbackpackers.co.uk

Westwood, Torrs Park. Helen and John Vowles have transformed a large Victorian house into 5-chic, luxurious rooms by using contemporary fabrics and furnishings. The bedrooms are spacious and full of the latest mod cons. Open all year. (K3) 01271 867443 west-wood.co.uk

WHERE TO EAT, DRINK & BE MERRY...

Espresso Café Bar & Grill, 1 St James Place. An unpretentious and hospitable café serving up freshly caught seafood. A warm welcome is guaranteed. (K3) 01271 855485 seafoodrestaurantilfracombe. co.uk La Gendarmerie, 63 Fore Street. A quality bistro serving fresh produce with a touch of Mediterranean flair. Comfy leather sofas, stripped floors and modern art provide a youthful flourish. (K3) 01271 865984 lagendarmerie.co.uk

No 11, The Quay. Damien Hirst's much lauded restaurant and bar has been feeding the local foodies with aplomb for sometime; Laid back Tapas for lunch downstairs, whilst Dinner is served overlooking the harbour, upstairs. Fish is naturally a speciality, as is local Devon beef. (K3) 01271 868090 11thequay.com

The Olive Room, 56 Fore Street. Thomas Carr is the first Michelin Star chef to land in Ilfracombe. Will it be a yoke around his neck, or a life-saver? Pitta-Patta, You know not what you will eat

Damien Hirst's Verity

until the boat comes in. No doubt dynamic. Open Tu-Sa 6.30-9. (K3) 01271 867831 thomascarrchef.co.uk

LEE
Set in a sheltered combe known as Fuschia Valley, for fuchsias grow wild in the hedgerows and stone banks. The lane leads to Lee Bay, a beach of special marine biological interest overlooked by the empty Lee Bay Hotel, an eyesore in a spectacular position that requires millions to bring it back to its former (if ever) glory. Low tide provides sand and rock pools, and steps to Sandy Cove. Beware of getting stranded by the inrushing tide on left-side beach. Note the special patterns of slate made by the swirling currents. Park opposite the church. C14 Grampus Inn/Micro-Brewery for lunch, dinner and friday music nights. Smugglers Cottage Beach Café opens for Easter and overlooks the Bay. (J3)

PLACES TO STAY...RENT

Grey Cottage. Julia Waghorn's slate clad cottage will charm you. The views from the steep hillside garden are stupendous. The bedrooms are bright and comfortable; Egyptian cotton sheets and deep baths. Ideal for house parties of 6 out of season, min 2-nights. or for weekly hire in season. (J3) 01271 864360 greycottage.co.uk

614
Battle at "Beandum", Bindon near Axmouth. Between the Saxons and Dumnonia.

680
St Boniface born in Crediton (approximate date).

35

MORTEHOE

A pretty, isolated hilltop village overlooking Woolacombe and Morte Bay. Surrounded by four campsites. Local beaches are either Rockham Bay, reached by a footpath on the North Morte road, or Grunta, below the Old Chapel. There's a lovely circular family walk out to Morte Point, and back, via the Cemetery. Two uninspiring pubs. (H4)

PLACES OF INTEREST...

Borough Farm. Working Sheepdog demonstration by TV celebrity, David Kennard and Falconry display by Jonathon Marshall from the North Devon Birds of Prey Centre. Shepherd Experience. Farmyard Show on Tu in season. (G4) Displays late May to early Sept, W 6 pm. 01271 870056 marshallfalcons.co.uk

Morte Point. Scene of many shipwrecks and loss of life. Beware of the Morte Race, a notorious and treacherous current. In full flow, an amazing site. An exhilarating spot on windy days. Look out for the razor-sharp rocks, sculptured by wind, rain and the sea. (G4)

Mortehoe Museum. Maritime history, local flora and fauna, farming and country skills. 'Hands on' games and puzzles for children. Tractor and trailer rides in July & Aug, Tu & W. Open East-Oct. except M /F, daily July/Aug. (H4) 01271 870028

St Mary Magdalene, Mortehoe. Founded in 1170 by William de Tracey. Superb Norman doorway. 48 magnificent bench ends. (G4)

WHERE TO STAY...

Bull Point Lighthouse. Built in 1879 to protect shipping from the dangers of Morte Point. Now an automatic station. 4 self-catering cottages to rent. 01386 701177 (H3) ruralretreats.co.uk

Town Farmhouse. Listed building belonging to the National Trust converted into a comfortably furnished and centrally heated B & B close to **Morte Point** and **Coastal Footpath**. Cream teas in summer. Ample parking. (H4) 01271 870204 townfarmhouse.co.uk

Watersmeet Hotel. This seaside hotel overlooks one of Britain's finest beaches. A relaxed, informal atmosphere pervades this bright and colourful hotel. Sea views. Swimming pool. Restaurant (open to non-residents). No pets. (G4) 01271 870333 watersmeethotel.co.uk

LIGHT BITES...

Mor-shellfish-t-eat, 2 Rockleigh House. The Huelin family run a Lobster-Crabber boat, The Walrus, out of Ilfracombe, and supply various restaurants in the North Devon area. They have recently opened this cafe and takeaway, and you won't find fresher lobster or crab anywhere better than this. And, for the beach, they provide Seafood Platters. Open daily East-Sept. (H4) 01271 870633 mor--shellfish-t-eat.co.uk

Rockleigh Takeaway, Rockleigh House. It's all cooked on the premises; Thai curry, Moroccan Tagine, Peas mash. Opens East-Sept. (H4) 01271 870704.

Mor-shellfish-t-eat, Mortehoe

722
Saxons defeated at the Battle of Hehil, probably near Jacobstowe.

739
Minster founded at Crediton.

WOOLACOMBE

One of the purest beach resorts in the UK, and the world. For the coast is untouched by campsite and bungalow. All about you is National Trust land protecting it from unsavoury development. A busy family holiday village with a two-mile long sandy beach extending to Putsborough Sands. Excellent for swimming, surfing and sandcastles. Invigorating coastal path to Baggy Point (popular with rock climbers) and Ilfracombe. (G5)

WHERE TO STAY...

Woolacombe Bay Hotel. A family hotel of the old-school run by the Lancaster family for the past 40- years. Spacious and suitable for children and grandparents of all ages. Squash, tennis and pools. Grounds lead down to beach. Special Autumn and Spring Breaks (2 nights for price of 1). Apartments. (G5) 01271 870388 woolacombe-bay-hotel.co.uk

SPECIAL PLACES TO VISIT...

Fremington Quay Café. An exceptionally popular destination café on the Tarka Trail next to the Cycle Hire depot. Coffee, cakes and soups/lunches featuring exhibitions of this historic quay. Open daily, all year. (K10) 01271 268720 fremingtonquaycafe.co.uk

Marwood Hill Gardens. A magical 20-acre garden with many rare trees and shrubs. Rock and alpine garden, 3-lakes, large bog garden, famous collection of camellias (largest in country), clematis, Australian plants. Tea Room. Nursery with plant sales. Garden open daily Mar-Sept, Oct F & W/Es from 10. Nursery open daily 11-5. (M8) 01271 342528 marwoodhillgarden.co.uk

Mike Taffinder Woodcrafts. Wood-framed mirrors, candle-holders and original items crafted from ancient oak by a man with a passion for wood and an eye for the unusual. Best phone before visit, he may be walking his dog. (J6) 07974 391228 miketaffinderwoodcrafts.com

BEACHES & SURFING...

Rockham Bay. Sand at low tide. Isolated. Rock pools. Interesting rock formations and wreck remains. 3/4 miles walk from North Morte campsite. (G3)

Hele Bay. Shingle and rocks. R/WC/D. (L2)

Rapparree Cove. Shingle, sand and rocks. R/D. (L3)

Lee Bay. Shingle. Rock pools. A marine biologist's delight. Cut out steps at low tide to **Sandy Cove.** P/WC/Hotel Bistro in summer. (J3)

Grunta Beach, Mortehoe. Named after pigs landing. Sand at low tide. Rock pools. Access via coast path. (G4)

Combesgate, Woolacombe. New steep steps descend to expansive sandy (wet) beach at

Noel Corston, Woolacombe ss

LIGHT BITES...AND MORE...

Bar Electric. These guys are keen to give the Red Barn some much-needed competition. Its cleaner, sparkier and the food is better. Burgers, pizzas, quiches, and 80s music nights, too. Opens 9-late. (G5)

Beachcomber Cafe, The Esplanade. Access through main car park. The view straight up the beach will provide the heartiest appetite for their burgers, pizzas and stuffed jacket potatoes. (G5) beachcombercafe.co.uk

NC (Noel Corston), South Street. This is the Business. If you seek first-rate tucker from an award-winning chef, look no further. The menus are multi-course, original, seasonal and delicious. Booking essential. (G5) 01271 871187 noelcorston.com

Red Barn. With some imagination this could be one of the greats. Yet, 'cos it makes money easily it sits on its laurels. But, it remains the heart and soul of Woolacombe welcoming surfers and families, alike. Friendly atmosphere, a full range of beers and lagers, and unimaginative, solid food to fill empty tummies, but don't expect gastronomic cuisine. Longboards are displayed like Old Masters from the V & A. Live music nights. Open all year. (H5)

The Boardwalk Restaurant & Cafe Bar, The Esplanade. One of the great views in England can be had whilst you sip your drink or tuck into your lunch or dinner. Freshly prepared meals. Open daily in season. (G5) 01271 871351 theboardwalkwoolacombe.co.uk

Woolacombe Sands

low tide. Rock and sand pools. Good surfing with nice peaks at low tide. Protected from north winds. Beware of strong tidal flow/undercurrents. No dogs May-Sept. P on road. (G4)

Barricane, Woolacombe.
Sand at low tide. Safe family beach. Good for shells and rock pools. Keep an eye out for children. Natural swimming pool at high tide. Asian café (evening meals in summer). Short walk from P. (G4)

Woolacombe Sands.
Two miles of flat sand. Popular family beach. Water sports all year; surfing, windsurfing, kayaking. Life Savers School. Former Longboard centre - northern end produces Rights at half-tide. Beach casting for bass. R/WC/D/LG/P. (G5)

Putsborough Sand (Vention). Superb, flat family beach with spacious sand and dunes. Popular with young families. Water sports. Beach casting for bass. Short walk from P (charge). Dogs allowed on R side. Café/WC/ Camping (advised to pre-book). Narrow lanes leading to beach best avoided during bank holidays. (G6)

Croyde. Flat sand at LT. Sand dunes and rocks at north and south sides. Surfing for experienced only - can be crowded. Rated as one of England's best beach Breaks, especially "Oyster", off Downend. Surf School. R/LG/ WC/P. (F7)

Saunton Sands.
Sand dunes (**Braunton Burrows**), rocks, water sports, bracing walks. Surf popular with longboarders and beginners - slow breaks. At extreme low tides it's possible to see rock forms that came down from Scotland in the Ice Age. Sands Café Bar/LG/Surf Survival Club/Board hire/P. (G8)

SAUNTON SURF SCHOOLS...

Surf South West. Surf school on Croyde Bay and Saunton Sands. Surf lessons, surf courses and surf holidays. Normal sessions 10.30-12.30 and 1.30-3.30. Open daily Apr-Oct. (F7) 01271 890400 surfsouthwest.com

Walking On Waves. Sarah Whiteley's school is based at Saunton Sands and holds individual, group and family lessons. BSA registered. Alspo, Glamping/luxury camping available. (G8) 07786 034403 walkingonwaves.co.uk

CROYDE SURF SCHOOLS...

Surfing Croyde Bay, 8 Hobbs Hill. Courses for all abilities, from two hours, equipment supplied; wetsuits etc. Coasteering. (F7) 01271 891200 surfingcroydebay.co.uk

COASTAL FOOTPATH...

Combe Martin to Ilfracombe (5 miles). Much of this section inevitably follows the main road, but there are interesting diversions around Napps Hill, Widmouth Heath and Rillage Point, and a final climb over Hillsborough with its prehistoric fort and fine views.

Ilfracombe to Woolacombe (8 miles). The path ascends through Torrs Walk and continues along an easy level track and down to the village of Lee. From here the going becomes more difficult, keeping close to the cliff edge past Bull Point Lighthouse, and to the promontory of Morte Point, notorious for its wrecks - then past the shell beach of Barricane and down to the wider sands of Woolacombe.

Woolacombe to Braunton (12 miles). From Woolacombe the path traverses 2 miles of sand dunes, though some may prefer the easier going along the beach. From Vention the path rounds Baggy Point, famed for rock climbing and sea birds, and descends to the main road as far as Saunton. From here the path crosses Braunton Burrows Nature Reserve along the Tarka Trail towards Crow

838
Battle of Hingston Down, near Tavistock.
Saxons defeat the Celts and Vikings

877
The Danes occupy Exeter

Point, then strikes north east beside the estuary to Velator, and follows the old railway line to Barnstaple which has been renamed as the Tarka Trail. It's now possible to follow the Tarka Trail on foot, or by bicycle all the way to Bideford without the encumbrance of the motorcar.

LUNDY ISLAND (NT)

A romantic and historic island, and one-time fortress and home to pirates. A place of great contrast and beauty, it lies nineteen miles west of Morte Point.

Just three miles long and half a mile wide. Lundy's western cliffs, popular with rock climbers, rise to 400 ft (the Devil's Slide is ever-popular), whilst in the east there are small valleys filled with woodland, bracken, rhododendrons and hydrangeas. The footpath running between these shrubs can be difficult, and it is easy to trip up over their roots. So beware. Soft walking boots or trainers are advised. The small community includes a Victorian church, a pub - the Marisco Tavern, the Marisco Castle and two lighthouses plus a shop. Campsite for 40 people and 23 self-catering properties (landmarktrust.org.uk).A short break or holiday here will contrast sharply with your average city lifestyle. The peace and solitude, the exposure to weather and the lack of cars apart from the farmer's Land Rover will appeal to many. It may take a day or two to get used to the slow pace of life.

Those who find it difficult to adjust may gravitate to the Marisco Tavern. A splendid place; great jollity and friendships to be made here. The home made pies and fine ales are difficult to refuse. Not a bad place to be stuck in foul weather. A return trip on the Oldenburg in a Force 6 is not to be recommended.

Basking sharks can be seen during the months, July to September, puffins May to mid July, and seals all the year, and the best places to see them: Landing Bay, Frenchman's Landing, Gannets Bay, Rat Island and the North End, or always away from rough water.

Visitors can take a day trip aboard the MS Oldenburg from Bideford, or Ilfracombe. Herewith some telephone numbers detailing more information. Sailings: 01237 470422, and accommodation from the Landmark Trust: 01628 825925, or call Lundy on: 01237 431831. Lundy Booking Office: 01271 863636. lundyisland.co.uk

Braunton Burrows from Saunton Down

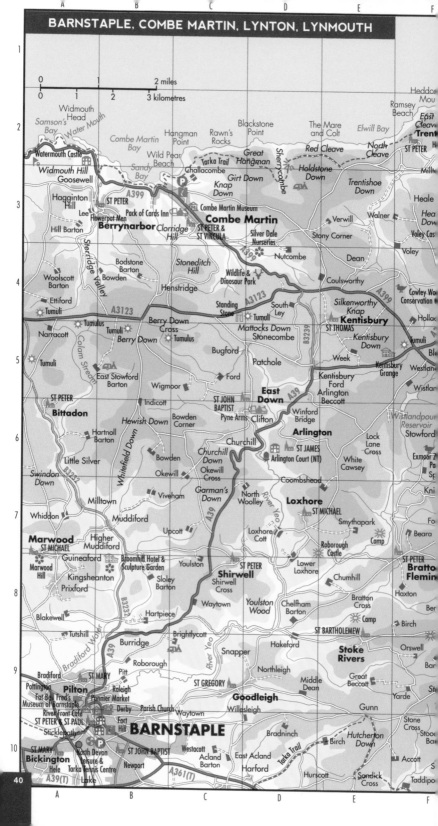

BARNSTAPLE, COMBE MARTIN, LYNTON, LYNMOUTH

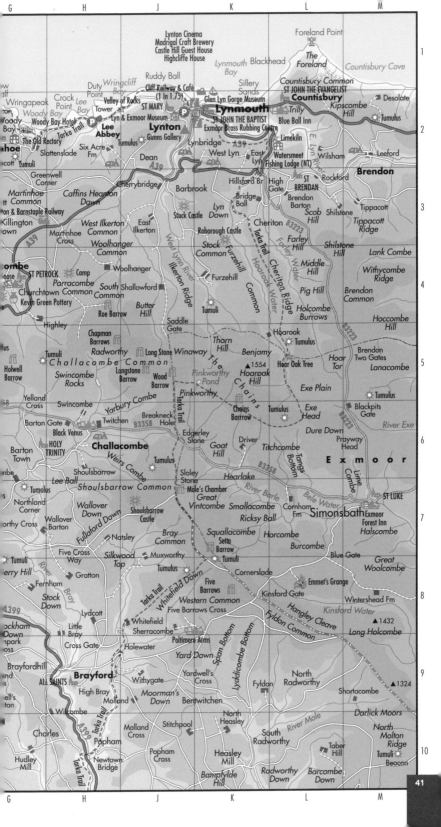

Barnstaple Church Spire Reflections

BARNSTAPLE

The principal town (and former port) of North Devon is undergoing a transformation from sleepy market town to busy route centre. A controversial development on Shapland's warehousing site beside the River Taw has caused grief to many, and the new bridge crossing from Sticklepath to Pottington has eased the bottleneck of traffic. C16 bridge, crook-spired church. Pannier Market (Friday farmer's market). Queen Anne's Walk (C16 colonnaded arcade). Guildhall. Remains of Castle beside Market car park. Cinema. Fair in Sept. Guided Town walks from Museum/TIC. Tarka Tennis & Leisure Centre. E/C W. (B10)

PLACES TO VISIT...

Butcher's Row & Pannier Market. No visit to Barnstaple can be made without stepping into the Pannier Market. All sorts of odds and sods on sale, and over the road, Butcher's Row, selling a medley of cheeses, meat, fish and bread. Café. (B10)

The Museum of Barnstaple and North Devon, The Square. Victorian gothic building houses this fascinating local museum; history, geology, archaeology, local pottery and the Regimental Collection of the Royal Devon Yeomanry. Tarka Gallery. Undersea World. Teas. TIC. Open all year M-Sa 9.30-5. (B10) 01271 346747 devonmuseums.net/barnstaple

LIGHT BITES...

Head for **The Strand** overlooking the **River Tamar** and beside the **Tarka Trail** is **Tea By The Taw**. A vintage tea room with an extensive menu. Breakfasts, lunch and tea parties. Popular with families of cyclists. Licensed. (B10) 01271 370032. Obsessed with the perfect coffee? Head for the Bus Station, and opposite is **Beatsworkin**, a skateboard shop proudly serving the best coffee in town. Seriously. An alternative is the **Boston Tea Party** overlooking the Market car park. The coffee and cakes, and all-day breakfasts are top notch. Beware of the sinking seats!

TO DINE...TO SUP FINE WINES...

Fatbelly Fred's, 16 Maiden Street. Geoff, the chef, trained with the Michelin Star Mark Dodds at the Mason's Arms, Knowstone. He is passionate about his seafood dishes and lets the fish do the talking. It's cosy and Geoff will spoil you. Lunch F & Sa, Dinner Tu-Sa. 01271 345700 fatbellyfreds.co.uk

Next door, the brilliant curry house (according to Geoff), **Everest Gurkha Chef** serving authentic Nepalese and Indian dishes. Winners of the prestigious British Curry award. Takeaways, too. 01271 376863 everestgurkha.co.uk

BERRYNARBOR

A beautiful, ancient village with a history going back to the Bronze Age. The Domesday Book (1085) listed four other manors in the vicinity. St Peter's church, Ye Olde Globe Inn (improving) and tea rooms to visit. A web of footpaths and walks connects the village; see Community shop and Post Office for details. (B3) berrynarborvillage.co.uk

901 King Edward the Elder holds a "Witan" or Saxon royal council at Axminster.

905 Copplestone. Putta, the Bishop of Devon is murdered. A granite cross marks the spot.

COMBE MARTIN

A long, straggling village bordered by some of the most beautiful countryside in England; rich, undulating pastures that lead down to a small harbour, and beach. Nearby, Trentishoe Downs and the Heddon Valley, and beyond, the wild combes of Exmoor. Former silver mining centre. Fine Parish Church of St Peter ad Vincula. Wildlife Park and Dinosaur Park up the hill, south of the village. Curious C18 inn; 'Pack of Cards'. Aug carnival. E/C W. (C3)

PLACES OF INTEREST...

Combe Martin Museum, Cross St. Illustrates old village industries. Newly designed displays. Shop. Open East to mid-July & school hols, 10.30-5, Su 11.30-2. (C3) 01271 889031 combemartinmuseum.co.uk

Silver Dale Nurseries, Shute Lane. National Collection of Hardy Fuchsias with over 300 varieties. Shrubs, alpine, perennials, herbs and bedding plants. Worth visiting for the stupendous views. Open daily 10-6 (Tea Gardens East-Oct). (D4) 01271 882539

St Peter Ad Vincula, Combe Martin. A magnificent Perpendicular church with fine C12 medieval Tower decorated with pinnacled battlements and a superb collection of gargoyles. It stands at over 100 ft and was built from the wealth of the silver industry. A typical Devon wagon roof, carved English rood screen, medieval windows, C14 paintings on the wainscotting and C15 font. Sunday services. Open afternoons. (C3)

Watermouth Family Theme Park & Castle. C19 castellated house with the accent on family entertainment; mechanical music, 'Granny Kitchen'. Explore the Dungeon Labyrinths and Adventure Land. Open daily Apr-Oct except Sa. (A2) 01271 867474 watermouthcastle.com

Wildlife & Dinosaur Park. Set in 28 acres of a Sub-tropical paradise. Home to Snow Leopards, Timber Wolves, Sea Lions, Primates and Meerkats, to name a few. Of special interest for children are the many dinosaurs, some are animated and appear to be alive! Open daily mid-Mar to end Oct & Xmas hols 10-3(5) (last adm). (D4) 01271 882486 wildlifedinosaurpark.co.uk

Barnstaple's New Bridge

Cloudy Waterfalls, East Lyn River

LYNTON & LYNMOUTH

Twin villages in a spectacular setting; Lynton on its cliff edge overhangs the small port of Lynmouth. The two are linked by a steep, wooded hill connected by footpath, road and funicular railway powered by water tanks. The rivers East and West Lyn fall rapidly to the sea through picturesque wooded gorges.

On the night of the 15th August, 1952 a freak cloudburst on Exmoor turned the East and West Lyn rivers into raging torrents destroying all that lay before them; 31 died, 93 houses were destroyed, power lines, bridges, cars and caravans were swept into the sea (similar to Boscastle's recent tragedy). Amazingly the Rhenish Tower c.1860 overlooking the harbour survived.

The area is proud of its literary connections; Percy Bysshe Shelley honeymooned here in 1812, and Samuel Taylor Coleridge conceived the idea of "The Ancient Mariner" whilst on a walking tour with Dorothy and William Wordsworth.

These valleys, and the surrounding country provided the setting for Blackmore's Lorna Doone. Popular walking centre with easy, waymarked trails up to Watersmeet and Countisbury Hill. The steep, coastal road up to Countisbury, and on to Minehead, which overlooks the Bristol Channel and South Wales, is not to be missed and is arguably one of the most scenic drives in England. (J2)

PLACES TO VISIT...

Cliff Railway. Built by the publisher of the Strand Magazine, Sir George Newnes. He wanted to create a little Switzerland, an Alpine-style village in North Devon. This Victorian invention is operated by water ballast tanks and it connects the two villages. You can't visit these two villages without a ride on this extraordinary contraption. Superb sea views and woodland walks. Clifftop Café. Open mid-Feb to early Nov from 10. (J2) 01598 753486 cliffrailwaylynton.co.uk

Exmoor Coast Boat Trips. Daily trips from the Quay depending on the tide; to Woody Bay, Valley of Rocks and Lee Abbey. Also, Mackerel drift fishing. (K2) 01598 753207

Glen Lyn Gorge. Dramatic ravine that carried much of the flood water during the 1952 disaster. Hydro-Electric plant and exhibition on water-power; Britain's first tidal current turbine. Open daily East-Oct 10-5 (-6 July/Aug). (K2) 01598 753207 theglenlyngorge.co.uk

Lee Abbey. Christian Centre for holidays, retreats and conferences. The house was built in 1859 and stands on the site of the old Manor of the de Wichelhalse family. A small natural history museum is open displaying the work of Ursula Kay. There's an Honesty Box toll on the road through the estate leading to the picturesque coastal road to Woody Bay. leeabbey.org.uk

Lee Abbey Nature Trail. Passes through the private estate down a wooded valley to cliff girt beaches with rock pools. (H2)

Lyn & Exmoor Museum, Market Street. Herewith, the oldest surviving domestic house in Lynton displaying old Exmoor crafts, implements and a way of life. Open East-Oct Tu W Th & Sa 10.30-1.30, 2-5. Su 2-5. (J2) 01598 752225

Lynton Cinema. An independent and award-winning cinema adds the personal touch to this art form. (J2) 01598 753397 lyntoncinema.co.uk

Madrigal Craft Brewery, Lynmouth Manor, Countisbury Hill. Hear ye, all scholars of yeast and fine ales will be tempted to make a judicious path to this haven of liquid fare. Tours (book) are second Saturday every month at 12pm. (K2) 07857 560677 madrigalbrewery.co.uk

974
Benedictine Abbey of Tavistock founded.

1001
Danes landed at Exmouth.

LYNTON LIGHT BITES...

There is no end of choice. My favourite is **Charlie Friday's Coffee Shop**, on **Church Steps**. It's fun and friendly for humans (and dogs), and the coffee/hot choc is made with gusto. The decor is all-colour and a little crazy. Open 9-5. 07544 123324.

Nartnapa Thai Kitchen@The Cottage Inn, Lynbridge. The locals love the fusion of Thai food, homage to Buddha and the choice of English ales and ciders. 01598 753496 thairestaurantlynton.co.uk

LYNMOUTH LIGHT BITES...

You are here for the sea (and countryside), and sea views so there is only one choice. **The Pavilion Cafe** above the **National Park Centre**. A full range of food on offer: breakfasts, burgers, salads, toasties, quiches, vegan and home-made cakes. But, it's the view, darling. Impressive, for you can watch surfers at play through the massive window. Open daily 10-5.

Middleham Gardens. On the site of cottages washed away in the 1952 Flood. A Memorial with a rose and fuchsia garden, Californian redwoods and evergreen oaks. Albeit, somewhat overgrown, but charming. Open daily, all year. (K2)

Polly Skye Gallery, Castle Hill, Lynton. If it's colour, form and style you're after then Polly has an artwork for you. Paintings, ceramics, glassware and homewares all breathe colour and life in this airy gallery with its friendly artist-owner. (J2) 01598 753452 pollyskye.co.uk

Valley of Rocks. A place of legend and dramatic scenery tempered by a micro-climate of swirling mists and brazen winds. The geologist will tell you it's a rock-strewn elevated valley created in the Ice Age, a mere collection of massive sandstone outcrops inhabited by Cheviot goats imported from Northumberland. They have become quite an attraction and a talking point in the local press when yet another tourist has her handbag snatched. A great place to scramble on the rocks, the more refined walker will follow the coastal path. Below the rocks, nestling in a bowl, a Cricket Ground, and just along the road, Mother Meldrum's Tea Gardens. (H2)

Watersmeet Fishing Lodge (NT). Built in 1832 and set in a picturesque valley at the confluence of the East Lyn and Hoar Oak Water. Focal point for many lovely walks. NT shop and tearoom. Open daily mid-March to Oct 10.30-dusk. (L2) 01598 753348

Watersmeet (NT). Five miles of wooded valleys of the East Lyn River and its tributary, the Hoar Oak. A spectacular landscape of fast-flowing rivers, ancient woodland and steep-sided hillsides. Waymarked trails with two fine high-level walks up Myrtleberry Cleave and Lyn Cleave (easiest ascent from Hillsford Bridge). Easy riverside walk up from Lynmouth. All dog walkers (and those wearing shorts) beware of tics! (L2) nationaltrust.org.uk

Woody Bay. Worth the steep descent off the coastpath to this glorious pebbled (slippery) beach with waterfall and tidal pool. Lime kiln and remains of pier storm damaged in 1902, the dream of bankrupted entrepreneur, Benjamin Lake. (G2)

Lynton & Barnstaple Railway. Train rides along the first mile re-opened of Former Woody Bay Station, closed in 1935. Open daily Apr-Oct 11-4, W/Es & Su in winter. Steam W/Es, Sch Hols & Christmas. (G3) 01598 763487 lynton-rail.co.uk

PLACES TO STAY...

Castle Hill Guest House, Lynton. The reviews are ecstatic, the 7-bedrooms have ensuite bathrooms, Egyptian cotton covers the duvets and the pillows are hypoallergenic. All leads to nights of blissful sleep. And, a stones throw to the coastpath. (J3) 01598 752291 castlehillguesthousedevon.co.uk

Highcliffe House, Sinai Hill. This is a new, enthusiastic venture. A classy B&B affording spectacular views of the coast. Stylish beds with intricately carved headboards. No children or dogs. 01598 752235 highcliffehouse.co.uk

Ancient Woodland, East Lyn River

Illustration of the Poltimore Hunt, Poltimore Arms

SIMONSBATH

Situated in the very heart of Exmoor in a sheltered valley beside the River Barle. Popular angling and walking centre. Two hotels. Farmer's Den for riding and outdoor gear. Exmoor Forest Inn (recently refurbished) to assuage your thirst following a walk beside the River Barle to Cow Castle. Free parking. (M7)

NATURAL PLACES OF INTEREST...

Foreland Point, Countisbury & Watersmeet. 13,000 acres of National Trust land, including the East Lyn River up to Rockford Bridge, and several miles of coast and cliffs to the east of Lynmouth. Many footpaths (details from excellent National Trust leaflets). Foreland Point Lighthouse is open weekday afternoons. Footpaths ascend to Watersmeet from Lynmouth and continue in many directions. (L1)

Great Hangman. Imposing hill rising to 1044 feet which drops precipitously to the sea. An impressive coastal landmark. Remote place inhabited by skylark, wheatear, raven and stonechat. On coastal footpath. Named after a sheep rustler who mistakenly hanged himself. (D2)

Heddon Valley and Mouth. A beautiful, thickly wooded valley sided by steep hillsides. Arguably one of the most enchanting valleys in England. A path leads from behind the right side of the Inn down a tricky slope to the riverbank and follows the river to Heddon Mouth, a rock strewn beach with a massive old limekiln. The river is only fordable in dry months. The valley has numerous walks in all directions. National Trust shop opposite car park.

Hoar Oak Tree. Ancient boundary mark of Exmoor Forest. The present tree was planted in 1917, and is the third in more than three centuries. To reach it, follow the wall westwards from Brendon Two Gates for two miles across rough country. (L5)

Kevin Green Pottery, Parracombe. A simplicity of style, individual pieces in stoneware often with unique motifs set Kevin's work apart. Open daily. 01598 763516 (G4) kevingreenpottery.co.uk

River Barle. The source begins in the north-west corner of Exmoor beside the man-made Pinkworthy Pond. The Barle winds a diagonal course in a south-easterly direction meeting the River Exe just to the north of Exebridge. A walk beside this river provides a key insight into the magic of Exmoor. (K5)

Rockford Bridge. Popular beauty spot on the East Lyn River. (L3)

Shoulsbarrow Castle. Iron Age fort on remote moorland. (J7)

The Chains. Central area of Exmoor; the source of the rivers Barle, Exe and West Lyn. Remote, desolate and waterlogged. (K5)

Trentishoe. A strategic hamlet with farmstead, church and mill overlooking the Heddon Valley. The church mainly dates from 1861, yet there's documentary evidence of Rectors back to 1260! Worth a detour.

Wistlandpound Reservoir. Fishing available for natural brown trout and larger rainbows. Season 15 Mar - 12 Oct. Permits from Post Office, Challacombe, The Kingfisher, Barnstaple and Fishing Tackle, Combe Martin. (F6)

SPECIAL PLACES TO STAY...

Emmetts Grange (Holiday Let), Simonsbath. A small, isolated hamlet with farmstead amidst a stunning Exmoor landscape. For those who enjoy country pursuits (riding, fishing, hunting), antiques and old-style luxuries EG has accomodation for 15-persons. Stabling available. Dog friendly. Your hostess is a Master of Foxhounds and mother of young children. Tennis court and Spa Pool + The Linhay for 2. (L8) 01271 377432 emmettsgrange.co.uk

Kentisbury Grange. This is a Victorian manor house combining country house style with over-the-top luxurious bedrooms. The Coach House restaurant, on opening, was a talking point amongst North Devon folk given its opulence and unusual style. Michael Caines oversees the restaurant so expect a nourishing evening. (E5) 01271 882 295 kentisburygrange.co.uk

The Old Rectory Hotel, Martinhoe. Small C19 Country House hotel set in

1050
Bishop's see of Crediton transferred to Exeter.

1068
Exeter besieged by William the Conqueror, Rougemont Castle built.

3-acres of mature, tranquil gardens. Rooms are cosy and tastefully furnished. Romantic candlelit dinners from local organic produce. In superb walking country. No children under 14. No dogs. Closed Nov to end March. (G2) 01598 763368 oldrectoryhotel.co.uk

Woody Bay Hotel. Few hotels in Britain are so magnificently situated. I would describe this as a Restaurant With Rooms, such is the joy of the food created by the proprietors. A mere 4-bedrooms, well apppointed with seaviews, so prepare your boots for coastal walks and woods clothed in moss, your soul for wild swimming and adventures. (G2) 01598 763264 woodybayhotel.com

PUBS SERVING FOOD...

Blue Ball Inn, Countisbury. In spectacular position with stupendous views to be gained in summer from their outside seating area. Log fires, comfy sofas and a changing selection of dishes. Real Ales. Friendly towards walkers and their dogs. B&B. Start off point for many circular walks. (L2) 01598 741263 blueballinn.com

Fox & Goose, Parracombe. Fresh fish in season supplied by local boats, and on the menu the day I visited; bass, fish stew, tiger prawns, red mullet fillets, and game in season.... all the walls are covered in bric-a-brac; lobster pots, badger and fox heads, hunting prints and paraphernalia. A good time feel factor. Local Exmoor brews. Foremost, a dining pub rather than a local inn. B&B. (G4)01598 7633239 foxandgooseinnexmoor.co.uk

Brendon Fields

1086
Domesday Book compiled. About 20,000 persons out of a total Devon population of some 70,000 accounted for.

1137
Exeter Castle besieged by King Stephen.

47

White Cottage, Woody Bay

Hunters Inn, Heddon Valley. An imposing (Swiss-style) hostelry set in a valley of great beauty. Heddon Valley is a centre for walking and riding. Home cooked, seasonal fare, and real ales. B & B. Beer & Music Festival 2nd W/E in Sept. Open daily. (F2) 01598 763230 thehuntersinnexmoor.co.uk

Poltimore Arms, Yarde Down. Isolated little country pub popular with Exmoor folk. Serves real ales and good, honest fare at a reasonable price. Opens for breakfast at 7am. Beer garden and dogs welcome. Village shop & Gallery, next door. (J9) 01598 710381 poltimorearms.co.uk

Pyne Arms, East Down. This is a cracking little pub with 3-spanking new bedrooms providing first-rate food. Husband and wife team, Ellis (chef) and Amie (front of house and pastry chef), are a great team. Well located for Exmoor, the North Devon beaches and Hartland. 01271 850055 (C6) pynearms.co.uk

The Exmoor Forest Inn, Simonsbath. Hostelry caters for walkers and fishermen who may well have flogged the Barle all day, and are in dire need of sustenance. Restaurant/pub food uses local produce. B&B. Dog friendly. (M7) 01643 831341 exmoorforestinn.co.uk

SPECIAL PLACES TO VISIT...

Arlington Court & The National Trust Carriage Museum (NT). Elegant house built in 1822 by Thomas Lee. Home of the Chichester family; the present contents consist largely of the collections of Rosalie Chichester (aunt of Sir Francis), who died in 1949. Fascinating medley of objets d'art, model ships, pewter, costumes and furniture. Watercolours by William Blake. Costume displays. Famous collection of horse carriages (rides available), including Queen Victoria's pony bath chair. Victorian formal garden. Extensive park and nature trail. Garden open daily mid-march to Oct & BHs 10.30-5 (House 11-5) except Sa. Footpaths through Park and woodland open all year. NT shop and licensed restaurant. (D6) 01271 850296 nationaltrust.org.uk

Arlington Court. Two-mile nature trail through the park. Lakeside and woodland scenery, Shetland ponies, Jacob's sheep, botanical and ornithological interest. Buzzards and ravens. Heronry and bird hide. Open daily 11-6. Small admission charge to Park. (D6) 01271 850296

Blakewell Fishery. Trout fishery. Family fun, catch your own trout. Farm shop, tackle room, ornamental fish and water garden. Tea room/Café - open 11-5, East/May until September. Fishery and Visitor Centre open daily 9-5. (A8) 01271 344533 blakewell.co.uk

Broomhill Hotel & Sculpture Garden. One of the great attractions of North Devon: With 300 sculptures, set in 10-acres of gardens (charge) in a most glorious valley. Contemporary Art Gallery (free), award-winning restaurant (W-W/Es) and hotel. Open daily all year 11-4. Hotel closed 20 Dec-15 Jan. (B8) 01271 850262 broomhillart.co.uk

Chapman Barrows. Eleven Bronze Age burial mounds on Challacombe Common. Fine views towards North Devon. (H5

Exmoor Zoological Park. Over 12-acres of landscaped gardens on the edge of the National Park with mammals, exotic birds and the Exmoor Beast, a black leopard! Open daily; summer 10-6, winter 10-4. (F6) 01598 763352 exmoorzoo.co.uk

SHORT WALKS ON EXMOOR...

1. **Lynmouth** to **Countisbury** and **Foreland Point Lighthouse**. (H1)

2. **Lynmouth** to **Watersmeet** via **Lyn Cleave and Myrtleberry Cleave**. (H1)

*1156
Earliest recorded reference to tin mining in Devon.*

*1196
Torre Abbey founded.*

Broomhill Sculpture Garden

COASTAL FOOTPATH...

County Gate to **Lynmouth**. (8 miles). Follow the path back to Glenthorne House where it continues along the coast towards Foreland Point, above some of the highest cliffs in England. After a steep climb to Countisbury Common there are two alternative routes; one following the coast, with fine seaviews towards Lynmouth, and the longer route crossing over to the wooded valley of the East Lyn.

Lynmouth to Combe Martin (13 Miles) The path starts with the beautiful North Walk leading to the Valley of the Rocks. From here to Woody Bay the route runs along a minor road, but there is an alternative way through the woods higher up. From Woody Bay the path follows a level elevated track with fine views, then descends to the River Heddon and zig-zags its way up Heddon Mouth Cleave. The path ascends to Trentishoe Down and follows a course over open grassland, culminating in the ascent of Great Hangman and the final descent past Little Hangman into Combe Martin.

3. **Watersmeet** to **Rockford Bridge** beside the **East Lyn River**. (H1)

4. **Arlington Court Nature Trail**. (D6)

BEACHES...

Lynmouth. Shingle, sand and rocks. Boating pool. Breaks for experienced surfers only. R/WC/D. (K1)

Lee Abbey. Sand and rocks. Short walk from P/R/WC. Toll. (H2)

Combe Martin. Pebbles, rocks and pools. Some sand at LT. Boating pool. R/WC/D. (B3)

Watermouth Castle. Protected inlet popular for mooring light craft. Sand at LT/P. (A2)

Two Moors Way. This is a Long Distance footpath, although not officially designated as one, which runs from Lynton to Ivybridge, linking the Exmoor and Dartmoor National Parks. The Way makes use of footpaths, bridleways and public roads. From Lynton to Watersmeet then southwards along the Cheriton Ridge to Hoar Oak Tree and Exe Head, crossing the B3358 at Cornham Farm. Then striking south-east to meet the River Barle below Pickedstones Farm. Cross country to Withypool, the Way proceeds down-stream beside the Barle to Tarr Steps. Then south towards West Anstey

Coastal View, Woody Bay

1205
First mayor of Exeter recorded - second only to Winchester in provincial cities.

1205
Totnes issued with a Charter. Possibly the oldest Municipal Borough in England.

49

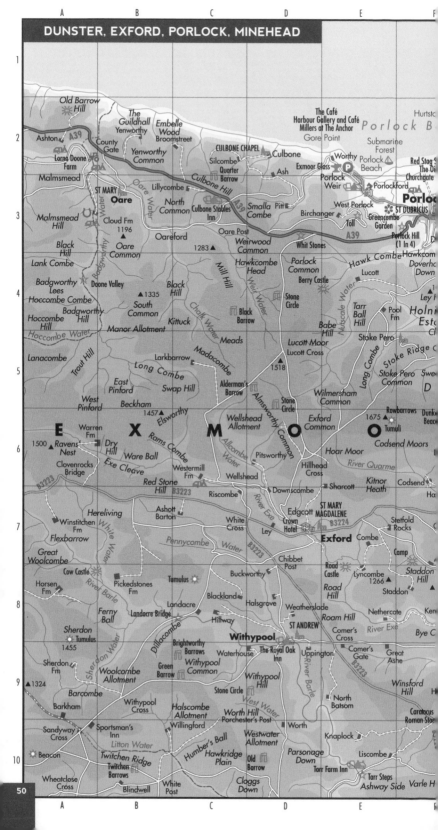

A B C D E F

1

Old Barrow Hill
The Guildhall
Yenworthy
Embelle Wood
Broomstreet
Porlock B
Hurtstc
The Café
Harbour Gallery and Café
Millers at The Anchor
Gore Point
Ashton
A39
County Gate
Submarine Forest
Red Stag
The Oi
Churchgate
Lorna Doone Farm
Yenworthy Common
CULBONE CHAPEL
Silcombe
Culbone
Worthy
Exmoor Glass
Porlock
Porlock Beach
Malmsmead
Oare Water
Lillycombe
Quarter Barrow
Ash
Porlock Weir
Porlockford
Porloc
ST MARY Oare
North Common
Culbone Hill
Smalla Combe
Pitt
West Porlock
ST DUBRICUS
Malmsmead Hill
Cloud Fm
1196
Culbone Stables Inn
Birchanger
Greencombe Garden
Porlock Hill
(1 in 4)
Black Hill
Oareford
Oare Post
Weirwood Common
Whit Stones
Toll
Lank Combe
1283
Hawkcombe Head
Porlock Common
Hawk Combe
Hawkcom
Doverho
Down
Badgworthy Lees
Doone Valley
Black Hill
Mill Hill
Weir Water
Berry Castle
Lucott
Ley H
Hoccombe Combe
1335
South Common
Kittuck
Black Barrow
Stone Circle
Babe Hill
Tarr Ball Hill
Pool Fm
Holn
Esto
Cl
Hoccombe Hill
Badgworthy Hill
Manor Allotment
Meads
Lucott Moor
Lucott Cross
Stoke Pero
Lanacombe
Trout Hill
Long Combe
Larkbarrow
Madacombe
1518
Alderman's Barrow
Stone Circle
Wilmersham Common
Long Combe
Stoke Ridge C
Stoke Pero Common
Swe
D
East Pinford
Swap Hill
Beckham
1457
Elsworthy
Wellshead Allotment
Exford Common
1675
Rowbarrows
Tumuli
Dunk
Beac
West Pinford
E X
Warren Fm
Dry Hill
Rams Combe
M
Alcombe Water
O
Pitsworthy
O
Hoar Moor
Codsend Moors
1500
Ravens Nest
Ware Ball
Exe Cleave
Westermill Fm
Wellshead
River Quarme
Hillhead Cross
Kitnor Heath
Codsend
Clovenrocks Bridge
B3223
Red Stone Hill
B3223
Riscombe
Downscombe
Sharcott
Ha
Hereliving
Ashott Barton
White Cross
River Exe
Ley
Edgcott
ST MARY MAGDALENE
B3224
Stetfold Rocks
Winstitchen Fm
Flexbarrow
White Water
Crown Hotel
Exford
Combe
Camp
Great Woolcombe
Pennycombe Water
B3223
Chibbet Post
Road Castle
Lyncombe
1266
Staddon Hill
Cow Castle
River Barle
Pickedstones Fm
Tumulus
Buckworthy
Road Hill
Staddon
Horsen Fm
Ferny Ball
Landacre
Landacre Bridge
Blackland
Halsgrove
Hillway
Weatherslade
Roam Hill
Nethercote
Ken
Bye C
Sherdon
Tumulus
1455
Dilacombe
Brightworthy Barrows
Waterhouse
Withypool
ST ANDREW
Withypool
The Royal Oak Inn
Uppington
River Exe
Comer's Cross
Comer's Gate
Great Ashe
Sherdon Fm
Green Barrow
Withypool Common
Withypool Hill
River Barle
B3223
Winsford Hill
H
1324
Woolcombe Allotment
Withypool Cross
Halscombe Allotment
Stone Circle
West Water
North Batsom
Caratacus Roman Sto
Barcombe
Barkham
Willingford
Worth Hill
Porchester's Post
Worth
Knaplock
Liscombe
Sandyway Cross
Sportsman's Inn
Litton Water
Humber's Ball
Westwater Allotment
Old Barrow
Parsonage Down
Tarr Farm Inn
Beacon
Twitchen Ridge
Twitchen Barrows
Hawkridge Plain
Cloggs Down
Tarr Steps
Ashway Side
Varle H
Wheatcloss Cross
Blindwell
White Post

A B C D E F

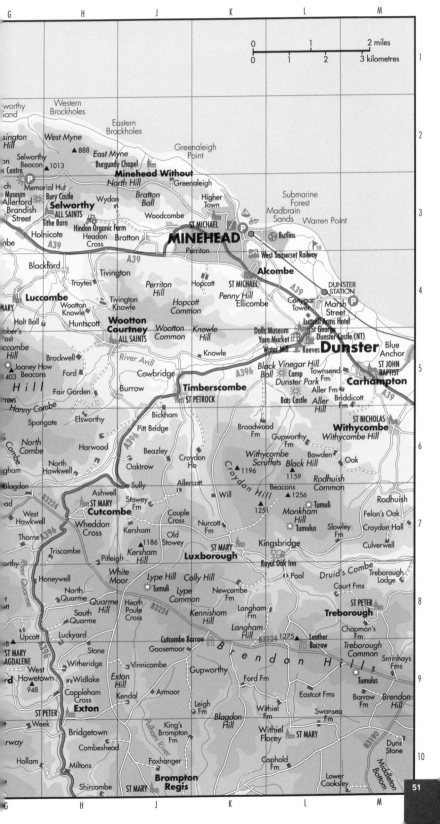

0   1   2 miles
0   1   2   3 kilometres

1

worthy
and

Western
Brockholes

sington
Hill

West Myne

Eastern
Brockholes

▲888
East Myne
Burgundy Chapel

Greenaleigh
Point

2

Selworthy
Beacon ▲1013

North Hill
Minehead Without

Greenaleigh

n
Centre

Memorial Hut

Bury Castle

Wydon

Bratton
Ball

Higher
Town

Submarine
Forest
Madbrain
Sands

Warren Point

Museum
Allerford
Brandish
Street

Selworthy
ALL SAINTS
Tithe Barn
Holnicote

Hindon Organic Farm
Headon
Cross

Woodcombe

ST MICHAEL

MINEHEAD

Butlins

3

mbe

Blackford

A39

Bratton

Perriton

Alcombe

West Somerset Railway

18

Luccombe

Troytes

Tivington

Perriton
Hill

A39

A39

DUNSTER
STATION

4

MARY

Holt Ball

Wootton
Knowle

Tivington
Knowle

Hopcott

ST MICHAEL

Penny Hill
Ellicombe

Conygar
Tower

Marsh
Street

ober's
ost

Huntscott

Hopcott
Common

Luttrell Arms Hotel
St George

ccombe
Hill

Wootton
Courtney
ALL SAINTS

Wootton
Common

Knowle
Hill

Dolls Museum
Yarn Market
Water Mill

Dunster Castle (NT)
Reeves

Dunster

Blue
Anchor

Joaney How
403 Beacons

Brockwell

Ford

River Avill

Cowbridge

Knowle

Black
Ball

Vinegar Hill
Camp
Dunster Park

Townsend

ST JOHN
BAPTIST

Carhampton

5

Hill

Fair Garden

Burrow

A396

Timberscombe
ST PETROCK

Aller Fm

Bats Castle

Aller
Hill

Briddicott
Fm

rows

Hanny Combe

Spangate

Elsworthy

Bickham

Broadwood
Fm

Gupworthy
Fm

Withycombe Hill

ST NICHOLAS
Withycombe

6

Combe

North
Combe

gham

North
Hawkwell

Harwood

Pitt Bridge

Beazley

Croydon
Ho

Withycombe
Scruffets

Black Hill
1159

Bowden
Oak

Rodhuish
Common

Blagdon

ad

West
Hawkwell

B3224

Ashwell
ST MARY

Oaktrow

Sully

Allercott

Croydon Hill
1196

Beacons
▲1256
1251

Rodhuish

Felon's Oak

Croydon Hall

7

Thorne

Cutcombe

Wheddon
Cross

Stowey
Fm

Couple
Cross

Will

Nurcott
Fm

Monkham
Hill
Tumulus

Tumuli

Slowley
Hill

Culverwell

A396

Triscombe

Kersham

Old
Stowey

ST MARY

Kingsbridge

orthy

Pitleigh

▲1186
Kersham
Hill

Luxborough

Royal Oak Inn

Pool

Druid's Combe

Court Fms

Treborough
Lodge

8

River Quarme

Honeywell

North
Quarme

White
Moor

Lype Hill
Tumuli

Colly Hill

Lype
Common

Newcombe
Fm

Langham
Fm

ST PETER

Treborough

t
ett

Upcott

South
Quarme

Quarme
Hill

Heath
Poule
Cross

B3224

Kennisham
Hill

Langham
Hill

B3224 1275▲

Leather
Barrow

Chapman's
Fm

8 ▲

ST MARY
MAGDALENE

West
Howetown
948

Luckyard

Stone

Witheridge

Vinnicombe

Cutcombe Barrow

Goosemoor

Gupworthy

B r e n d o n

Ford Fm

H i l l s

Treborough
Common

Sminhays
Fms

9

d

Coppleham
Cross

Exton

Widlake

Exton
Hill

Kendal

Armoor

Leigh
Fm

Withiel
Fm

Eastcot Fms

Swansea
Fm

Barrow
Fm

Tumulus

Brendon
Hill

ST PETER

Week

Bridgetown

King's
Brompton
Fm

Blagdon
Hill

Withiel
Florey

ST MARY

B3190

rway

Hollam

Combeshead

Miltons

Foxhanger

Cophold
Fm

Duns
Stone

10

Shircombe

ST MARY

Brompton
Regis

Lower
Cooksley

Middleton
Bottom

51

Dunster Castle

DUNSTER

Arguably the most picturesque of Exmoor villages overlooked, and dominated, by the Castle. You can park on the north, and south end, of the village, or on the High Street, next to the C17 Yarn Market. Do explore on foot and visit the Gallox bridge, the Water Mill and admire some of the 200 listed buildings. The beautiful Parish Church is quite outstanding. Always a popular centre from which to explore Exmoor and the coast. Hobby Horse Dance, 1st May. It is becoming a centre for fine cuisine, and there are a number of tearooms. Waymarked circular walks lead off into Vinegar Hill, to Bat's Castle, but the more adventurous climb up Knowle Hill which can on a clear day provide expansive views. (L5)

SPECIAL PLACES TO VISIT...

Conygar Tower. A rich man's folly built in 1775 rises to 59ft. It can be walked to through woodland from the Castle in 1.5 mile circuit. (L5)

Dunster Castle (NT). Imposing C13 building with many additions through the years, and major remodelling from 1868-72. Home of the Luttrell family for 600 years. Notable staircase, ceilings, family portraits and stables. Terrace walk with sub-tropical plants. Garden and park open daily Feb-December, from 11 to dusk 10-5. Castle open Mar-31 Oct daily 11-5, Dec W/Es 11-4. (L5) 01643 821314 nationaltrust.org.uk

LIGHT BITES...AND MORE...

If you have entered from the A39 and are in dire need of coffee, tea and cakes or more, the Luttrell Arms Hotel will furnish your needs. Enter via a glass door into a haven of wood panelling, pargetting, log fires and ancient beams. Open all day for food. Perhaps, after a walk around the village you will have passed the Church and entered West Street. On your right is **Chapel House**, a craft shop and tea room. Comfy chairs and a warm welcome will usher you in to stay to sample their home made cakes and west country cheeses. 01643 822343 chapelhousedunster. co.uk A few doors down, **Hathaways**, an Italian restaurant recommended by their peers. All is cooked to order; fish (in season), meat and vegetarian dishes for dinner. 01643 821725 hathawaysofdunster.com

Reeves, 20-22 High Street. This has gained a well deserved reputation. Cosy and intimate, with a flair for interior design, the food is prepared by Justin who trained in Oxford and at country house hotels in the Cotswolds. Open Tu-Sa for dinner, and lunch weekends 12-2 pm. (L5) 01643 821414 reevesrestaurantdunster.co.uk

Dunster Museum & Doll Collection, 17 High St. Home to over 900 dolls from all over the world. Open daily Easter to end Sept 11-3. (L4) 01643 821220 dunstermuseum.co.uk

Dunster Working Waterwheel (NT), Mill Lane. This is a fully operational C18 mill, a rare example of a double-overshot mill. Oats and stoneground flour produced, and on sale. Riverside tea-room. Open daily Mar-Oct 10-5. (L5)

Parish Church of St George. Priory church built in the C14 shared by the monks and parishioners. Bell tower is open on Th evenings during bell ringing practice. (L4)

WHERE TO STAY...

The Luttrell Arms Hotel. Small, C15 hotel used in medieval times as a guesthouse for the Abbots of Cleeve. 4-poster beds and high ceilings, log fires and the choice of bar snacks all-day, or the more formal restaurant with al fresco dining. (L5) 01643 821555 luttrellarms.co.uk

Spears Cross Hotel, 1 West Street. Award-winning B & B in much demand. Fabulous oak door leads into a lounge with Inglenook fireplace. The bedrooms are top notch with contemporary fittings, and massive beds. No dogs. (L5) 01643 821439 spearscross.co.uk

Porlock Weir

MINEHEAD

Seaside resort on the Bristol Channel developed in the C19 from an old fishing port sheltered by high cliffs to the west. The sandy beach is extensive at low tide but the grey Bristol Channel does not invite a leisurely bathe, better to drive west to Woolacombe. The town has some fine Georgian houses and the picturesque Old Town with its fine C14 church is not to be missed. The town's situation makes for a convenient centre from which to explore Exmoor, the Quantocks and Brendon Hills. It is possible to walk up to North Hill through the Old Town, and onto Selworthy via the coastal footpath. On May 1st, the Minehead Sailors' Hobby Horse parades through the streets in commemoration of a phantom wreck that entered the harbour without Captain or crew, and has done so for years. (J3)

SPECIAL PLACES TO VISIT...

Butlins Minehead, Seafront. Sub-Tropical sunsplash waterworld; funfair, family fun and daytime entertainment, Odeon cinema and bowling alley. Quite an experience now with New Style Chalets! Open daily. (L3) 01643 703331 butlins.com

West Somerset Railway. One of the major railway preservation schemes - 20 miles from Bishops Lydeard to Minehead. Trains (steam but sometimes diesel) run daily May-Oct, and some days in April.

Connecting buses between Bishops Lydeard and Taunton. All trains steam-hauled from mid-July to end Aug & BHs. Ten restored stations along the line. (K4) 01643 704996 westsomersetrailway.vticket.co.uk

PORLOCK

Picturesque village set back from the coast in a beautiful **Exmoor** valley protected on three sides by heather covered moors. An abundance of flora and fauna, and pure air plus a temperate climate makes for a relaxing ambience. Fine church

with interesting tombstones. A popular walking centre with many shops selling gear. It's just off the coastal footpath, and close to many fine **Exmoor** walks.

SPECIAL PLACES OF INTEREST...

Churchgate Gallery, High Street. Their Mantra is Just Beautiful Art, in all its guises; paintings, ceramics, jewellery and natural history. 01643 862238 churchgategallery.co.uk

Dovery Manor Museum. Quaint little museum displaying the history of the locality. Open M-Sa May-Sept. (F3) 01643 862645 doverymanormuseum.org.uk

Greencombe Gardens. Enchanting old garden on the edge of woodland overlooking Porlock Bay. Choice rhododendrons, azaleas, camellias, maples, roses, hydrangeas, ferns and small woodland plants. Completely organic with compost heaps on show. Plant sales. No dogs. Open W/Es, M, Tu & W 2-6 Apr-July. (E3) 01643 862363 greencombe.wordpress.com

---

LIGHT BITES...

The **Big Cheese** is just that, with a full panoply of West Country cheeses and careno coffees. Picnics made up for you. Chutneys and jams.. and **Eastwards the Home Cook Cafe** for breakfasts, soups of the day, special burgers, homemade cakes and cream teas. Open daily from 10.

The small hamlet at **Porlock Weir,** 2-miles north-west has a charming harbour overlooked by fishermen's cottages. Much of this area is owned by the National Trust and the Blathwaite Estate (Owners of Dyrham Park, Bath) who have thankfully retained a continuity of lifestyle by renting to the same families over many generations. E/C W. (F3)

On your left as you enter, **The Cafe, Porlock Weir Run** by passionate chef Andrew and his wife, Sarah.

High quality food is available all day, from lobster to simple fare. Al fresco dining. Opens at 12.00. Accommodation. 01643 863300 thecafeporlockweir.co.uk

If you seek something less ambitious there's **The Harbour Gallery & Cafe**. A healthy concoction of coffee, cakes, ceramics, paintings, smoked fish and shellfish platters in the Porlock Estate's former stables. All with a view and a sea breeze. Open daily at 10. 01643 863514 harbourgalleryandcafe.co.uk

Next door, **Ziangs** for Far Eastern street food, and fish and chips. Open M-Sa 12-7. Now, if antiques are your passion you may have noticed **Miller's at the Anchor** as you passed it by. Worthy of a look-see. The decor is something else. The owners are usually absent and the food can be lacklustre. 01643 862753 millersattheanchor.co.uk

---

1303
First recorded mayor of Barnstaple.

1307 Introduction of Stannary Towns for the administration of tin mines; Tavistock, Ashburton, and Chagford. Later, Plympton was added in 1327.

53

The Oily, High Street.
This rarely open former
motor museum epitomises the
eccentricity and charm of this
Somerset town. Now run as a
hobby rather than a business,
so if you are in luck it may be
open. Inside, old advertising
signs, manuals, a black Rolls
Royce, Morris Minors, forlorn
motorcycles and a kindly old
gentleman in his Sanctuary.

SPECIAL PLACES OF INTEREST...

Exmoor Glass. Glassblowers
create top quality decanters,
goblets, vases and jugs. Regular
demos. Gallery open daily
10-5, Studio M-F 9-4. (E3)
Harbour Studios 01643 863141
exmoorglass.co.uk

VILLAGES OF INTEREST...

Allerford. Pretty village noted
for the Packhorse Bridge and
thatched cottages. Fine walks to
Selworthy, Bossington Hill and
Porlock Bay. (G3)

Culbone. Hamlet with the
smallest church in England.
Once home to charcoal burners
and a leper colony. Reached
via car, or the coastal footpath
from Porlock Weir, or County
Gate. (D2)

Horner. Quaint hamlet of
thatched cottages and running
water. A steep ascent leads off
into the woods. Walking centre.
Tea shops. (G4)

Exford. Bright, attractive
village astride the River Exe
with a village green, and two
sportsmen's inns. Exmoor's fox
and stag hunting centre now
in decline following the recent
hunting ban. (E7)

Luccombe. Quiet little village
with white-washed thatched
cottages which overlook a
peaceful churchyard. Amidst
superb walking and trekking
country. (G4)

Oare. Scattered village in
steep wooded country. The
church was immortalised in
R D Blackmore's novel Lorna
Doone as the setting for Lorna's
wedding. (B3)

Selworthy. National Trust
village with many picture-
postcard thatched cottages.
Superb views across the
Holnicote Estate towards
Dunkery Beacon. Fine wagon
roof to church. Short, easy
waymarked walks lead into the
woods. (H3) Periwinkle Cottage
Tea Rooms. Home-made
cakes and soups, light lunches
and cream teas. Open daily in
season. (H3) 01643 863341

Winsford. One of Exmoor's
prettiest villages and well
known for the thatched Royal
Oak Inn, and as the birthplace
of Ernest Bevin in 1881, the
Labour Statesman. (G9)

Withypool. Unspoilt village in
the centre of Exmoor spanned
by a beautiful five-arched
bridge. R D Blackmore wrote
much of Lorna Doone while
staying at the Royal Oak Inn.
Fine country to the south-west,
and riverside walk beside the
Barle to Tarr Steps. (D8)

NATURAL PLACES OF INTEREST...

Badgworthy Water. A beautiful
little valley associated with the
Lorna Doone story. Convenient
parking at Malmsmead for
the easy-going walk, or pony
trek beside the riverbank to

Badgworthy Wood, an ancient
place with tangled oaks, moss and
lichen. (A4)

Brendon Hills. Rolling hills of
patchwork fields and woodland
in varying shades of greens and
brown. Often overlooked as a
place of great beauty because of
their close proximity to Exmoor
and the Quantocks. The walk
across Exmoor through these
fields to the Quantock Hills was
considered by John Hillaby,
the great long distance walker
and author, to be "the most
beautiful part of England". (K9)

Caractacus Stone. Inscribed
ancient stone of the Dark Ages
set in a shelter on Winsford
Hill. (F9)

Clatworthy Reservoir.
Artificial lake of 130 acres
created in 1960. trout fishing.
Viewing area and nature trail.

**Coastal Road; Porlock to
Lynmouth**. One of the most
spectacular and awe-inspiring
coastal drives in England.
It begins, or ends, with a
warning more reminiscent of
the "Golden Age of Motoring"
when cars were not given to
good brakes and trenchant
tyres: "Stay in First Gear". It
remains a steep, and hazardous
ascent (for an under-powered
vehicle) up Porlock Hill, a 1 in 4
gradient. There is an alternative
route: the toll road through
the Blathwaite Estate, a less
dramatic route, but blessed with
the buzzard and raven, and wild
flowers. Once up on the brow of
the hill, there are superb views
seawards and inland across the
rolling patchwork landscape.
On a clear day you can spy the
South Wales coast all the way
to Worms Head on the Gower
Peninsula. It is worth turning
around and driving back the
route you came, for it will look
very different.

Cow Castle. Iron Age
stronghold in commanding
position. Fine viewpoint
overlooking the River Barle.
Reached via a flat, easy walk
from Simonsbath running
parallel with the Barle. (A8)

Dunkery Beacon. Rises
to 1,704 feet, and is the
highest place on **Exmoor**.
Formerly the site of a fire

Red Stag Safari ss

Selworthy

beacon. Wonderful views in all directions. Short-easy walk from road. (F6)

Holnicote Estate (NT). Over 12,000 acres given over to the National Trust by Sir Richard Acland. Extends from the coast to the summit of Dunkery Beacon, including the picturesque villages of Allerford, Bossington, Selworthy, Tivington and Luccombe. Three packhorse bridges and several prehistoric sites plus Selworthy Tithe Barn, the Horner Valley, Selworthy Beacon, Hurlstone Point and North Hill. The footpaths crisscross in all directions and can be quite mind boggling to navigate around. They have crazy names based on Acland's children and grandchildren. Booklets of walks available from the National Park. (F4)

Horner Wood. Ancient and secluded woodland below Dunkery Hill. The little stream, the Snorer (Hwrnwr), saxon named because of its gurgling sound, winds its way around the knobbly oaks. Now one of Britain's National Nature Reserves. (G4)

Landacre Bridge. Medieval bridge in excellent condition. Popular picnic spot beside the River Barle. Walks beside Barle to Cow Castle, a fine viewpoint. (B8)

North Hill. Lovely scenic drive from Minehead to Selworthy Beacon. Nature trail. Campsite. (J3)

Tarr Steps. Ancient clapper bridge crossing the River Barle, and one of Exmoor's most visited attractions so beware

of large crowds on weekends and bank holidays. Walks up riverbank. It's possible to cross the river in a 4 x 4, or on horseback but not in a saloon car. Car park and toilets in close proximity. Best approached from the B3223 on Winsford Hill. Tarr Farm Inn provides teas and refreshments. (E10)

Webber's Post. Popular spot below Dunkery Hill with fine views over Stoke Pero Common and Selworthy Beacon. Nature trails and bridleways lead off in all directions, and can cause havoc with your map reading skills. Paths to Stoke Pero church and Dunkery Beacon. Car park. (G5)

SPECIAL PLACES TO VISIT...

Exmoor Owl & Hawk Centre, Allerford. Flying displays; owls to hawks at 2pm. Feed the animals. Hawk walk. Falconry tuition. Shop and tea garden. B&B. Pony trekking across Exmoor. Open Mar-Oct Su-F 10.30-4.30, & BH Sa. (G3) 01643 862816 exmoorfalconry.co.uk

Discovery Safaris of Porlock. This Exmoor safari views the National Park in a specially designed Land Rover Defender to explore the stunning scenery of Exmoor by using off-road routes. Available all year. Trips last 2-3 hours. (K3) 01643 863444 discoverysafaris.com

Lorna Doone Farm, Malmsmead. C14 farmhouse known as Plovers Barrow Farm in Blackmore's Lorna Doone, the home of John Ridd. Now an artsncrafts and gift shop, next door The Buttery tea rooms. Open daily late Mar-Oct 10-6, Nov-Christmas 11-4.30. (A2) 01598 741388

Red Stag Safari. In the comfort of a Land Rover Discovery you will be whisked around the delights of Exmoor; wildlife, panoramic viewpoints, fast-flowing rivers, and more. 01643 841831 redstagsafari.co.uk

West Somerset Rural Life Museum, Allerford. Victorian schoolroom, laundry and dairy. Craft workers' tools. Croquet lawn. Picnic area. Open Apr-Oct Tu-Su 10.30-4, Su & BHs 1.30-4.30. (G3) 01643 862529 allerfordmuseum.org.uk

PUBS SERVING FOOD...

Royal Oak Inn at Luxborough. Hidden away in the Brendon Hills, this little cosy, flagstoned pub has built a reputation for good, honest fare and real ales. Luxurious cottage-style accommodation with bathrooms. (L7) 01984 641408 theroyaloakinnluxborough.co.uk

Tarr Farm Inn. C16 farm set in its own 40-acres overlooking Tarr Steps, and the River Barle. Modern bedrooms with all mod cons. Restaurant provides meals from local farms. Activities and Events organised. Opens at 12am. (E10) 01643 851507 tarrfarm.co.uk

SPECIAL PLACES TO STAY...

Crown Hotel. This family-run C17 Coaching Inn and sporting hotel delivers a warm welcome to you, your dogs and horses. Log fires and luxurious bedrooms. Impressive food in Restaurant. Cosy country bar and meals. Shooting Party rates. (D7) 01643 831554 crownhotelexmoor.co.uk

Hindon Organic Farm. Lovely old creaking farmhouse at the end of a long, long lane. Be prepared to reverse! An organic farm for many years producing fresh organic meats; Aberdeen Angus beef, Gloucester Old Spot pork, Hindon hams, sausages and pies. (H3)01643 705244 hindonfarm.co.uk

WALKING ON EXMOOR...

Walking is the most satisfying way to experience Exmoor's many virtuous delights. Her charms will seduce you into returning again, and again, and whether you are a naturalist, geologist or botanist, fresh air fiend, or just a keen horseman. You will always be in her debt. We are privileged to walk her beautiful paths.

The National Park is dissected by scores of footpaths and bridleways (about 650 miles in total). Most signposted and waymarked. There are many publications available giving detailed plans for walks, including some excellent leaflets published by the Exmoor National Park, the National Trust and local tourist offices. Guided, and special interest walks can also be arranged throughout the season through several Tourist Information Centres. The recommended walks listed below are only a small indication of some of the areas, and routes worthwhile exploring. All start within easy reach of a car park.

Gloucester Old Spot (weaners), Hindon Organic Farm

1346
Devon ports provide 88 ships for Crecy and Calais campaign.

1348
Black Death reaches Devon, about one third of population dies. Nearly half the clergy die.

Saunton Sands

1. **Bossington** to **Selworthy**, either via **Hurlstone Point** or **Selworthy Beacon**. (G2)

2. **North Hill** 3-mile trail. (J3)

3. **Webber's Post** to **Stoke Pero Church** and **Dunkery Beacon**. (G4)

4. Cloutsham Woodland Trail. (F5)

5. **Horner** to **Webber's Post** via **Horner Wood**. (G4)

BEACHES & SURFING...

Blue Anchor. Sand and shingle. R/WC/P. (M4)

Dunster Beach. Shingle and sand. R/WC/P. (M4)

Minehead. Shingly sand. R/P/WC. (K3)

Porlock Weir. Pebbles. HZ swimming. Fast waves for experienced surfers. P/WC/R. (E2)

COASTAL FOOTPATH...

Minehead to **County Gate** (9 miles). The path begins fairly easily from the end of Minehead Quay, passing gently through woodland onto North Hill. For about three miles there is wonderful high level walking towards Selworthy Beacon, a fine viewpoint at 1013 feet, and

worth a slight detour. Then down the hill to Bossington, a pretty village, and a short length of road work before following the beach to Porlock Weir, a delightful little harbour overlooked by a row of fishermen's cottages.

The path then climbs up beside Yeanor Wood towards Culbone Church, set secluded in a wooded glade. The path continues with slight elevations to Glenthorne House. From here the path ascends to County Gate where there is a car park and National Park Centre.

Saunton Sands

1356 Watercourse, or leat (clean water for cleanliness and health) provided for the inhabitants of Cullompton by the Abbot of "Bokland".

1390 Exeter Cathedral's great East Window is rebuilt by Robert Lyen.

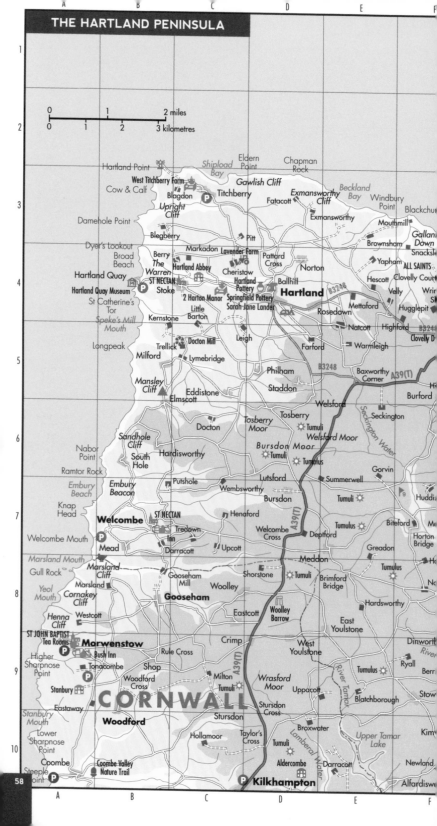

THE HARTLAND PENINSULA

0 1 2 miles
0 1 2 3 kilometres

Hartland Point
Shipload Bay
Eldern Point
Chapman Rock
West Titchberry Farm
Gawlish Cliff
Cow & Calf
Blagdon
Titchberry
Fatacott
Exmansworthy Cliff
Beckland Bay
Windbury Point
Blackchu
Upright Cliff
Exmansworthy
Damehole Point
Mouthmill
Gallan Down
Blegberry
Pitt
Markadon
Lavender Farm
Brownsham
Snacksl
Dyer's Lookout
Berry
The Warren
Hartland Abbey
Cheristow
Pattard Cross
Norton
Yapham
ALL SAINTS
Hescott
Clovelly Court
Broad Beach
ST NECTAN
Hartland Pottery
Ballhill
Velly
Wrir
S
Hartland Quay
Stoke
2 Harton Manor
Hartland
Clovelly D
Hartland Quay Museum
Springfield Pottery
Hartland
Rosedown
Mettaford
Highford
Hugglepit
St Catherine's Tor
Little Barton
Sarah Jane Lander
B3248
St Catherine's Tor
Kernstone
Leigh
Farford
Natcott
Speke's Mill Mouth
Trellick
Docton Mill
Warmleigh
Highford
B3248
Longpeak
Milford
Lymebridge
Clovelly D
Mansley Cliff
Eddistone
Philham
B3248
Elmscott
Staddon
Baxworthy Corner
A39(T)
Welsford
Burford
Hi
Docton
Tosberry Moor
Tosberry
Tumuli
Welsford Moor
Seckington
Sandhole Cliff
Hardisworthy
Bursdon Moor
Tumuli
Tumulus
Gorvin
Nabor Point
South Hole
Putshole
Lutsford
Summerwell
Tumuli
Huddi
Ramtor Rock
Wembsworthy
Bursdon
9
Embury Beach
Embury Beacon
Henaford
Tumulus
Biteford
Me
Knap Head
Welcombe Cross
Tumulus
Horton Bridge
Welcombe
ST NECTAN
Tredown
Deptford
Greadon
H
Welcombe Mouth
Inn
Upcott
Meddon
Tumulus
Nc
Mead
Darracott
Shorstone
Tumuli
Brimford Bridge
Hardsworthy
Marsland Mouth
Marsland Cliff
Gooseham Mill
Woolley
Gull Rock
Yeol Mouth
Marsland
Gooseham
Eastcott
Woolley Barrow
East Youlstone
Henna Cliff
Cornakey Cliff
Westcott
ST JOHN BAPTIST
Tea Rooms
Marwenstow
Crimp
West Youlstone
Dinwort
River
Higher Sharpnose Point
Bush Inn
Rule Cross
Tumulus
Ryall
Berr
Tonacombe
Shop
Milton
A39(T)
Wrasford Moor
Stow
Stanbury
Woodford Cross
Tumuli
Uppacott
Blatchborough
Eastaway
CORNWALL
Sturdson Cross
Stanbury Mouth
Woodford
Sturdson
Broxwater
Upper Tamar Lake
Kim
Lower Sharpnose Point
Hollamoor
Taylor's Cross
Tumuli
Darracott
Newland
Coombe
Aldercombe
Alfardiswe
Steeple Point
Coombe Valley Nature Trail
Kilkhampton

58

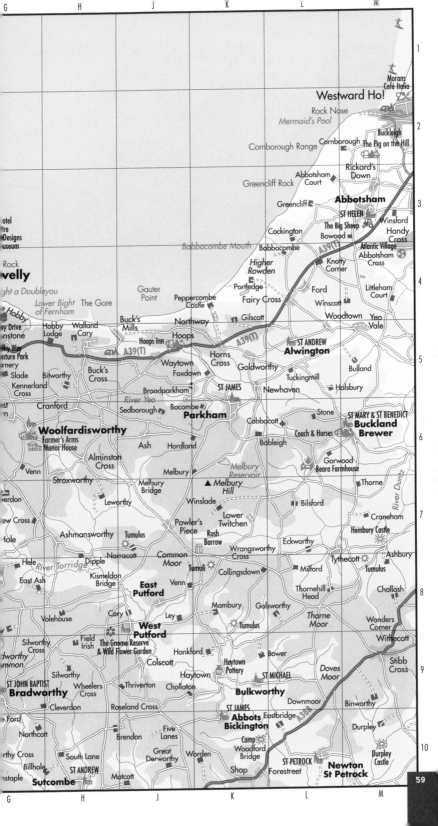

Three views of Clovelly

1403
Plymouth burned by Breton raiders.

1404
Breton raiders land on Slapton Sands prior to invading Dartmouth.

BUCK'S MILLS

Name derived from the Saxon "Bussac Hewise", meaning homestead. An isolated hamlet of romantic cottages (most are second homes, and are usually empty) at the bottom of a steep combe protected by high cliffs to either side, and from behind, thick woodland. In times gone by, the villagers made a living from fishing; herring, mackerel, lobster and prawn, as well as coastal lime burning needed for the fertilising of inland farms, so as to neutralise the acid soil. The steep, wide road from the beach was built to transport lime shipped in from South Wales. Hence, the massive lime kilns above the beach. As the fishing declined, the villagers sought new employment in the quarries on Lundy, sailing daily to and from work. Bygod, they were tough, in them, thar days. (J4)

CLOVELLY

A timeless village of cobbled streets and quaint cottages descend steeply to a harbour and backdrop of rich blue sea. Set in a superb position amidst beautiful scenery Clovelly belongs to the Rouse family who take great care to maintain the buildings in traditional materials. It's a former fishing port whose major wealth came from catching mackerel and herring. Today, it's a centre for small fishing trips, and visiting day-trippers.

When the fishing dried up Clovelly men would seek employment digging the quarries on Lundy. Clovelly folk were a hardy breed. It was not just the men who worked their socks off, the women got stuck in, too. With the quarrying, and the making of fishing nets.

Visiting Clovelly is an unforgettable experience and loved by children and folk of all ages. Take sensible shoes, the descent on cobble stones can be slippery. It is also steep, and the unfit or elderly would be wise to either take a ride on a donkey, or seek a lift in the Land Rover to the harbour.

Cliff Edge Cottages, Buck's Mills

On arrival, park in the parking area provided and enter via the Visitor Centre where there is a charge which helps maintain the village for future generations. Open daily. (G4) 01237 431781 clovelly.co.uk

WHAT TO SEE, AND WHOM TO VISIT IN CLOVELLY...

Ann Jarvis Designs. Scarves, ties, cushions and accessories designed and handprinted onto silks, velvets and fine wools. Commissions and day courses undertaken at workshop. Open Summer, daily 10-5. Winter, M-F 10.30-3.30. (G4) 01237 431033 clovellysilk.com

Clovelly Court Garden. These gardens have undergone a major restoration programme. A classic example of a Victorian kitchen garden with magnificent greenhouses. The unique maritime microclimate provides exotic flower borders and fruit. Open daily, all year 10-4. (F4) 01237 431200

Clovelly Pottery. Variety of exhibits from different ceramicists. Resident Caroline Curtis hand throws slip decorated earthenware pots. Open summer M-Sa 10.30-5, Su 11-5. (G4) 01237 431042 clovellypottery.co.uk

Hobby Drive Walk. Follow the signs from Clovelly. This was laid out between 1811-29 by Sir James Hamlyn Williams, as a celebration of nature. One of the schemes that came to mirror the Romantic Movement of the early C19. The pathway was designed to accommodate carriages, and it features four gently curving bridges. The panoramic views peer down on Clovelly, and westwards towards Lundy and West Wales. They are unforgettable. There are a number of caves just off this drive that were used to store the C19 smuggler's contraband. But, beware of ghostly forms. (G4)

St Nectan's, Stoke

HARTLAND PENINSULA

An isolated corner of Devon full of interest. The village of Hartland is a popular centre for the arts and crafts and has a number of pubs and tearooms. The church is strangely two miles westwards at Stoke.

SPECIAL PLACES TO VISIT IN AND AROUND HARTLAND...

Hartland Abbey & Gardens. Founded in 1157, the current building has been an historic family home since 1539. Furnished in Queen Anne, Georgian and Regency splendour; pictures, murals, furniture, porcelain. Beautiful informal gardens designed by Gertrude Jekyll with a woodland walk to the Atlantic Ocean. Cream teas. Open 26 Mar to 1 Oct Su-Th House 2-5, Gardens & Tea Room 11-5. (C4) 01237 441496 hartlandabbey.com

Hartland Quay. A wild and windswept corner of England forever associated with smugglers of contraband, and a favourite landing for Sir Francis Drake and Sir Richard Grenville, Devon men. It's set on a treacherous coastline, and little wonder that the quay was swept away in 1841, 1887 and 1896. The present quay was rebuilt in 1979. The former harbour master's house is now the hotel and inn. A wide road leads down to the slipway

built for the transport of lime imported from South Wales. (B4)

Hartland Quay Museum. Features four centuries of local shipwrecks, old coastal occupations, shipping, smuggling and fishing. A wonderful introduction to this corner of Britain. Gift shop. Open daily. (B4) 01237 441371

Sarah Jane Lander, No.39 Pottery, Fore St. Sarah uses red earthenware clay and stoneware clay to produce decorated domestic ware. Open Sa-Th. (B4) 01237 441883 sarahjanelander.com

Springfield Pottery. Established in 1979 by Philip Leach, grandson of Bernard Leach. He and his wife, Frannie produce earthenware pottery hand-made from local clays; tiles, garden pots, domestic ware and individual pots. Open M-Sa 9-5. (D4) 01237 441506 springfield-pottery.com

St Nectan's Church, Stoke. A sailor's landmark for miles around, and one of the finest churches in Devon and the West Country. The 128 foot tower is the tallest in North Devon. Perpendicular, and largely built in the mid C14. The tower is in four stages with buttresses and massive gargoyles. The interior is large and lofty, indeed spacious with

Early Jacobean pulpit, C15 Rood Screen, C20 stained glass by Christopher Webb. A simple plaque to Sir Allen Lane, the founder of Penguin Books whose family have a long association with Hartland. There's a little museum with all manner of pieces that gives this church that extra wow factor.

PLACES TO STAY...

2 Harton Manor B & B, The Square. C16 building set in the heart of the village. Comfortable bedrooms and lounge are decorated with original art. Your hostess, Merlyn Chesterman runs printmaking Woodcut Workshops. Open all year. (D4) 01237 441670 twohartonmanor.co.uk

Hartland Quay Hotel. Without doubt one of the most spectacularly sited hotels in Britain. Set on dramatic, rugged cliffs overlooking the Atlantic. Book in when a Force 8 is forecast. Experience some real weather, and if the wind and drama doesn't blow you away, get stuck into some fine food and beer in the Wrecker's Retreat Bar (and hopefully, you'll sleep through the storm). Simple, pine furniture in bedrooms with bathrooms, and stupendous views. (B4) 01237 441218 hartlandquayhotel.com

The Painted Ceiling, St Nectan's, Stoke

1494
Great Court of tinners meets at Crockern Tor.

1496
Devon and Cornwall men rebel against taxes.
Defeated at Blackheath.

MORWENSTOW

No visit to this area will be complete without a visit to this historic village. The village is only made up of a few farms and cottages, but it is to the church, pub and tearoom that one is drawn.

Church of St John the Baptist. Famous for Richard Stephen Hawker, 1803-75, the eccentric and original vicar-poet, and originator of harvest festivals. A compassionate man, he would stalk the wild coast in beaver hat, fisherman's long boots and yellow cloak in search of shipwrecked sailors. Many of those he failed to save, he laid to rest in his churchyard. To stimulate and awaken his congregation he sometimes dressed as a mermaid! His original hut made of driftwood clings to the cliffs. Opposite, the Rectory Tea Rooms, open daily in season. (A9)

The Bush Inn. C13 freehouse revitalised into a contemporary gastro-pub on the Devon-Cornish border. Cosy, authentic snug bars plus a more spacious, modern dining area. Local fish and steaks, a speciality. B&B/Holiday Let. (A9) 01288 331242
thebushinn-morwenstow.com

SPECIAL PLACES TO VISIT...

Cheristow Lavender Farm. Grows over 100 varieties of lavender and many English roses. Soaps and oils. Tearoom. Campsite. Breeders of Devon Red Ruby cattle (Beef on sale). Open Mar-Sept W-Sa 12-5. (C4) 01237 440078
cheristow.co.uk

Docton Mill Gardens & Tea Room. Historic site of former flour mill now a flourishing and captivating garden with water features; leat, head weir and tailrace. 8 acres encompass bog garden, orchard and woodland. Walk to coastal waterfall and beach at Spekes Mill Mouth. B & B. Plant sales and award-winning tea room. Open daily mid-Mar to early Oct 10-5. (C6) 01237 441369
doctonmill.co.uk

Haytown Pottery. Domestic earthenwares and humorous individual animals made by David Cleverly. Open East-Sept, Tu-Th 11-7 but call beforehand 01409 261476 (K9)
david-cleverlyceramics.co.uk

Milky Way Adventure Park, Nr Clovelly. Great family fun; Rides, large indoor adventure play area, sports hall, narrow gauge railway, collection of farming and agricultural equipment, dodgems and Birds of Prey. Open daily Mar-Nov, W/Es & 1/2 terms Nov-East. (G5) 01237 431255
themilkyway.co.uk

The Gnome Reserve & Wild Flower Garden, West Putford. Set in a 4-acre reserve of woodland, stream, pond, meadow and garden is the home of more than 1,000 gnomes and pixies! Approx. 250 labelled species of wild flowers, herbs, grasses and ferns. Open daily mid-Mar to Oct, 10-6. (H9) 01409 2411435
gnomereserve.co.uk

Woolfardisworthy (Woolsery). The Farmer's Arms and Manor House are in the process of being restored to their former glory. The mission of Americans, Michael and Xochi Birch, founders of Bebo to revitalise the village.

1497
Perkin Warbeck besieges Exeter.

1525
Boethius Consolation of philosophy printed at Tavistock, the first recorded Devon printing.

Hartland Quay

His spiritual home where his ancestors lived and where he holidayed as a youth. (G6) woolsery.com

SPECIAL PLACES TO STAY...

Beara Farmhouse. The Dorsets know a thing or two about the comforts of home, interior design and building skills. Their fabulous home has been converted from a ruin into a rural idyll at the bottom of a rough track. Self-catering cottages, too. (L6) 01237 451666 bearafarmhouse.co.uk

Red Lion Hotel, Clovelly. Waking up to the sounds of an ancient harbour is a blissful experience. The rooms are all modern and comfortable with nautical themes, and have superb harbour or sea views. All with bathrooms and mod cons.   The restaurant serves fish directly off the local boats. (G4) 01237 431237 stayatclovelly.co.uk

West Titchberry Farm. A traditional farmhouse B & B. Clean and comfortable, a little old fashioned. Don't expect "Country Living"

decor. All rooms have their own bathroom. Packed lunches and pick-up off the Coast Path can be arranged. Self-catering, too. (C3) 01237 441287 westtitchberryfarm.co.uk

Coach & Horses, Buckland Brewer. Popular "local" providing fine ales and excellent grub; skate, bass, monkfish, and local vegetables in season. Themed nights. 01237 451393 (M6)

Hoops Inn & Country Hotel. Thatched hostelry dating from the C13. Log fires, real ales and seasonal produce have made this a popular inn down the years. More a Dining Pub with Rooms. Dogs welcome. In former times, a meeting place for smugglers and seafarers. Sir Richard Grenville, Drake, Raleigh and Hawkins, all met here and planned their adventures. 01237 451222 (J5) hoopsinn.co.uk

NATURAL PLACES OF INTEREST...

Coombe Valley Nature Trail. Start from Combe

Cottage and follow a green and peaceful wooded valley rich in oak woods, honeysuckle and birdlife; buzzards, woodpeckers, dippers. Nearby, Stowe Barton, home of Sir Richard Grenville who was immortalised in Tennyson's poem, "The Revenge". (B10)

Peppercombe. The section of the coastal path from this hamlet to Buck's Mills is wonderful, and a detour to the beach is worth considering for its geological interest; triassic marl colours in reds, browns and bright yellow. The castle was demolished by fierce storms and eroding cliffs around 1900. (K4)

Peppercombe

1538 Dissolution of the monasteries begins in Devon with priories in Barnstaple, Cornworthy, Exeter, Frithelstock and Pilton.

1549 Crediton occupied by 10,000 Catholic insurgents demonstrating against The Reformation.

65

The Beach, Hartland Quay

Shipload Bay. If you have the legs for it, descend the 260+ steps to a beach of grey shingle, and if your luck is in you can watch Grey seals laze here in early summer. (C3)

COASTAL FOOTPATH...

Westward Ho! to **Clovelly** (12 miles). For the first mile the path makes use of the old railway track beneath the Kipling Tors, but soon becomes more arduous with many ups and downs following the rock coast to the tiny fishing village of Bucks Mills. A few miles further on the path joins the 'Hobby Drive', and by an easy twisting route through beautiful woodlands it reaches Clovelly. (M2-G4)

Clovelly to Hartland Quay (10 miles). Probably the finest section of the whole path. From Clovelly the route ascends the windswept headland of Gallantry Bower, then drops down to the little rocky cove of Mouth Mill. There follows some 4 miles of fine walking

along the cliff tops to Shipload Bay, one of the rare sandy beaches of this coast, and onward to Hartland Point. The coastline now turns sharply to the south and the seascapes increase in magnificence with their fantastically contorted geological formations. There is some hard but rewarding walking over these last few miles to Hartland Quay. (G4)

Hartland Quay to Marsland Mouth (6 miles). The spectacular scenery continues with some fairly stiff walking. At Spekes Mill Mouth there is a fine waterfall, from which the path ascends once again to the cliff tops. From here the path maintains a fairly steady altitude until descending to the small beach at Welcombe Mouth. A further half-mile leads the traveller, at last, to the Cornish border. (H4)

Forest Trails. The Forestry Commission have organised waymarked trails scattered throughout the county. Most have information centres

where detailed booklets can be obtained. Locations include Eggesford, Hartland Forest, Holsworthy, and Melbury in the north west. forestry.gov.uk

BEACHES & SURFING...

Bucks Mills. Small harbour with sand and rocks. 1/2 mile from P (J4).

Clovelly. Shingle and pebbles. Boating pool. R/WC, 1/2 mile walk from P (G4).

Shipload Bay. Shingly sand and rocks 1/2 mile from P (C3). Hartland Point. Shingle, rocks, cliffs. Short walk from P.R (B3).

Welcombe Mouth. Haunt of Cruel Coppinger, an C18 smuggler. Pebbles, rocks and a sandy beach at LT. Short walk from P/R. (A7)

Marsland Mouth. Rocky. Not conducive to bathing unless you are a hardy surfer. Poet's hut on north hillside set up by the late Ronald Duncan, playwright and novelist.

1563
Exeter Ship Canal opened, the first canal with
locks in England.

1568
Drake and Hawkins attacked at San Juan de Ulua in the
Spanish West Indies.

Images from The Mortehoe Heritage Centre and The Hartland Quay Museum

1571
Crediton hit by the Plague with 540 deaths.

1575
The first county map of Devon produced by
Christopher Saxton.

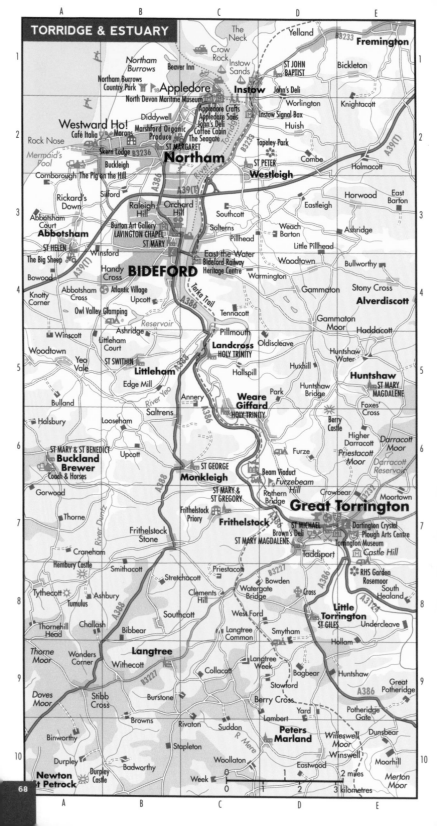

TORRIDGE & ESTUARY

The Neck
Yelland
B3233
Fremington
Crow Rock
Beaver Inn
Instow Sands
Northam Burrows
ST JOHN BAPTIST
Bickleton
Northam Burrows Country Park
Appledore
John's Deli
Knightacott
North Devon Maritime Museum
Instow
Worlington
Diddywell
Appledore Crafts
Instow Signal Box
Westward Ho!
Appledore Sails
John's Deli
Huish
Café Italia
Morans
Coffee Cabin
Rock Nose
Marshford Organic Produce
The Seagate
Tapeley Park
Mermaid's Pool
Skern Lodge
B3236
ST MARGARET
ST PETER
Combe
Holmacott
Buckleigh
Northam
Westleigh
Cornborough
The Pig on the Hill
Silford
A39(T)
Rickard's Down
Raleigh Hill
Orchard Hill
Southcott
Eastleigh
Horwood
East Barton
Abbotsham Court
Burton Art Gallery
LAVINGTON CHAPEL
Salterns
Weach Barton
Ashridge
Abbotsham
ST MARY
Pillhead
Little Pillhead
ST HELEN
East-the-Water
Woodtown
Bullworthy
The Big Sheep
Winsford
Bideford Railway Heritage Centre
Warmington
Bowood
BIDEFORD
Handy Cross
Tarka Trail
Gammaton
Stony Cross
Knotty Corner
Abbotsham Cross
Atlantic Village
Upcott
Tennacott
Gammaton Moor
Alverdiscott
Owl Valley Glamping
Reservoir
Haddacott
Winscott
Ashridge
Pillmouth
Oldiscleave
Huntshaw Water
Woodtown
Littleham Court
Landcross
HOLY TRINITY
Huxhill
Huntshaw
Yeo Vale
ST SWITHIN
Hallspill
ST MARY MAGDALENE
Bulland
Littleham
Edge Mill
River Yeo
Annery
Weare Giffard
HOLY TRINITY
Park
Huntshaw Bridge
Foxes' Cross
Halsbury
Looseham
Saltrens
Berry Castle
Higher Darracott
Darracott Moor
Buckland Brewer
ST MARY & ST BENEDICT
Upcott
Furze
Priestacott Moor
Darracott Reservoir
Coach & Horses
ST GEORGE
Beam Viaduct
Gorwood
Monkleigh
Furzebeam
Crowbear
Moortown
Thorne
ST MARY & ST GREGORY
Rothern Bridge
Hill
Great Torrington
Craneham
Frithelstock Priory
Frithelstock
ST MICHAEL
Dartington Crystal
Plough Arts Centre
Hembury Castle
Frithelstock Stone
ST MARY MAGDALENE
Brown's Deli
Torrington Museum
Castle Hill
Tythecott
Smithacott
Priestacott
Taddiport
RHS Garden Rosemoor
Tumulus
Ashbury
Stretchacott
Bowden
Cross
South Healand
Thornehill Head
Challash
Southcott
Clements Hill
Watergate Bridge
Little Torrington
ST GILES
Undercleave
Thorne Moor
Wonders Corner
Bibbear
West Ford
Smytham
Hollam
Langtree
Withecott
Langtree Common
Doves Moor
Langtree Week
Bagbear
Huntshaw
Stibb Cross
Burstone
Collacott
Stowford
Great Potheridge
Binworthy
Browns
Rivaton
Suddon
Berry Cross
Yard
Potheridge Gate
Durpley
Durpley Castle
Badworthy
Stapleton
Lambert
Peters Marland
Dunsbear
Newton St Petrock
Woollaton
Eastwood
Willeswell Moor
Winswell
Moorhill
Week
Merton Moor

A386
B3227
A3124

0   1   2 miles
0   1   2   3 kilometres

68

Sunset Over The River Torridge

BIDEFORD

A lively and busy town on the Torridge Estuary, and to this day, cargo ships load and unload on the quay. In the C16 and C17, one of Britain's major seaports, handling cargoes from, and to, the New World. A favourite haunt of Drake, Grenville, Hawkins and Sir Walter Raleigh, who it is claimed brought his first cargo of tobacco to Bideford. Furthermore, in the late C17, local merchants traded wool with Newfoundland sending out more ships than any other apart from London and Topsham.

The fine 24-arch C15 bridge is one of the longest (677 ft) in the country, but now overshadowed by the new bridge down river. New Year's Eve attracts over 20,000 revellers to celebrate the New Year who dress up in all manner of garb. Pannier Market on Tuesdays and

LIGHT BITES...

Start you visit at the **Cafe du Parc** set within the **Burton Art Gallery**. A little bit of France, for the Patron and the Waiter are both French, and **Les Petit Plats du Maison** will provide you with the energy to wander the streets of **Bideford**. 01237 429317 On leaving with the river on your left hand side walk yo the High Street. Just past the bookshop is **Barkers Fish and Chips**, for takeaway or sitting in. Then ascend to **Cafe Collective**, 9 Grenville Street. Its funky, dog friendly, quirky...gluten free cakes and fresh pizzas. Open 10-4 and summer evenings. 01237 473999 cafecollectivebideford.co.uk

Saturdays. Trips to Lundy Island. Regatta in Sept. E/C W. (B4)

SPECIAL PLACES TO VISIT...

Bideford Railway Heritage Centre, Former Railway Station. Visitor Centre in restored railway carriage. Refreshments. Hibberd 0-4-0 "Planet" Diesel loco No. 3832 built in 1957. Open East - Oct Su & BHs 2-5. Nov-East Su 2-4. (C4) 01237 423585

Burton Art Gallery & Museum, Kingsley Road. The Museum of Bideford; with three exhibition spaces; museum, craft gallery, shop, workshop and lecture theatre and Café du Parc. TIC. Open M-Sa 10-4, Su 11-4 (B3) 01237 471455 burtonartgallery.co.uk

Pannier Market. One is never sure what will turn up here; antiques, works of art, sculptures, home-made bread. Indeed, a fine mix of entrepreneurs and artists. At 15 Butcher's Row is the Curious Creatures Gallery. Pieces made from tin, steel and iron cast offs.

WHERE TO STAY...

Owl Valley Glamping, Bideford. Three Bell tents set in a secluded valley amongst wild animals, birds and flowers. Environmentally friendly with compost loo and eco shower. 01237 239204 (B4) owl-valley.co.uk

The Old & New Bridges, Bideford

1578
Queen Elizabeth 1 grants Sir Humphrey Gilbert Letters Patent to found an English Colony with Sir Francis Drake and Thomas Carew they amass seven vessels.

69

Appledore

Instow

1580
Sep 26. The Golden Hinde sailed into Plymouth after Sir
Francis Drake's three year voyage round the world.

1581
Buckland Abbey passed to Sir Francis Drake.

APPLEDORE

One of the most attractive villages in North Devon. It's set on the Torridge Estuary, and has ancient inter-connecting streets with rows of colour-washed cottages reminiscent of the Greek, Cycladean islands. A thriving fishing and trading village since the C14. Many of the fishermen's cottages date back to the Elizabethan period. The centuries old shipbuilding tradition has had a precarious existence. Many pubs, craft shops, and home to many artists. The view out to sea from the RNLI Station & Museum is memorable. It is worth exploring the little streets and watching the boats come and go. Like a lot of holiday places the cottages are often sadly empty but for a few months of the year. Instow Ferry. (C2)

SPECIAL PLACES TO VISIT…THINGS TO DO…

Appledore Crafts Co, 5 Bude Street. Co-operative gallery founded by local craftsmen who produce fine furniture, lighting, paintings, ceramics, glass, textiles and jewellery. Open: Jan-Mar W/Es 10-4, Apr-Oct daily 10-5, Nov-Dec W-Su 10-4. (C2) 01237 423547 appledorecraftscompany.co.uk

Appledore Sails, 1 The Quay. Charter a two-mastered 15ft lug boat with skipper and sail the Torridge-Taw Estuary, and beyond if desired. For 4-persons and dog. (C1) 01237 423163 appledoresails.co.uk

North Devon Maritime Museum, Odun Road. North Devon's nautical history displayed with paintings, models, tools and photos. Shipbuilding through the ages. Wrecks and rescues. World War 11. Fishing and navigational exhibits. Open daily Apr-Oct 10.30-5. (C2) 01237 422064

Skern Lodge. Adventure activities for all ages and abilities. Climbing, powerboats, abseiling, surfing, archery, rafting. canoeing and tunnels. (B2) 01237 475992 skernlodge.co.uk

---

LIGHT BITES…
As you enter the village, on your left is **John's Deli & Cafe** where you can refresh yourself with a coffee, pastry and perhaps prepare a picnic hamper.

Moving north you come to **The Coffee Cabin**, another pleasant venue for a coffee and homemade cakes.

If you seek a proper Devon Cream Tea bear left down a side street to **Susie's Tea Rooms.**

Perhaps, you require steak and chips, a pint of ale, a comfy chair and a bed for the night, **The Seagate** overlooking the **Quay**. 012137 472589 theseagate.co.uk

There are two fish and chip takeaways; **The Royal Plaice** and Sylvesters.

Untainted by time, untouched by tide or no man stands the **Beaver Inn** on **Irsha Street**. A popular, unpretentious Freehouse that provides seafood and meat dishes. And, has up its sleeve superb panoramic views of the Estuary. Jazz nights. Dogs welcome. (C2) 01237 474822 beaverinn.co.uk

---

INSTOW

A popular holiday village with sandy beach, pedestrian ferry to Appledore and fine views of the Torridge Estuary.

Sailing Club. Unique thatched cricket score box and pavilion. Stopping off point for riding the Tarka Trail. The Commodore Hotel is a civilised destination, popular with golfers and the retired. (C2)

WHAT TO SEE & DO…

Instow Signal Box, Level Crossing. Built in 1873, now restored to its former glory with levers, gate wheel and instruments. Open East-Oct Su & BHs 2-5, Nov-East Su 2-4. (D2) 01237 423585

LIGHT BITES…
You won't go hungry or thirsty in **Instow**. At the top (north) end of the village, a cluster of inns, **The Wayfarers**, **Instow Arms** and eatery **The Boathouse**. It's a question of your style and choice, not much in it… Further down the seafront you come to **John's Deli and Café**. They have everything you need, a coffee, pastry, cheeses and now meals, breakfast, brunch and lunch. Fill you knapsacks if cycling the Tarka Trail. And, Bon Voyage!

Appledore viewed from Instow

1583   June. The Golden Hind sails from Plymouth with five vessels for the New World. Sir Humphrey Gilbert lands at St John's Newfoundland and founds the first British colony. Later to drown on return voyage aboard the Squirrel off the Azores.

71

GREAT TORRINGTON

An ancient hilltop town set in a strategic position overlooking the River Torridge and rolling, green countryside. The English Civil War's Battle of Torrington in 1646 ended the Royalists' resistance to the Parliamentarian cause in the West Country. The TV series "Down To Earth" was shot around the town and vicinity. Note the fine Market Square with Town Hall and other interesting buildings. Twenty miles of footpaths on The Commons, a public area of 365-acres with flora and fauna. The town is the centre for many Sealed Knot re-

LIGHT BITES...

Park in the large space (charge) beside **Torrington 1646** (closed) overlooking fabulous country, and great for exercising your dogs.

For a full English breakfast it has to be the Cafe in 1646. On leaving P turn L and you come to **Browns Deli & Café, 37 South St.** For a full range of cheeses, quiches, pies and pates, chocolates, and afternoon cream tea. Open Tu-Sa 9.30-5.30. brownsdelicatessen.co.uk

On the other end of town is the Café in **The Plough Arts Centre, 9-11 Fore St**. A loyal following stop here for their toasties and savouries. Relaxing before or after intellectual stimulae.

To the north-west of the town is the **Puffing Billy** beside the **Tarka Trail**, open from 9-5 for breakfast. The homemade food is basic pub-grub sourced from local suppliers; Soups, quiches, jacket potatoes. Railway afficionados will feel at home here. 01805 623050 puffingbilly.co.uk

Next door, **Torrington Cycle Hire, Station Yard** 01805 622633 (D7)

enactments of the Civil War. Pannier Market on Thursdays and Saturdays. May Fair, first Th. (E7)

Dartington Crystal. Handmade lead crystal ware. Viewing galleries and guided tours. Historic glass exhibition. Family Activity Centre. Open daily; tours M-F 9-3.15, Shop/Restaurant daily from 10. (D7) 01805 626242 dartington.co.uk

Great Torrington Museum. Collection of local historic interest including the Coronation Coronets and robes of the last Earl and Countess Orford of Torrington. Open May-Sept M-F 11-4, Sa 11-1. (E7) 01805 626146 great-torrington.com

The Plough Arts Centre, 9-11 Fore St., Lively centre with special workshops, galleries, live events, film shows and more. Café. Open daily. (E7) 01805 624624 theploughartscentre.org.uk

SPECIAL PLACES TO VISIT...

Frithelstock Priory. Commanding ruin of C13 Augustinian priory with adjoining church. (C7)

Kenwith Nursery. Specialists in dwarf and rare conifers. Mail order. Tu-Sa, 10-4.30. (E8) 01805 603274 kenwithconifernursery.co.uk

Marshford Organic Produce, Churchill Way. For the past 30-years they have Specialised in varieties of mixed salads and greens; oakleaf, spinach and rocket, plus little gems, caesars and more. Open daily. 01237 477160 (C2) marshford.co.uk

Northam Burrows Country Park. 253 hectares of grassy plain, saltmarsh, dunes and a notable pebble ridge. Access to two miles of safe, sandy beach. Walks and trails. Burrows Centre has exhibitions and displays. Shop. Toilets for disabled. Centre open daily May to early Sept 10-5, Park open all year. (B2) 01237 479708 torridge.gov.uk/northamburrows

RHS Garden Rosemoor, Nr Great Torrington. An enchanting 65-acres of gardens and woodland, including 2,000 roses in 200 different varieties, colour theme gardens, herb garden and potager, stream and bog garden, cottage garden, fruit and vegetable garden, and semi-tropical areas. Plant Centre, Restaurant and shop. Picnic area. Open daily Apr-Sept 10-6 (-5 Oct-Mar). (E7) 0845 265 8072 rhs.org.uk/gardens/rosemoor

Tapeley Park Gardens, Nr Instow. With magnificent views out to sea, these fascinating gardens offer a variety of exciting terrains; wooded lakes, pleasure grounds, new Organic Permaculture garden, traditional walled kitchen garden, and beside the unique Italian terraces rare plants flourish in the warm Devon climate. Home since 1700 to the Christie family who built the Opera House at Glyndebourne. Also, pigs and pets, pug's graves, ilex tunnel, grotto, croquet, bowls, plant sales, lunches and cream teas in the Queen Anne Dairy. Health & Harmony Festive Weekends Open daily late Mar to early Nov Su-F, 10-5. (D2) 01271 860897 tapeleygardens.com

The Big Sheep. Sheep in all shapes, sizes and disguises, combining to create the bizarre, the entertaining and the unexpected. Sheep dairy and sheep milking. Mountain Boarding. Open daily Apr-Oct & winter W/Es & school hols, 10-6. (M3) 01237 472366 thebigsheep.co.uk

WESTWARD HO!

Unusually, a seaside resort named after a book - it was established in 1863 in recognition of Charles Kingsley. Rudyard Kipling was educated at United Services College (some buildings survive as guest houses), and set 'Stalky & Co' in the hills to south, now named 'Kipling Tors'. Interesting pebble beach to north. A quieter beach (but can be muddy) to surf becoming increasingly popular, away from the hordes of Croyde and Saunton. Of late, much building development in the shape of apartments overlooking the sea, and a posh hotel is in the planning stages. Fine bass fishing, and excellent fishing tackle shop. Major tennis club in North Devon. E/C W. (B2)

BEACHES & SURFING...

Westward Ho! Wide expanse of sand. Pebble ridge behind. Water sports. R/WC/LG (B2).

Instow. Flat, estuary sand, fine for sun bathing and ball games, but not conducive for bathing. R/P. (C1)

LIGHT BITES...

Just off the Green is **Morans**, a restaurant and bar fusing Thai cuisine with English country fare, add a spectacular Cocktail, its a recipe for success. Opens at 11.30 M-F Sa 10.30, Su 12.00 til late. 01237 472070 moransrestaurant.co.uk Just along from there is **Cafe Italia Pizzeria** knocking out stonebaked pizzas. A little distance away (by car) is **The Pig On The Hill.** This is a popular dining pub in a great pastoral location. The food is above average pub-grub but let down by poor service. On site, three self-catering Cedar cabins. (B3) 01237 459222 pigonthehillwestwardho. co.uk

1585
War with Spain declared. Plymouth became Naval Base.

1585
Sir Richard Grenville departs Bideford for the New World, to colonize Virginia.

Various Coastal Views of Westward Ho!

1587
The first engraved plan of Exeter produced by Remigius
Hogenberg after John Hooker

1588 Jul 20. The Spanish Armada sighted off Plymouth
(131 ships with 17,000 armed soldiers
and 180 Catholic priests)

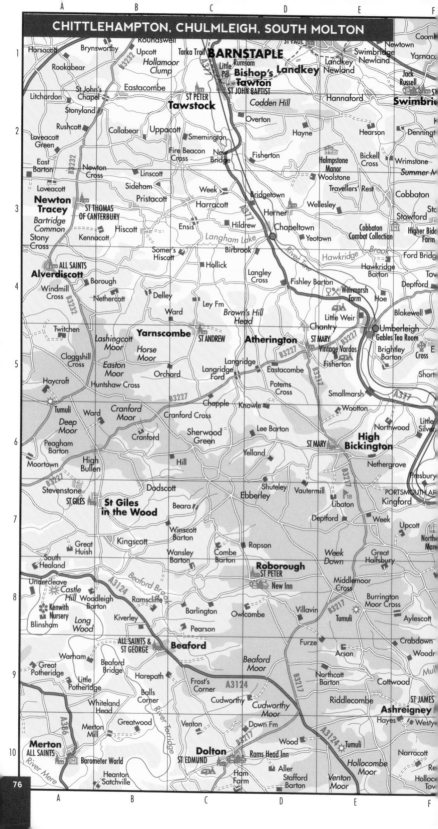

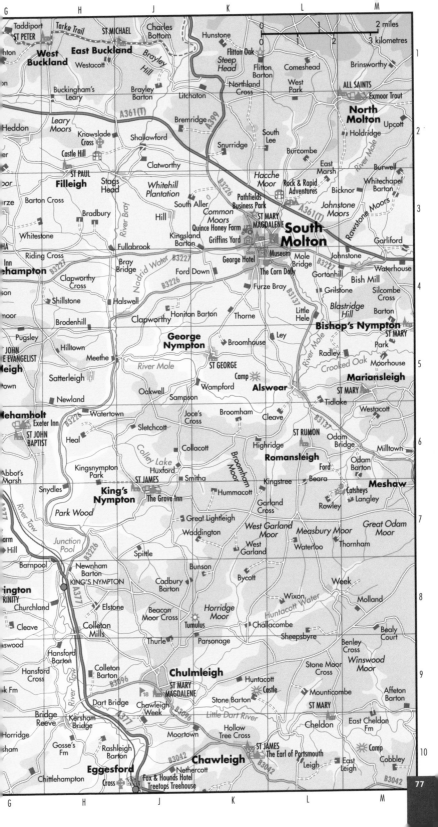

Treetops Treehouse, Eggesford

SOUTH MOLTON

Busy Market town for North East Devon, and route centre for Exmoor. Wide main street. C18 Guildhall and Museum. As the town's prosperity grew from the wool and cloth trade in the C17, and as several of the mills were powered by the River Mole, processing wool and corn, the town became an important thoroughfare for merchants, gaining a riotous reputation employing some 500 Ladies of Ill Repute (see Museum). Sheep Fair - end Aug. E/C W. (L3)

SPECIAL PLACES TO VISIT IN THE TOWN...

Quince Honey Farm, North Rd. Britain's largest honey farm and home to a million bees. Unique exhibition of observation hives. Honey and beeswax products for

Castle Hill

1591
Men of Bideford fight fifteen French galleons off Flores,
for fifteen hours.

1593
Sir Richard Hawkins departs Plymouth for South
America, and ultimate disaster off Chile.

sale. Open daily Apr-Oct from 9. (K3) 01769 572401 quincehoneyfarm.co.uk

South Molton Museum, The Guildhall. Glimpses into the domestic life, trades, industry, mining and farming of the town and district's past. Open late Mar to early Nov M & Tu 10.30-4. Th & Sa 10.30-1. (L3) 01769 572951 southmoltonmuseum.org

LIGHT BITES...

Corn Dolly, 115a East Street. Real tea shop providing breakfast, light lunches and cream teas. Home baked fare. Gifts. Open daily. (K4)

Griffin's Yard, North St. An organic and natural foods emporium, as well as a Cafe serving lunch, teas and coffees. 01769 572372 Also, KK Design, a personal service creating curtains, clothing and soft funishings. 01769 572299. Open M-Sa from 9am. (K3) griffinsyard.co.uk

SPECIAL PLACES TO VISIT...

Castle Hill. Grade 1 Palladian mansion built in 1730 by Hugh Fortescue, Lord Clinton, as his family home is set in 5,500 acres of prime agricultural land. Home of the late Sir John Fortescue, historian and the Queen's Librarian at Windsor Castle and good friend to Henry Williamson who lived

for seven years at Shallowford where he wrote Salar the Salmon and raised many children. Now the home of the Earl and Countess of Arran. House open by appointment only, Gardens all year Su-F from 11am. An impressive sight from the road. Public access is permitted along two paths from Feb-Sept inclusive, starting from Filleigh Village Hall (3/4 hour) and Filleigh Sawmill (1/2 hour). (H2) 01598 760336 castlehilldevon.co.uk

Cobbaton Combat Collection. British and Canadian fighting vehicles of World War 11. Field guns, radios and other equipment. Home Front section, Women's Land Army. Children's play area. Militaria shop. Open Su-F Apr-Oct & Su July-Aug, Nov-Mar M-F, 10-5. (E3) 01769 540740 cobbatoncombat.co.uk

SPECIAL PLACES TO STAY...

Catsheys, Nr Romansleigh. A quite stunning rural hideaway brimming with artwork; sculptures, ceramics and paintings, overlook eleven acres of gardens and woodland. Massive beds with modern bathrooms. Light, airy spaces furnished with pieces handcrafted by your host. Bookings by prior arrangement only. (L7) 01769 550580 catsheys.co.uk

Fox & Hounds Hotel, Eggesford. Former Victorian

Coaching Inn set amidst the beautiful Taw Valley. Roaring fires and comfy leather sofas will relax you. The bedrooms have been refurbished. Fishing rights on five beats; Ghillie services and fly fishing tuition available. Day tickets available to non-residents. Bar foods and restaurant. The **Treetops Treehouse** set within a 250-year old oak tree may be more your thing. It's over-the-top (sic) luxury. No dogs. All set within the North Devon Biosphere Reserve and the River Taw, below. (J10) 01769 580345 foxandhoundshotel.co.uk

Higher Biddacott Farm, Chittlehampton. B&B in C12 farm house. Large bedroom with 1680 pargetted ceiling by the famous Abbot Brothers. Jonathan Waterer is a Devon-style Horse Whisperer, training Heavy and Light Horses. Wagon tours. Pre-arranged Dinner available. Also, a Self-catering cottage and a Wildlife Trail. (F3) 01769 540222 heavy-horses.net

Northcote Manor, Nr Burrington. C18 manor house set in 20-acres of mature woodland with outstanding views overlooking the Taw Valley. Classic English Country House hotel provides luxury and comfort at a relaxed pace. Great bathrooms and big beds. Boasts one of North Devon's finest restaurants (open to non-residents for lunch and dinner). If your conversation is at a loss then admire the Murals of monks past. (F7) 01769 560501 northcotemanor.co.uk

Higher Biddacott Farm

ARTS & CRAFT INTERESTS...

Chittlehampton Pottery. Roger Cockram creates handmade pots and jars based on a Natural World theme. Open M-F 10-1, 2.25-5 (F4) 01769 540420 rogercockramceramics.co.uk

COUNTRYSIDE INTERESTS...

Higher Hacknell Organic Farm. An award-winning food supplier farming organically since 1985; South Devon beef, Lleyn and Lenx Texel lamb, pork sausages. Food Boxes (and Ready Meals) to satisfy all carnivores. (F7) 01769 560909 higherhacknell.co.uk

Rock and Rapid Adventures South Molton. Indoor climbing wall and outdoor activities galore; rock climbing, coasteering, swimming, caving, jumping, survival training and more, all with qualified instructors. Café. Outdoor gear/hire shop. Open daily 10 til late. (L3) 01769 309003 rockandrapidadventures.co.uk

WHERE TO EAT, DRINK & BE MERRY...

The Earl of Portsmouth, Chawleigh. Leading dining pub who pioneered sourcing its materials from the local farms. Soups and bread made on premises. Specials may include Aberdeen Angus braised steaks, lambs liver and bacon. (K10) 01769 580204 earlofportsmouth.co.uk

The Grove Inn, Kings Nympton. Gracious and friendly hospitality awaits you in this traditional country pub serving fine Devon cuisine and real ales. No wonder we keep hearing encouraging reports about this dining pub. (J7) 01769 580406 thegroveinn.co.uk

The New Inn, Roborough. A traditional C16 thatched Inn bestows a warm hospitality and a snug ambience. Good, wholesome pub-grub. (D8) 01805 603247 thenewinnroborough.co.uk

Vintage Vardos, Fisherton Farm. Have you ever wished to really, yes really, get away from it all? To immerse yourself in nature, the sound of birdsong, a trickling stream, waving trees, and a firepit to cook and to eat like never before. Fresh lamb and beef supplied from this farm. To sleep, to dream...to rid yourself of stress and the outside world. For groups only. Sleeps 8 in luxury mode (or 12/14 cosy mode) in vintage gypsy vans. 07977 535233 fishertonfarm.com

The Rams Head Inn, Dolton. This is a welcome new hostelry on the North Devon stage. Their young chef was trained by a Michelin-starred chef, and the food is an exponent of this. The decor is a kaleidoscope of form. The B&B is luxurious. (A10) 01805 804255 theramsheadinn.co.uk

Weirmarsh Farm Restaurant, Nr Umberleigh. Popular and amazing value-for-money restaurant. 5 course dinner for around £28.50. per person. Advance booking essential (by at least two weeks). Special room for parties of 8 or more. Licensed. Open F & Sa. (E4) 01769 560338 Yurt available for Glamping adventures. weirmarshfarmrestaurant.co.uk

The Lake, Castle Hill

Vintage Vardos, Atherington ss

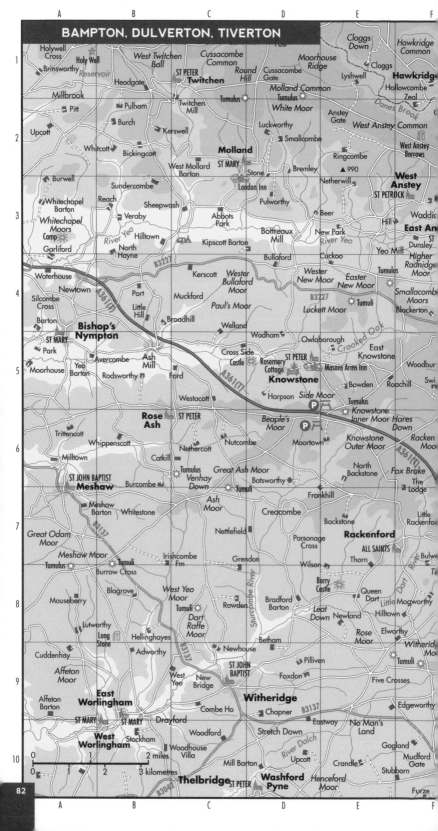

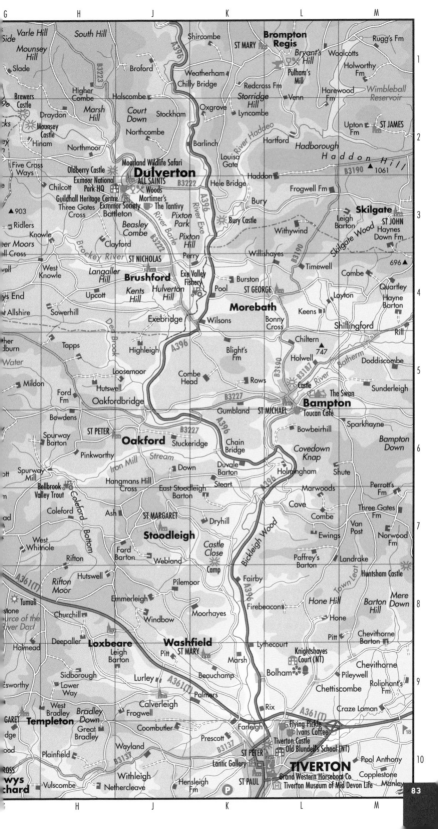

BAMPTON

A natural route centre set in a sheltered wooded valley. Fine C13 and C16 church and Heritage Centre (that should be your first stop-off) with Saxon Cross. A thriving wool centre in the C18 and by the 1800s the largest sheepfair in the South West, for over 14,000 sheep were sold at Bampton Fair. Today, the town is famous for the annual October Fair, on the last Thursday. In the 1880s it became, for the next one hundred years, the famous Bampton Pony Fair trading in Exmoor ponies. The locality is rich in wildlife encouraged by the conservation policy in the town.

LIGHT BITES...

The **Toucan Café** on pretty **Brook Street** has had a loyal following for many years. Open M-Sa 9-5 for breakfast and light lunches, and across the road is **Lucy Lou's** for homemade cakes and coffee. I am not impressed by awards for best pub or best cafe but **The Swan** behind the **Churchyard** has been in the news, of late, as a Pub of the Year. It has a mixed clientele; rustic artisans pop in for an after work drink, or two followed by a more refined crowd in search of fine dining and good-value pub-grub. Bampton has been crying out for such a venue.

DULVERTON

Often described as the gateway to southern Exmoor but it is much more than that. It's a thriving community with all sorts of buildings and interesting shops, plus antiques, galleries, tearooms, pubs and restaurants. An old-fashioned country town happy with its lot. The National Park have their HQ here, and there are easy riverside walks beside the River Barle. It has the best shooting and fishing on Exmoor, the Barle is well stocked with Brown Trout and Salmon. The church tower dates from the C12, and inside are memorials to the colourful Sydenham family, and stained glass provided by the founder of

the YMCA, George Williams. Nearby is Pixton Park, former home of the Herbert family (Earls of Carnarvon) whom the Catholic novelist and travel writer Evelyn Waugh married into, and the Aclands of Killerton Park and Selworthy. (J3)

Guildhall Heritage & Arts Centre, Off Fore St.
Exhibitions of local artists and craftsmen, plus Touring Exhibitions. Open daily East-Oct 10-4.30. (J3) 07969 243887

The Exmoor Society, 34 High Street.
Their purpose is to protect and fight to maintain Exmoor's heaths, grass moors, ancient woodlands, tranquil landscapes and uncluttered skylines. They organise walks, talks, field visits and more. Independent of the National Park. Open daily. (J3) 01398 323335 exmoorsociety.com

WHERE TO STAY...

Northcombe Camping Barns. (J2)

ARTS & CRAFTS INTEREST...

Lantic Gallery, 38 Gold Street.
Gallery displaying a variety of artists and craftsmen; John Maltby, Les Grimshaw... and constantly changing exhibs. Open M-Sa 9.30-5. (L10) 01884 259888 lanticgallery.co.uk

Pulhams Mill, Nr Brompton Regis.
Solid timber furniture in English hardwoods, and hand painted English china and tiles with rural scenes. Tuition on-hand. Tea room and gardens. Barn Shop a showcase of British arts and crafts. Open M-Sa 10-5, Su 12.30-5. (L1) 01398 371366 pulhamsmill.co.uk

COUNTRYSIDE INTERESTS...

Bellbrook Valley Trout Fishery.
If you seek peace, wildlife and are of a mind to catch trout then visit this isolated haven. There are 7 lakes fed from 2 streams in a 40-acre valley. Fly fishing for Rainbows. Day fishing. Tuition available. Open all year. (H6) 01398 351292 bellbrookfishery.co.uk

Exe Valley Fishery, Exebridge.
Rainbow Trout are reared here where you will find a Farm shop and fly fishing lakes. Fly fishing courses. Open daily 8-6. (K4) 01398 323008 exevalleyfishery.co.uk

Wimbleball Lake.
A 370-acre reservoir housing the Outdoor & Active Centre that organises fishing, dinghy sailing, camping, waymarked walks, windsurfing, a nature reserve and trail. Circular cycle route with cycle hire. Café. Open daily, all year. Not accessible by public transport. (M1) 01398 371460

LIGHT BITES...

Dulverton is awash with pubs and tearooms. If in need of lunch and ale I always head for **Woods Bar & Restaurant, 4 Bank Square**. Genial, cosy and a relaxed ambience pervades this pub decorated with old prints. A log fire, British cooking with a French bias is all-enticing. (J3) 01398 324007 woodsdulverton.co.uk

Looking for coffee, cake and a newspaper, or walking map to tramp **Exmoor's** paths, you better start at **The Tantivy**. Breakfast is from 9.00. If a Welsh Rarebit is your salvation head down the **High Street** to **Mortimer's** where you can get a cream tea, and more. 01398 323850 mortimersfood.co.uk

WHERE TO EAT & DRINK...

London Inn, Molland.
Now thankfully back under new ownership. The tell-tale signs are positive and the Sunday lunches a treat. How a country pub in a rural idyll should be. 01769 550269 londoninnmolland.co.uk

Masons Arms Inn, Knowstone.
A thatched village inn with a small, cosy bar leading to the restaurant. Mark Dodson's cuisine has been lauded with awards. It will empty your pockets of change, and arrest your bank balance. The Dining Room extension has interesting murals on the ceilings,

Parish Church of St Peter, Tiverton

and fine countryside views. Masterclasses organized. Food Station. Booking advised. Just off the Two Moors Way. Open Tu-Sa 12-2.30, 6-11 pm. Su 12-2.30 pm. (E5) 01398 341231 masonsarmsdevon.co.uk

WHERE TO STAY...

Bulworthy Project, Rackenford. Stay in an off-the-grid cabin and experiment with low impact living. Forage for wild food and listen out for badgers, foxes and owls. No mains electricity. Barbeque Café Evenings, Courses and Events. (G8) 0759 4569441 bulworthyproject.org.uk

Rosemary Cottage B&B. Ideally situated for footsore folk in need of rest after a long trek. Two bedrooms. Book in advance. (E5) 01398 341510 rosemary-cottage.co.uk

TIVERTON

The Market Town for the Exe Valley, and main centre for the north-east corner of Devon. The major attractions being the imposing Castle, Old Blundell's School and the notable Parish Church next to the Castle. There is a Town Trail leading you to the most interesting aspects of this small, industrial town. The major employer, the Heathcoat lace factory, in operation since 1816 has a store selling all manner of lace and fabrics. The Luddites had forced John Heathcoat, inventor of the bobbinet lace machine, to leave Loughborough, so he headed south to friendly Devonshire. The Railway Station at Tiverton Parkway is a conduit for all rail travellers heading out into North/Mid-Devon

and Exmoor. Sadly, the town is not blessed with a surplus of eating emporia. However, the Flying Pickle at 40 Gold Street is where you can have a splendid repast, a deli and café of impressive heights. 01884 242661 flyingpickle.co.uk. Further down the street towards Tesco, on the corner opposite the ancient build that was Blundells, a Vietnamese noodle bar, Pho Nam opens 11-3, 6-9. (L10) phonam.co.uk

Ivan's Coffee at The Bike Shop on Leat Street (north side) is not to be missed. Enthusiasm for two-wheels and the coffee bean hath no bounds here. Cakes and brownies to set you up. 07796 1228057 vans-coffee.com

SPECIAL PLACES TO VISIT...

Grand Western Canal Country Park, Canal Hill. The canal meanders through eleven miles of beautiful Devon countryside. On either side a rich diversity of wildlife; wildflowers, plants, hedgerows, fields and small woodland. The towpath provides easy walking with good car parking and picnic sites available. The Canal today (Tiverton-Lowdeswells) is a remnant section of the intended route between Bristol and the English Channel. Work began in 1810, was completed in 1814, with the northern section completed in 1838. However, it was unprofitable and closed in 1869. (L10) 01884 254072

Grand Western Horseboat Co., The Wharf. The enchantment and tranquility of travel, at a slow pace; a painted barge pulled by heavy horses mingles with nature. Boat hire. Café-Bar. Picnics. Open daily Apr/East to end Oct. Reservations advised: (L10) 01884 253345 tivertoncanal.co.uk

Knightshayes Court (NT). Victorian Gothic house designed by two contrasting architects. Richly decorated interior. Paintings. Garden of interest at all seasons; specimen trees, formal terraces, unique topiary, rare shrubs, 'Garden in the

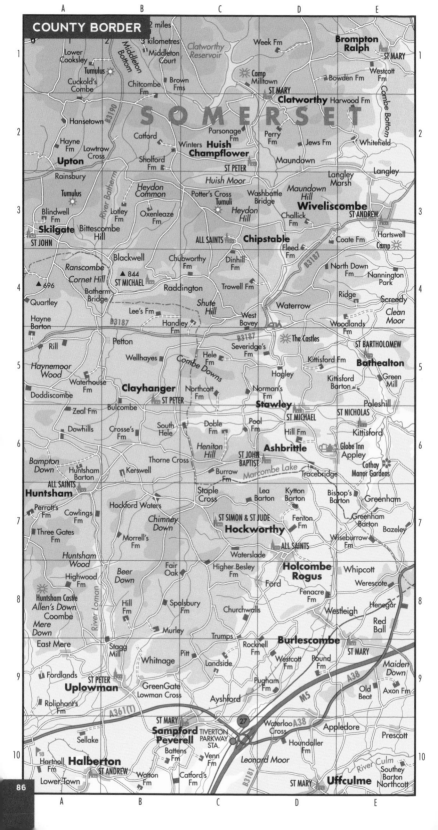

Wood'. Plant sales. Restaurant and NT shop. Parkland open all year, dawn to dusk. House/ Garden open daily from 10. (L9)01884 254665 nationaltrust.org.uk

Parish Church of St Peter. A grand building built from the proceeds of the wool trade. The intricate detail of sailing ships cut into the white limestone of the South Porch was the gift of the wool merchant, John Greenway in 1517. Inside, Tomb Memorials to the rich burghers of the town; George Slee and John Waldron. (L10)

Tiverton Castle. Historic fortress of Henry 1 built in 1106. Fine medieval gatehouse and tower. Romantic ruins of chapel, solar and curtain walls. Fine Civil War armoury, old wall and new gardens. Open East Su to end Oct, Su, Th & BH Ms, 2.30-5.30. Other times for parties of 12 or more. (L10) 01884 253200 tivertoncastle.com

Tiverton Museum of Mid Devon Life, Beck's Square. An award-winning museum that depicts local industries, a railway gallery, Victorian laundry, Great Western Canal relics, wartime history and model aircraft. TIC (01884 230878). Open Feb-Dec 21 M-F 10.30-4.30, Sa 10-1. (L10) 01884 256295 tivertonmuseum.org.uk

VILLAGES OF INTEREST...

Sampford Peverell. Fine church built by Sir Hugh Peverell, Lord of the Manor from 1241 to 1296. His monument lies on the north side of the Chancel. Restored in the mid C19.

WHERE TO EAT, DRINK & BE MERRY...

Globe Inn, Appley. Hidden away down narrow Somerset lanes is this popular C16 Freehouse with cosy, little rooms. Superb prints of ships. No dogs. Open Tu-Su. (D6)

COTHAY MANOR GARDENS

This is a magical garden of 12-acres laid out in the 1920s, which was redesigned and replanted within the original framework of the yew hedges. The Manor was built in 1480 and has, amazingly, remained virtually untouched. No dogs. Open first Su in April to end Sept Tu, W, Th, Su & BHs 11-5. House by appointment. (E6) 01823 672283 cothaymanor.co.uk

Three Views of Cothay Manor Gardens ss

1628
Sir Ferdinando Gorges establishes colony of
New Plymouth.

1638
Lighting strike over Widecombe church kills four of
the congregation.

87

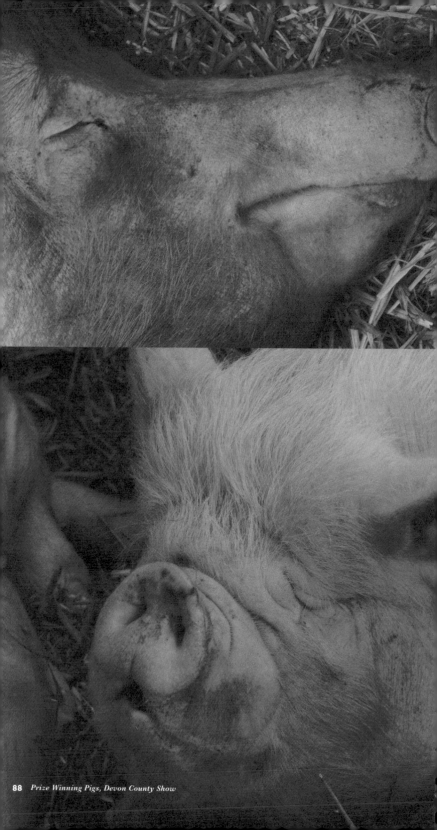

Prize Winning Pigs, Devon County Show

This stretch of country belongs to a Devon often neglected and forgotten. An undulating, pastoral landscape lying between the coastal resorts and medieval trade routes of North Devon, and to the south, the great expanse of Dartmoor.

Here are isolated villages and hamlets, sometimes made up of a single or secondary homestead originally built from the local earth, commonly known as cob. Connected by narrow country lanes set between high hedgerows, that with time, have grown in height and width. Built up by peasant farmers long since dead, who cleared the stone from the fields, a tapestry of a thousand natural colours; greens, reds, oranges and mauves.

Is this the rural idyll of an England long forgotten, and sought for, in glossy magazines? Not if you live and work here. The 45 parishes that surround Holsworthy and Hatherleigh have created the brand "Ruby Country" to market their towns following the disastrous foot n' mouth epidemic of 2001. The name is taken from the indigenous breed of cattle, Ruby Red Devon; a handsome beast, given to fine cuts of meat.

It was this Devon, in isolation, that so attracted the poet, Ted Hughes. He lived the last third of his life in the parish of North Tawton. Close to nature, he wrote about the natural world, as he saw it, and fished the upper reaches of the Taw and Torridge, for salmon and sea trout.

These communities have witnessed a great change since the development of the A30 and A36, now largely inhabited by commuters from Exeter and Taunton. Yet, despite this, there are still those whose lifestyle remains unchanged, where the major social event of the week is Market Day, or the village cricket match. The church, pub and village store continue to be the focal points of village life.

Mid Devon can be a charming place to visit. You will find that people have more time for you. Just watch the locals of Hatherleigh walk about their daily business, forever stopping to talk with their friends and acquaintances. You too will come across friendly pubs and churches offering solitude and fine craftsmanship.

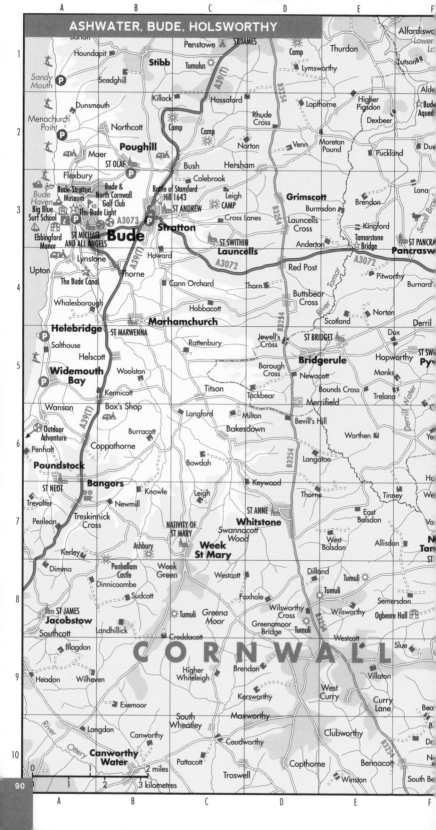

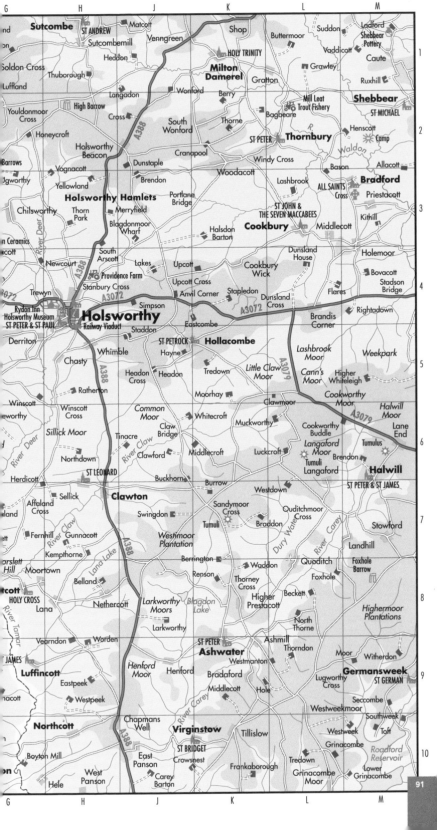

Grid references (top and bottom): G, H, J, K, L, M

Grid references (right side): 1, 2, 3, 4, 5, 6, 7, 8, 9, 10

Sutcombe
ST ANDREW
Matcott
Venngreen
Shop
Suddon
Ladford
Shebbear
Pottery
Buttermoor
Vaddicott
Caute
Sutcombemill
Heddon
HOLY TRINITY
Grawley
Soldon Cross
Thuborough
Milton
Damerel
Gratton
Ruxhill
Luffland
Langadon
Wonford
Berry
Mill Leat
Trout Fishery
Shebbear
ST MICHAEL
Youldonmoor
Cross
High Barrow
Cross
South
Wonford
Thorne
Bagbeare
Waldon R.
Honeycroft
ST PETER
Thornbury
Henscott
Camp
Barrows
Holsworthy
Beacon
Cranapool
Windy Cross
Bason
Allacott
Vognacott
Dunstaple
Woodacott
Lashbrook
Bradford
Jgworthy
Yellowland
Brendon
ALL SAINTS
Cross
Priestacott
Chilsworthy
Holsworthy Hamlets
Merryfield
Portlane
Bridge
ST JOHN &
THE SEVEN MACCABEES
Kithill
Thorn
Park
Blagdonmoor
Wharf
Halsdon
Barton
Cookbury
Middlecott
n Ceramics
cott
Newcourt
South
Arscott
Lakes
Upcott
Cookbury
Wick
Dunsland
House
Holemoor
Providence Farm
Stanbury Cross
Upcott Cross
Bovacott
Stadson
Bridge
Trewyn
Anvil Corner
Stapledon
Dunsland
Cross
Flares
Rightadown
Rydon Inn
Holsworthy Museum
ST PETER & ST PAUL
Holsworthy
Railway Viaduct
Simpson
Eastcombe
A3072
Brandis
Corner
Derriton
Staddon
ST PETROCK
Hollacombe
Lashbrook
Moor
Weekpark
Chasty
Whimble
Hayne
Tredown
Little Claw
Moor
Cann's
Moor
Higher
Whiteleigh
Ratherton
Headon
Cross
Headon
Moorhay
Clawmoor
Cookworthy
Moor
Halwill
Moor
Winscott
eworthy
Winscott
Cross
Common
Moor
Whitecroft
Muckworthy
Cookworthy
Buddle
Lane
End
Sillick Moor
Tinacre
Claw
Bridge
Middlecroft
Luckcroft
Langaford
Moor
Tumuli
Langaford
Tumulus
Brendon
Northdown
Clawford
ST LEONARD
Buckhorn
Burrow
Westdown
Halwill
ST PETER & ST JAMES
Herdicott
Sellick
Clawton
Swingdon
Sandymoor
Cross
Tumuli
Braddon
Ouditchmoor
Cross
Stowford
Affaland
Cross
Fernhill
Gunnacott
Westmoor
Plantation
Berrington
Waddon
Quoditch
Foxhole
Landhill
Kempthorne
Renson
Thorney
Cross
Beckett
Foxhole
Barrow
Higher
Moortown
Belland
Nethercott
Larkworthy
Moors
Blagdon
Lake
Higher
Prestacott
North
Thorne
Highermoor
Plantations
HOLY CROSS
Lana
Larkworthy
Ashmill
Vearndon
Worden
ST PETER
Ashwater
Westmanton
Thorndon
Moor
Witherdon
JAMES
Luffincott
Eastpeek
Henford
Moor
Henford
Bradaford
Middlecott
Hole
Lugworthy
Cross
Germansweek
ST GERMAN
nacott
Westpeek
Seccombe
Northcott
Chapmans
Well
Virginstow
Tillislow
Westweekmoor
Westweek
Southweek
Toft
Boyton Mill
ST BRIDGET
Crowsnest
Frankaborough
Tredown
Grinacombe
Roadford
Reservoir
Hele
West
Panson
East
Panson
Carey
Barton
Grinacombe
Moor
Lower
Grinacombe

Rivers and features: River Deer, River Tamar, River Claw, River Carey, Dury Water, Lana Lake

Roads: A388, A3072, A3079

91

View South towards Thornbury

HOLSWORTHY

Market town with a thriving cattle market, and Pannier Market every Wednesday in the Market Square. Be sure to visit "St Peter's Fair" in early July to catch the crowning of the "Pretty Maid". The centre of a rural idyll; scattered farms and hamlets, rolling, green pastures unintimidated by our crazy world. Hereabouts is real Devon for you. Unsophisticated, quiet, miles from the nearest motorway. A haven of peace. (H4)

SPECIAL PLACES OF INTERESTS...

Holsworthy Museum, Manor Offices. Housed in a C17 Parsonage. Themed rooms feature the area's heritage, traditions and bygones of rural life. Open M-F 11-1, (W to 3.30). (H4) 01409 259337

Providence Farm & Organic Farm Shop, Crosspark Cross. Full range of organic poultry, eggs, pork, beef and lamb produce. Open W-Sa 9-5.30. Tavistock Pannier Market every Sa 2nd/4th of month 9-4. (H4) 01409 254421 providencefarm.co.uk

Mill Leat Trout Fishery. Fresh and smoked trout. Children's fishing ('Catch your own') in two lakes and 1/2 mile of River Waldron 9-5.30, (dusk fly fishing). Three self-catering cottages. (L2) 01409 261426 millleat.co.uk

Shebbear Pottery. Clive Bowen is one of the country's leading ceramicists. He studied painting and etching before taking up an apprenticeship. He makes (often large) wood-fired earthenware pots in a variety of colours and styles. (M1) 01409 281271 clivebowen.co.uk

Tamar Lakes. Reservoirs in remote country near Tamar's source. Sailing, canoeing, lakeside walks and windsurfing. Fly fishing in upper lake. Lower lake has coarse fishing, bird sanctuary and hide. Camping. Shop and refreshments. (F1) 01288 321712 outdoorandactive. uk.com/location/upper-tamar-lake

ARTS & CRAFT INTEREST...

Mullin Ceramics. Studio and gallery showing variety of handmade ceramics. Self-catering cottage to let. Open daily, 10-6. (G3) 01409 253589

The Rydon Inn, Rydon Hill. Take the Bude Road out of Holsworthy. Inside, the barn-like wood construction based on a Devon longhouse glows with warmth. You can lunch or dine overlooking the lake and nourish yourself with better than average pub grub. They claim it's a dining-pub. It's certainly the place to eat, hereabouts. (G4) 01409 259444 rydon-inn.com

1643
Sep 5. Articles of surrender were signed and the Royalists took control of Exeter after a siege.

1643
Tavistock a Royalist stronghold.

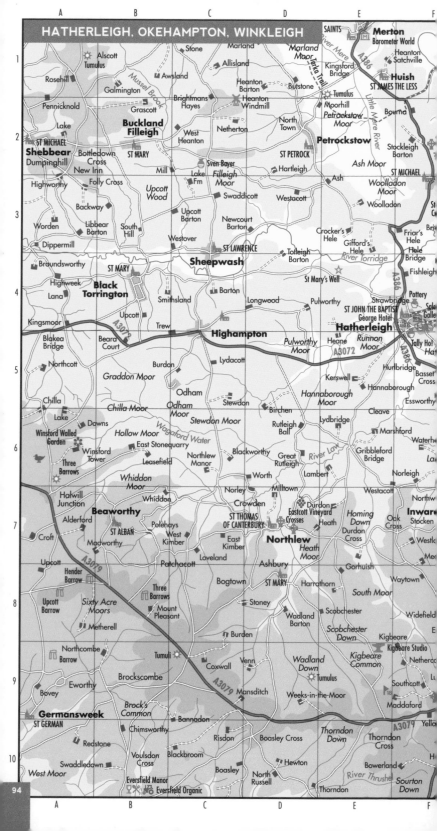

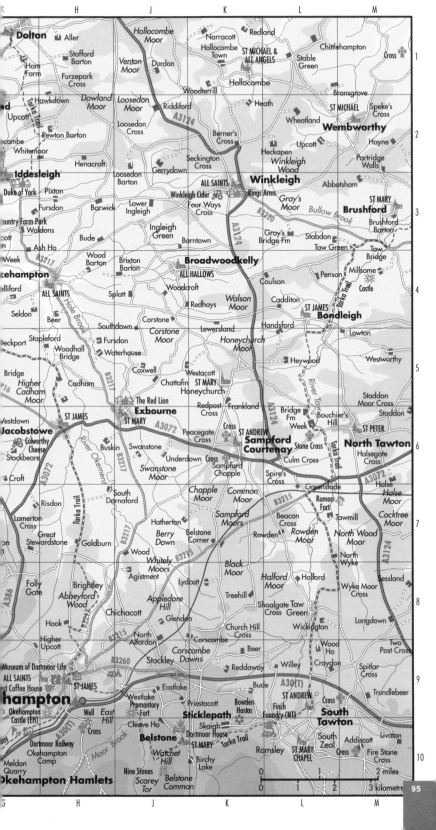

HATHERLEIGH

An ancient market town of thatched and cob cottages nestling in a rural landscape shaped by a thousand years of settlers and farming. This must be one of the most delightful little towns in Devon. The local community realize the privilege of living here and are always active in promoting regular events, from the Arts Festival in July to the Carnival in November. Artwork is exhibited about the town. The Livestock Market is famous. (E4) hatherleigh.net

SPECIAL PLACES TO VISIT IN AND AROUND HATHERLEIGH...

Hatherleigh Market. This is quite an attraction, from the Monday auction of ewes and lambs to the sales of live poultry (and furniture) on Tuesdays. Monthly horse sales. café. Phone for details: 01837 810496 (E4) vickshatherleighmarket.co.uk

Hatherleigh Methodist Chapel, High St. The beautiful stained glass was supplied by the monks of Buckfast Abbey. (F4)

Hatherleigh Pottery, 20 Market Street. A working pottery for 25-years with showroom displaying the work of Jane Payne and Michael Taylor, plus textiles and original prints from local craftsmen. Open Easter to New Year Tu-Sa 10-5. (F4) 01837 810624 hatherleighpottery.co.uk

Salar Gallery, 18/20 Bridge St. The Devon landscape and its occupants provide a never-ending source of inspiration for the painters, sculptors, photographers and craftspeople who show their work here. Regular exhibitions. Open Tu-Sa 10-1,2-5. Closed W. (F4) 01837 810940 salargallery.co.uk

St John the Baptist. Built at the top of the High Street its fine position provides splendid views. Early Norman church with C15 additions. In 1990 the medieval wooden spire collapsed during a great storm causing extensive damage and gaining national press coverage. Some interesting churchyard monuments. (F4)

War Horse Country Farm Park, Parsonage Farm. It was this valley and surrounding countryside that inspired Michael Morpurgo to write his book and play. WW1 Horse Exhibitions, Farm Trail, Kids play Area, A History of Farming 100 years ago. Cream teas. Open daily East-Sept 2-6. (G3) 01837 810318 warhorsevalley.co.uk

WHERE TO EAT, DRINK & BE MERRY...

Tally Ho! Country Inn, 14 Market Street. Traditional pub with oak beams and log fires serving home cooked food and real ales. Micro-Brewery. Beer garden. Open all day. B & B. (F4) 01837 810306

The George Hotel, Market Street. This medieval C15 Inn, that had been a sanctuary for monks, a brewery, law court and coaching inn burnt down a few years ago. What we now see is an extraordinary resurrection to its former glory. A hostelry of the old-school. One can imagine coaches coming through the arch to the inner courtyard. It is an Inn and a comfortable hotel. Coffees, bar food and Daily Specials. Pizzas, too. (F4) 01837 811755 thegeorgeinnhatherleigh.com

NORTH TAWTON

Interesting little town formerly the home of the poet, the late Ted Hughes where he had a farm nearby. More recently its claim to fame, as the setting for the TV series "Jam and Jerusalem". An elaborate clock stands in the Town Square to mark the 1877 jubilee. Interesting church, closed when I visited but there are remains of a Saxon or Roman cross, lovely bench ends and some C15 stained glass to look at if you have the opportunity. (M6)

WHERE TO EAT, DRINK & BE MERRY...

Duke of York, Iddesleigh. A friendly welcome awaits you in this C15 Devon Longhouse. Old photos, bank notes, low ceilings, small rooms and a large fireplace provide a fine ambience. Simple, honest food can be eaten in the bar and Dining Room, and a selection of real ales to succour the palate. The War Horse story has its origins from tales told in front of the fire by Wilfred Ellis to Michael Morpurgo. B&B. (G3) 01837 810253 dukeofyorkdevon.co.uk

Red Lion Inn, Exbourne. A traditional real ale pub (no lagers) of C16 origins where a sincere welcome greets you, and popular as a diversion just off the Tarka Trail for cyclists and walkers. Basic pub grub. (J6) 01837 851551 theredlionexbourne.co.uk

George Hotel, Hatherleigh

1645
Exeter besieged by Parliamentarians.

1646
Fairfax defeated Lord Hopton at Torrington.

Okehampton Castle

OKEHAMPTON

A finely situated town on the northern edge of Dartmoor, and well situated for exploring the "High Tors" and West Devon. The buildings are statuesque and remind one of the bygone Victorian age of steam and engineering excellence. Of late, has become a centre for family cycling and mountain biking on Dartmoor. The Granite Way starts off from the former Railway Station and YHA (Adventure Okehampton) and was extended in 2013 to expand the route to 18 miles of traffic-free cycling. Ideal for small families, or jaded city dwellers in search of peace and solitude. The arrival of Waitrose (that must surely serve a vast hinterland) brought amazement and great joy to the local chattering classes.

Light Bites...

Toast Coffee House on 2-4 Market Street for your coffees, smoothies and ciabattas, as well as the Dish of the Day. Free wifi. Open M-Sa 9.30-5. (H9)
01837 54494
eattoast.co.uk

PLACES TO VISIT...

Adventure Okehampton (YHA), Klondyke Road. You can try 15 different adventure activities suitable for all ages from 5; Archery to Climbing to Kayaking to Orienteering to Raft Building, and more. Ideal for families, groups, hen and stag parties, and individuals. Accommodation. (H9)
01837 53916
adventureokehampton.com

Museum of Dartmoor Life, 3 West St. Fascinating interactive displays on 3-floors illustrates the lives, work and beliefs of Dartmoor's people across time. Tearoom, gift and craft shops. TIC. Open M-F 10.15-4.15, Sa 10.15-1. (H9)
01837 52295
museumofdartmoorlife.org.uk

Okehampton Castle (EH). Ruins of the largest castle in Devon built in the C11. The square Norman Keep is all that remains of a seat of once great power in the hands of the Courtenays, Lords of Devon before Henry Courtenay upset Henry VIII, and subsequently lost his head. Its strategic position is, in effect, questionable. Open daily Apr-Oct 10-dusk. (G9) 01837 52844
english-heritage.org.uk

SPECIAL PLACES TO VISIT...

Bowden Hostas. The National Collection of over 1,000 hybrid Hostas in a 1-acre garden for 30-years. Chelseas RHS Gold Medal winners. Plant sales. Open Days. Visitors welcome. (K10) Cleave House, Sticklepath 01837 840989
www.bowdenhostas.com

Finch Foundry (NT). The last (C19) water powered-edge forge in England. 3 working water-wheels. Giant trip hammer and shears. Demonstrations of working machinery. Open daily Early-Mar to Oct 11-5, (L9)
01837 840046
nationaltrust.org.uk

Svend Bayer at Kigbeare Studio & Gallery. A much respected potter by his fellow Ceramicists. He produces wood-fired stoneware pots of great grandeur, deep, rich colours, and many are Anagama (cave kiln) inspired. Open daily in summer season. Be prepared for a long, grubby lane. (F9) 01409 231282

Winkleigh Cider Co., Hatherleigh Rd. Traditional cider pressed here since 1916. The apples collected from local orchards are fermented, and matured, in giant oak vats. Shop sells a range of ciders. Open M-Sa 9-5. (K3)
01837 835560
winkleighcider.co.uk

Winsford Walled Garden. A Victorian garden designed as an inspiration for artists and restored in the C21. A must-see for all garden enthusiasts. Open daily June-Sept W-Sa & Su BHs 10-5. Car park. Disabled access. Art Gallery of Dugald Stark's work (A6)
01409 221477
winsfordwalledgarden.org.uk

COUNTRYSIDE INTERESTS...

Culworthy Cheese, Stockbeare Farm. For 25-years hand-made cheeses in many varieties have bdeen made here. Milk sourced from the local farms. Beware of rough pot-holed track. (G6) 01837 810587
curworthycheese.co.uk

Eastcott Vineyard. A small 6-acre winery that has achieved remarkable success with their Sparkling and White Wines. 2-hour tours of the vineyard. Shop. Open June-Sept & 1/2 terms Tu-Sa, Oct-May Th-Sa, 9.30-5. Winter by appoint. (D7)
eastcottvineyard.co.uk

Eversfield Organic. 850-acre estate producing award-winning Aberdeen Angus beef, lamb, pork and chicken plus wild venison and game reared in the woods. (B10)
01837 871400
eversfieldorganic.co.uk

WHERE TO STAY...

Dartmoor House B&B, Belstone. There are 4-large and airy bedrooms. Crisp, light and fresh. Full English breakfasts. No pets/children U-12. 01837 840337
dartmoorhouse.co.uk

This is a family cycling trail, and Walkway, for 18 miles, otherwise known as National Cycle Network Route 27/Coast to Coast. The trail follows the former Okehampton to Lydford railway line and affords superb views of Dartmoor and the West Devon countryside. It crosses two spectacular viaducts at Meldon and Lake. Cycle hire is available at Okehampton's former station and the

1660
General George Monck (later Duke of Albermarle) of Great Potheridge, near Great Torrington organizes (The Restoration) the return of Charles ll from exile.

YHA 01837 53916 (and Devon
Cycle Hire & Café, Sourton
Down 01837 861141) where there
is ample parking space.

1670
Kingsbridge Grammar School built.

1682
Aug 14. Three Bideford women tried for witchcraft at
Exeter were convicted and sentenced to death.

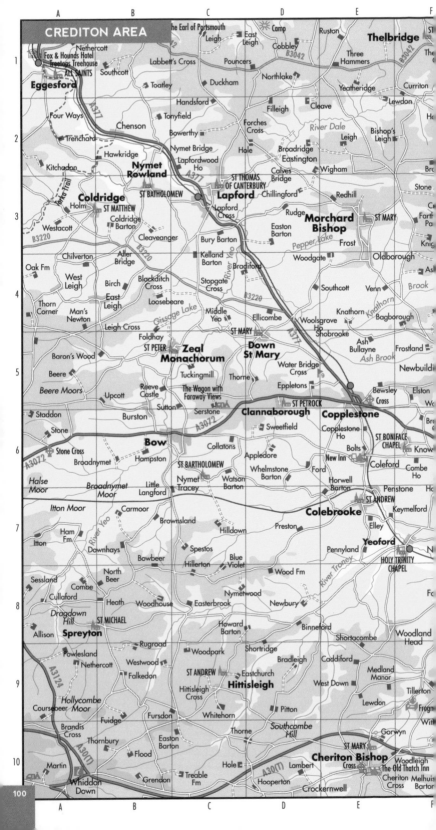

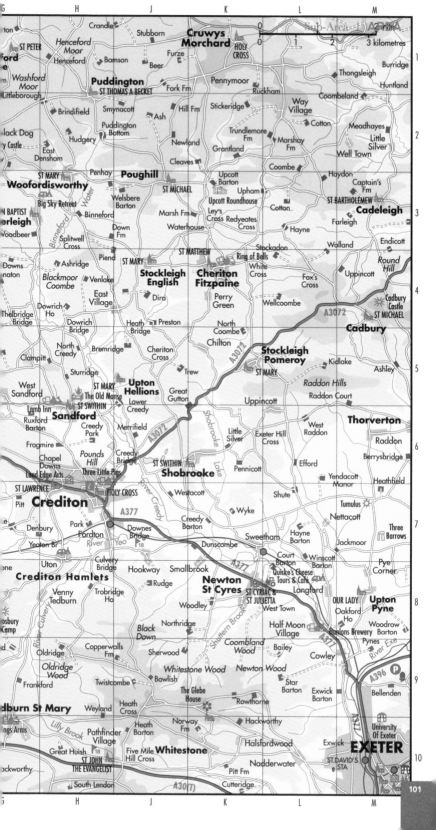

Upcott Roundhouse

CREDITON

The proximity to Exeter has created a resurgence and new dynamism in the town. Delis and eateries, as well as new galleries have recently opened. There is a welcome buzz about the town.

The ecclesiastical capital of the west before Exeter, and birthplace of St Boniface (Winfrith). There is a magnificent medieval church, but few other buildings survive due to disastrous fires. In 1743 all but a few of the C16 buildings were destroyed, also bringing ruin to many of the cloth makers and their looms. The woollen cloth industry was the major employer in the C16. Crediton serge was exported worldwide, and was very much a family industry; the children combing and carding the cloth, the mother spinning and the father weaving. In the C19, the cloth industry declined, and tanning leather became the staple industry of the town. The fertile countryside has affected the commercial output of the town. Smaller industries have thrived, and a number of trading estates are to be found on the outskirts. The soil is red, at times, crimson, and the cob walls on the farms bears witness to this phenomenen. A town trail is available to those seeking more information. (H7) crediton.co.uk

PLACES OF INTEREST...

Church of the Holy Cross. The grandest feature of this country town. A red, sandstone building dating from the 1130s. There was a church here before but it would have been made of wood, and was probably some short distance from this site. The birth of St Boniface in 680 together with records dating back to the C10 proves that a monastery was built here. As a Norman Collegiate Church it was the ecclesiastical centre of Devon until the Bishop's throne was removed to Exeter in 1050 under the command of Leofric. Apparently Exeter was easier to defend against the marauding Danes. Fine monuments survive, Tuckfield, Periam and others, and notable stained glass. The Chancel Roof, restored by John Hayward over 40 years in the Victorian Era is very fine. Small museum. St Boniface has been described as the first European. He took Christianity to Germany and the Netherlands, and is their Patron saint. He was martyred with 52 of his followers in 754 at Dokkum in Friesland which today is a place of pilgrimage and prosperity. (H7) creditonparishchurch.org.uk

Land Edge Arts, 99 High St., A gallery of Fine Art with a focus on ceramicists; Clive Bowen, Nicola Werner and painters Tim Salter. Open F & Sa from 10-5 (-2 Sa). (H7) 01363 775222 landedge.co.uk

Quicke's Cheese Tours, Newton St Cyres. 14 generations have ploughed and sown these fields, milked the cows, crafting and maturing their cheeses for you to enjoy. Two-hour tours from 9.30 M-F. Book first. Farm shop and café. (K8) 01393 851222 quickes.co.uk

Lamb Inn, Sandford ss

1685
The Devonshire Regiment raised in Bristol as the Duke of Beaufort's Musketeers to help crush Monmouth's Rebellion.

1685   Judge Jeffreys Bloody Assizes sent many West Country men to horrific executions – their bodies quartered before family and friends.

COUNTRY DINING PUBS...BREWERY...

Hanlons Brewery, Half Moon Village. Brewery tours, Friday nights welcome visitors from 5pm to drink ale and take supper in a warm atmosphere of fellowship and good cheer. Producers of 5-ales. (L8) 01392 8351160 hanlonsbrewery.com

Kings Arm, Tedburn St Mary. A traditional and substantial C16 inn offering B&B with 4-poster beds, open fireplaces, beams and a riotous history of ill-repute. (G10) 01647 61224 kingsarmsinn.co.uk

Lamb Inn, Sandford. This still remains a country pub (hostelry) despite its superb cuisine, par excellence, one of the finest in Devon that has garnered awards, galore. Lunch, dinner, a pint, or two, snacks, and a garden to linger in, or chew your baccy. Luxurious B&B. Cinema every F & W/Es. (H6) 01363 773676 lambinnsandford.co.uk

New Inn, Coleford. A C13 whitewashed cob pub in thatched village of great beauty. Good pub grub and craft beers. B&B. (E6) 01363 84242 thenewinncoleford.co.uk

Old Thatch, Cheriton Bishop.This inn typifies a picture postcard scene of an English pub. It's a Free House serving Devon ales and homespun pub-grub, and perfectly located as a stopover just off the A30. 01647 24204 theoldthatchinn.co.uk

Ring of Bells, Cheriton Fitzpaine. This is a stunning thatched Grade 11 listed Inn that provides good, Devon food simply done. Regular events: Cider & Beer Festival, Meat & Malbec Nights. B&B. 01363 860111 theringofbells.com

WHERE TO STAY...

Big Sky Retreat, Hookhill Plantation. A hand-crafted wooden yurt affording 180 degree views. Secluded in a former stone quarry, on a former grass farm. (H3) 01363 866146 big-grass.com

Frogmill B&B, Tedburn St Mary. Here you have an idyllic C16 thatched English cottage with garden, luxurious bedrooms and bathrooms, jaw-dropping food, and charming, old-fashioned hospitality. (G9) 01647 272727 frogmillbandb.co.uk

The Old Manse B&B, Sandford. A mere stone's throw from the Lamb Inn is this delightful C18 Grade 11 family home where you will be welcomed like a lost traveller and be treated to a superb breakfast. (H6) 01363 899423/07713 976578.

The Wagon With Faraway Views, Serstone Farm. As the name suggests the horizon and immediate views are stunning from this luxurious wagon. Sleeps 4-persons and a dog. Wood burner and more comforts.(C5) 01363 82366 wego.here.com

Upcott Roundhouse, Upcott Barton. Your chance to live like a Celtic King of the Dumnoni Tribe in C21 luxury. A quite magnificent thatched cob simulation of a Saxon/Viking homestead. Sleeps 9. (K3) 01363 866182 upcottroundhouse.co.uk

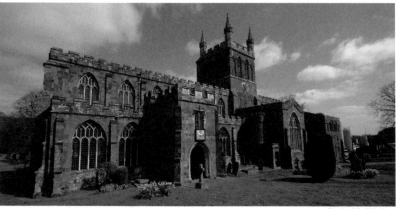

Church of the Holy Cross

1686
James 11 visits the West Country and pardons the dissenters. Later to grant freedom of worship with his Declaration of Indulgence.

103

COB

Cob has been in existence for many hundreds of years and has been the staple building material in many parts of the world. For British and European domestic (and agricultural) architecture, as well as Africa and Asia, Canada and the United States of America.

It is undergoing a strong revival, not least because of its eco-friendly properties. It is a non-pollutant, far more environmentally friendly than bricks and mortar. Recyclable? Yes. An old cob wall can be taken down and remixed with the new matter.

What is Cob? A "ready mix" of sub-soil, sand, clay, straw and water. The ingredients are stirred, or stamped upon, like porridge.

Its strengths are that it is an indigenous material, pliable, and can be sculpted and styled by hand or a spade. Its drawback, heavy and labour intensive. Walls are built on top of a plinth of stone, at least two feet in height, and two feet thick, to prevent rising damp. Preparation is slow; each handmade block (patties) is put in place, piece by piece with a pitchfork. Once a section is lumped on top of the section below it is left to dry for at least three days in summer before the next batch can be made up. Moulding can take place while the cob is still damp. Each layer is then compressed by a thwacker; a flat piece of wood. Cob is cool in summer, warm in winter. It can be protected with lime plaster and painted with a lime wash of at least six coats. This instils a breathable quality and an aesthetic appearance.

Crucial to its survival is that the top, and bottom, of the wall are protected from the elements otherwise the building will, with time, wither away. Witness the many farm sheds and buildings left to disintegrate. The natural roof covering was historically straw. Devon is a county with an abundance of cob buildings. Explore the villages to the north and west of Crediton and you will find some good examples. In some cases, the bare cob will differ in colour from red and yellow, to crimson, as per the indigenous material of its locale.

Thatch is not unique to Devon. It may just appear to be. There can be few counties in England with such a vast panoply of thatch buildings. In the following pages, we have illustrated a cross section of thatch designs to be found across Devon and Exmoor.

Many are enchantingly beautiful and blend in perfectly with their surrounding landscape. Thatch, too, is undergoing a revival and many of our Master Thatchers are now in demand overseas.

The preparation of thatch is a labour intensive process. Thatchers prepare their own materials or they buy in from East Anglia or Eastern Europe, namely Romania.

The process is as follows:-

1. Cut the harvest with the reaper and binder.

2. Let the sheaves dry in stooks (bundles) for 5 days.

3. Form a rick (a large pile) out of the sheaves.

4. Feed the sheaves into a combing machine to dry and separate (see below for details).

5. On leaving the combing machine the sheaves are trussed (tied) up into bundles ready for the thatcher.

Thatch Materials
Combed Wheat Straw. In use since the 1880s, the time a comber machine was devised which was attached to the threshing machine, hence the name. The comber machine had four drums and their purpose was to knock the corn out of the ears, and the flag or leaf of the corn out of the butts, which is the lower end of the straw. The reed then passes through the comber to be threshed. This leaves the straw in one piece and is laid out in lines, then trussed. The thatcher lays out the straw on the roof with the butts facing outwards. This makes for a tight finish similar to water reed. A wire netting is then required to prevent birds from removing the straw. Expected lifetime is 40 years, although this may be reduced if nitrogen or fertiliser gets into the straw.

Long Straw (or Devon Reed). In use since early times. The harvesting process is similar to combed straw. The difference is that the straw does not leave the threshing machine organised in lines. It is threshed into its complete length, soaked in a bed and drawn out into yelms. Sparred to the roof like combed and water reed, it will last up to 20 years.

Water Reed. In use since the Iron Age and harvested in Norfolk and the New Forest. Recommended for use on new or refurbished properties. The life span can be 50 years and does not require netting.

Apron: Single sided section of ridge to protect thatch under chimney or window

Baby: see 'Roller'

Back Filling: Laid above battens and under main thatch, used to adjust the tilt of reed or straw

Band / Bond: Twist of straw, reed withy or bramble used to tie a bundle of thatch to roof

Barge: See 'Gable'

Barge Board: Solid board used as an alternative to turned gable

Batting / Bolting: Bundle of tied, threshed straw

Biddle: Working platform hooked into thatch

Binder: Reaper for cutting standing corn

Bolder Reed: Norfolk Reed bundle containing mostly bulrush

Bottle: Tied yelm of straw for setting eave of gable

Box Gutter: Leaded gutter formed behind chimney

Brotch / Broach: See 'Spar'

Brow: The course after the eaves course

Bunch: Bundle of water reed 2' circumference, 1' above butt, usually at the tie

Butt: Thicker end of a bundle of reed or straw

Butting: Arranging the ends of the reed by dropping bundles or nitches onto board

Cheek: Side of window

Coat: Layer of entire thatch

Cock Up / Cockscomb: Topmost bundle of straw turned to shed water back onto the ridge

Continental Bundle: Imported bundle of water reed 1m around circumference or butt, usually tied twice

Compty: Substandard materials or thatch

Combed Wheat Reed: Straw which has had the corn leaf and weed removed - varieties include Aquilla, Marris Wiggen and Marris Huntsman

Course: Layer of reed or straw laid across the roof

Crook: See 'Iron'

Dolly: See 'Roller' and 'Bottle'

Dressing: Pushing reed into final position

Drift: See 'Legget'

Dutchman: Type of Legget originating from the Netherlands

Eave: First course of thatch

Fathom: Six bundles of water reed

Fargle: A goodly handful of steel sways

Feather: Seed head on water reed

Flag: Leaf on straw

Fleaking: A weave of water reed laid over the rafters instead of timber battens

Gadd: Cut length of hazel between 1" and 3" in diameter

Gaddule: Bundle of gadds

Hazel: Corylus Aveliana (L) - used for spars, sways and rods - said to be hardier than withy

Iron: Thatching nail used to fix sway to rafter, trapping thatch

Knuckle: Handful of straw, bent double

Legget: Tool that grips the ends of the reeds and pushes them into position

Ligger: See 'Rod'

Long Straw: Straw thrashed but not combed. Varieties of wheat : Little Josh, Red Standard, Square Headed Master

Net: A galvanised wire or polythene used to protect thatch from bird damage

Needle: Used to stitch on the thatch

Nitch: Bundle of combed reed of weight 28lb or 14lb

Northampton Roll: Rolled and rodded gable end

Pinnacle: Topmost bundle of ridging material used to shed water back onto the ridge

Pricker: Length of gadd about a yard long, used to fix sways on rick thatches

Ridge: Covering of supple straw or sedge grass, laid along apex of roof to bind and protect the main thatch. Types include wrap-over, butt up, flush, straight cut and patterned. Patterns include dragons' teeth, diamond, scalloped, clubbed, herring-bone and crossed.

Reeding Pin: See 'Spragger'

Roller: Continuous parallel bundle of thatch used to build up ridge

Rod: Hazel or withy, used to hold down thatch on the surface. Types include split, unsplit, apex, kettle and muff.

Rutland Cap: Peaked end at gable

Rye: Type of soft straw used for thatching

Sedge: Marsh Grass (Cladius Mariscus) used for ridging

Server: Skilled labourer

Set: See 'Tilt'

Sheaf: Bundle of unthrashed straw - 8 sheaves make a stook, 16 make a stock

Slapping: First course of ridge

Skirt: See 'Slapping'

Spar: A split length of hazel or withy, pointed and twisted to form a staple

Spit: See 'Spar'

Spot Board: Board for 'butting up' of reed bundles

Spragger: Pointed length of steel used to temporarily hold materials

Springing: See ' Tilt'

Stalch: A strip of thatch worked from eave to ridge

Standing Crop: The thatching materials whilst growing

Stool: Clump of Hazel

Sway: Steel or hazel rod used with irons to secure thatch

Thrashing: Method of removing grain from straw

Tilt: The angle formed by tightening the sway between the top and the butt of the reed

Tilting Fillet: A 'V' section of timber fixed to the rafter to set the tilt

Twisle: A crank for twisting straw for grass bonds

Wadd: See 'Bottle'

Wand: Length of unsplit willow or hazel, less than 1" diam

Water Reed: Phragmites Communis obtained traditionally from East Anglia now additionally from European countries

Wimble: See 'Twisle'

Withy: Willow used for rods and sways - it is said to be less prone to woodworm - varieties include Black bar, Dicky Medoes, Swallow tail and Whissender

Yelm: Drawn and wet straw ready for laying

Lying between the western reaches of Dartmoor, and the River Tamar of the Cornish border, and to the south, the urban expanse of Plymouth, to the north the fast-burning A30. Within this triangle, an enchanting array of small rivers, wooded valleys, and a bevy of hamlets and villages connected by slow lanes.

Not a place to hurry. Be advised to carry a compass, for disorientation is the norm in the Lew and Lyd Valleys. Road signs are, at times, confusing, and your map skills will be sorely tested if you wish to take advantage of the many fine hostelries within this domain.

Often the edges of a county are the most interesting. It is our habit to rush to the centre, and then to explore outwards. But, if you look to the natural border, in this instance, the Tamar Valley, and its feeding lines there are

sweet names to conjure with; Sydenham Damerel, Horsebridge, Bere Ferrers, Weir Quay, Lopwell…into these conduits great ships passed by with their tonnage. Visit Morwellham Quay, and you will experience our rich, industrial past.

Explore this area and you will be forgiven a hearty appetite. For it is here that Tavistock was judged a worthy centre of fine produce and cuisine. And, not too far distant are the hotels noted for their fine cuisine and sporting endeavours; Hotel Endsleigh, Percy's, and the Arundell Arms, the supreme Restaurant With Rooms, the Dartmoor Inn, and the country pubs, the Elephant's Nest, and the Peter Tavy Inn that will nourish and tender your gastronomic desires. So, Bon Appetit, and a safe journey home.

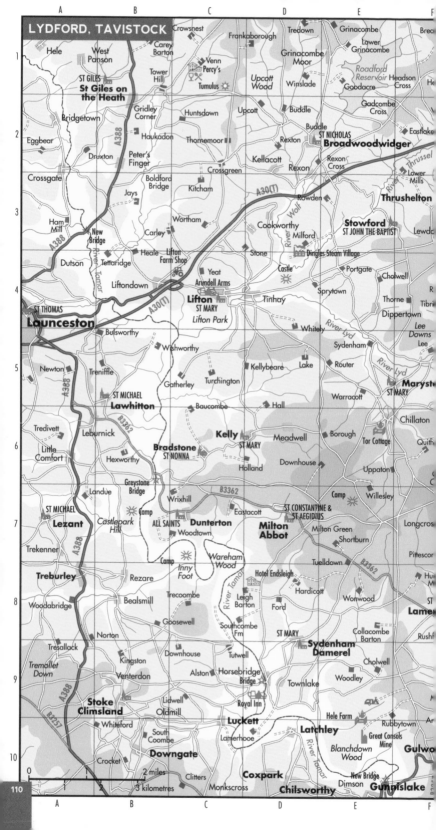

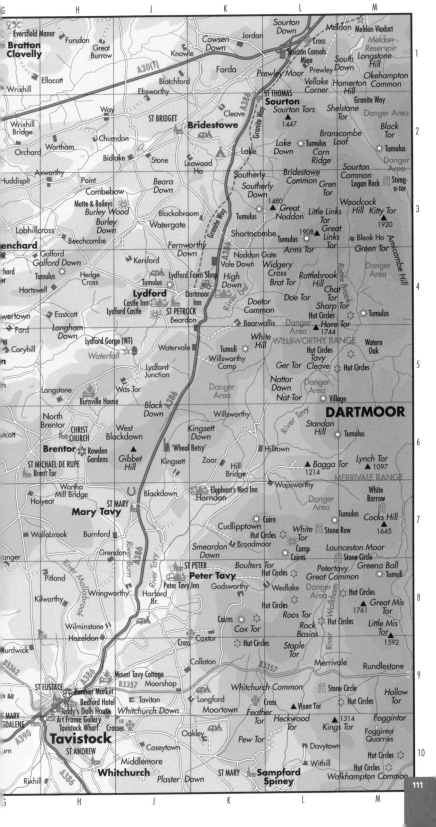

Towns and villages: Bratton Clovelly, Bridestowe, Sourton, Lydford, Brentor, Mary Tavy, Peter Tavy, Tavistock, Whitchurch, Sampford Spiney, Dartmoor

Selected place names and features:

Eversfield Manor, Fursdon, Cowsen Down, Jordan, Meldon, Meldon Viaduct, Meldon Reservoir, Great Burrow, Knowle, Sourton Down, Cross, Sourton Consols Mine, Longstone Hill, Wrixhill, A30(T), Forda, Prewley Moor, Prewley, South Down, Okehampton Common, Ellacott, Blotchford, Vellake Corner, Hamerton Hill, Granite Way, Ebsworthy, Cleave, St Thomas, Sourton Tors 1447, Shelstone Tor, Black Tor, Wrixhill Bridge, Way, St Bridget, Lake Down, Tumulus, Corn Ridge, Branscombe Loaf, Tumulus, Orchard, Wortham, Chumdon, Stone, Lake, Southerly, Bridestowe Common, Gren Tor, Sourton Common, Logan Rock, Steng-a-tor, Axworthy, Point, Combebow, Beara Down, Leawood Ho, Southerly Down, Woodcock Hill, Kitty Tor 1920, Huddispit, Motte & Baileys, Burley Wood, Blackabroom, Great Noddon 1480, Little Links Tor, Lobhillcross, Burley Down, Watergate, Tumulus, Shortacombe, Tumulus 1908, Great Links Tor, Bleak Ho, Green Tor, Beechcombe, Fernworthy Down, Noddon Gate, Arms Tor, Danger Area, Amicombe Hill, Galford, Kersford, Vale Down, Widgery Cross, Rattlebrook Hill, Chat Tor, Galford Down, Hedge Cross, Tumulus, Lydford Farm Shop, High Down, Brat Tor, Doe Tor, Sharp Tor, Tumulus, Hartswell, Lydford, Dartmoor Inn, Hut Circles, Hare Tor 1744, Castle Inn, St Petrock, Beardon, Doetor Common, Tumulus, Eastcott, Lydford Castle, Bearwallis, White Hill, Willsworthy Range, Watern Oak, Ford, Longham Down, Danger Area, Coryhill, Lydford Gorge (NT), Watervale, Tumuli, Willsworthy Camp, Hut Circles, Tavy Cleave, Ger Tor, Hut Circles, Waterfall, Lydford Junction, Nattor Down, Nat Tor, Village, Langstone, Was Tor, Burnville House, Black Down, Willsworthy, Dartmoor, North Brentor, Christ Church, West Blackdown, Kingsett Down, Standon Hill, Tumulus, Brentor, Rowden Gardens, Gibbet Hill, 'Wheal Betsy', Hilltown, St Michael de Rupe, Brent Tor, Kingsett, Zoar, Hill Bridge, Bagga Tor 1214, Lynch Tor 1097, Merrivale Range, Wortha Mill Bridge, Blackdown, Elephant's Nest Inn, Horndon, Wapsworthy, White Barrow, Holyeat, St Mary, Mary Tavy, Danger Area, Cocks Hill 1645, Wallabrook, Burnford, Cudlipptown, Cairn, White Tor, Stone Row, Tumulus, Pitland, Grendon, Smeardon Down, Hut Circles, Broadmoor, Camp Cairns, Stone Circle, Launceston Moor, Kilworthy, Wringworthy, St Peter, Boulters Tor, Hut Circles, Petertavy Great Common, Greena Ball, Peter Tavy, Peter Tavy Inn, Godsworthy, Wedlake, Danger Area, Hut Circles, Tumuli, Wilminstone, Harford Br., Hut Circles, Roos Tor, Hut Circles, Great Mis Tor 1761, Hazeldon, Cairns, Cox Tor, Rock Basins, Little Mis Tor 1592, urdwick, Cross, Coxtor, Hut Circles, Staple Tor, Merrivale, Rundlestone, Collaton, B3357, Mount Tavy Cottage, Moorshop, Stone Circle, Hollow Tor, St Eustace, Panther Market, Bedford Hotel, Taviton, Whitchurch Common, Hut Circles, Teddy's Dolls House, Whitchurch Down, Longford, Cross, Vixen Tor, Art Frame Gallery, Moortown, Feather Tor, Fogginter, Tavistock Wharf, Crosses, Oakley, Heckwood Tor, Kings Tor 1314, Fogginter Quarries, St Mary Magdalene, A390, Caseytown, Pew Tor, Davytown, Hut Circles, Tavistock, St Andrew, Middlemore, Withill, Hut Circles, A386, Rikhill, Whitchurch, Plaster Down, St Mary, Sampford Spiney, Walkhampton Common

TAVISTOCK

One of the four "Stannary Towns", established to control the production and distribution of tin from Dartmoor, and birthplace of Sir Francis Drake in 1542 at Crowndale Farm (now no more), south of the town. Later, developed by the Dukes of Bedford who lived in what is now the Bedford Hotel, and in the summer for six weeks at Endsleigh House (hotel) near Milton Abbot. The Bedfords were formidable, forward thinking town planners of their day, the early C19, and the impressive buildings have great dignity; the Town Hall and Pannier Market, and the long avenues were to their choosing. Drake's statue stands at the west end of the town's entrance, whilst at the end of the same road, stands a statue of Bedford. The Parish Church of St Eustace is formidable, too, and the Abbey, founded in 974, destroyed by Henry V111 in 1539 has a few surviving walls beside the riverbank. Tavistock is an attractive town, and a popular one to live in. It has plenty of smart, independent shops, good schools and a lively food culture. The area is noted for its abundance of smart hotels, restaurants and gastro-pubs. To offset your indulgences, Dartmoor is a few steps to the east. Plymouth is within commuting distance, and the Cornish border not too distant, either. (H10)

SPECIAL PLACES OF INTEREST...

Artframe Gallery, 17 Duke St. Broad range of paintings, ceramics bronzes and studio glass. Original art, limited editions. Open M-Sa 910-8. (H10) 01822 611091 artframegallery.co.uk

Drake's Trail. This is a 21-mile cycling and walking route linking Tavistock with Plymouth. Ideal for family and elderly cyclists keen to enjoy fresh air, fine views and free of traffic. It is part of the NCN Route 27, the "Devon Coast to Coast." It travels through tunnels and over bridges, and a viaduct. Just a couple of short road sections to be aware of. (H10) drakestrail.co.uk

Pannier Market. Purpose built in the 1850s. Markets held daily Tu-Sa 9-4.30. Crafts and antiques Tu, Mixed W, Fresh produce F, All sorts on Sa. Dukes Coffee House. (H10)

Parish Church of St Eustace. A fine, C15 construction with pinnacle tower and wide nave. A roof of carved beams and bosses, bench ends and C16 font. Tomb monuments to many local dignitaries; Sir John Glanville and John Fitz. William Morris stained glass in the north-east Chantry window and a clear reflection of the wealth created by the wool and tin merchants of west Devon. (H9)

Tavistock Wharf, The Wharf. Tavistock's art centre featuring cinema, live music, theatre and an art gallery. Bar and coffee shop. Open daily. (H9) 01822 611166 tavistockwharf.com

Teddy's Dolls House, Village Shopping Arcade, Brook St. Collection of dolls and teddies. Dolls & Teddies Hospital. (H10) 01822 612128

LIFTON

The new A30 (sadly) by-passes this charming old settlement founded by the Saxons as an admin centre. The C15 church with C12 and C14 origins is particularly fine, and the countryside around to the East is a gem. And, popular with fishers of men (and their ladies). (C4)

SPECIAL PLACES TO VISIT...

Dingles Fairground Heritage Centre, Nr Lifton. An all-weather attraction with a hands-on approach to machinery suitable for all children from 5-70+. Traction Engines. Café. Riverside walks. Open daily mid-Mar to end Oct 10-5 & half-terms. (D3) 01566 783425 fairground-heritage.org.uk

Lewtrenchard Manor. A C17 manor house that became the home of the Victorian squire and parson Sabine Baring-Gould. He inherited the estate in 1872 that comprised some 3,000 acres and the gift

of a living at Lew Trenchard parish. In 1865 he published his hymn "Onward, Christian Soldiers" with music composed by Arthur Sullivan. Nearby is Galford the site in the C9 of a battle involving the West Welsh and the Defnas tribes. Today, the house is a country house hotel where you can enjoy afternoon tea, and the full complement. (G4) 01566 783222 lewtrenchard.co.uk

Lifton Farm Shop. Always busy, popular with locals and day-visitors to the restaurant, bakery, fruit and veg stalls, and the butchery. A great family breakfast stop for those coming to and from Devon-Cornwall. (C4) 01566 784605 liftonfarmshop.co.uk

LYDFORD

From the C9 when Lydford was laid out in a grid system, visible today, where it has been an important centre on the

Western reaches of Dartmoor. Today, it is well located for visiting Dartmoor and the beautiful pastoral countryside of the Devon/Cornwall border. Off the beaten track and credited with country inns and charming places to stay. (J4)

Lydford Castle (EH). A C13 Tower remains above the C12 predecessor built during the Saxon and Medieval period when Lydford was an important centre of the tin trade and administrative centre for the forest of Dartmoor. From the Middle Ages to the C18 the Castle became a prison for those who disobeyed the Stannary laws. Open daily. (J4)

Lydford Farm Shop. Just the place to stock up for your picnics and adventures with their cakes, meats, fruit and veg, plus tea and coffees. Open daily, all week.(K4) 01822 820737

Lydford Gorge (NT). The beautiful woodland walk leads you down the deep wooded ravine 1.5 miles long carved out by the River Lyd as it plunges into the 'Devil's Cauldron'. The White Lady Waterfall is quite spectacular at 90 ft high. Open daily Apr-Oct from 10. Refreshments. Admission charge. Waterfall only rest of year 10.30-3. Tea room. (J5) 01822 820320 nationaltrust. org.uk

Merrivale Stone Circle. Remains from one of the earliest settlements in Devon. Clearly visible are boulders from Hut Circles, square dwellings, and Stone Rows from funeral burials. Two of the standing stones have markings indicating an A and a T, as an early road sign for crossing the Moor. A stream of pure water crosses the area. Park in car park. (L9)

Rowden Gardens, Brentor. World famous for their range of rare aquatic plants, especially irises. Consultancy service available. (H6) 01822 810275 rowdengardens.com

Wheal Betsy. Former tin mine in the care of the National Trust. You can spy the mine from the main road. (J6)

Lydford Castle

CHURCHES OF INTEREST...

St Mary, Bratton Clovelly. C15 with many attactive Norman features. (G1)

St Michael De Rupe, Brent Tor. Built by the monks of Tavistock Abbey in the C14, and romantically poised on an extinct volcano at 1130 feet. Like Glastonbury Tor, a favourite with children to clamber up, and witness the fine views across to Dartmoor, and west to Brown Willy, on Bodmin Moor. (G6)

QUALITY B & B...

April Cottage, 12 Mount Tavy Road, Tavistock. Friendly accommodation overlooks the River Tavy. All bedrooms with bathroom. Easy walking distance to town centre. (H10) 01822 613280

Burnville House, Nr Brentor. Large, comfortable Georgian house with views across to Dartmoor offers solitude and farmhouse cuisine. 4 self-catering cottages. (H5) 01822 820443 burnville.co.uk

Hele Farm, Nr Gulworthy. Grade 11 listed farmhouse with organic dairy dating back to 1780. Somewhat old fashioned dÈcor. Steeped in history of mining – see Great Consols Mine. Nature walks down to Tamar. Self catering, too. (E9) 01822 833084 dartmoorbb.co.uk

Mount Tavy Cottage. Lovely old gardener's cottage just ten minutes walk from Tavistock. Family room and 4-poster bedroom with bathrooms. Organic breakfasts. All set with 10 acres of paradise. Self catering, too. (H9) 01822 614253 mounttavy.co.uk

Tor Cottage, Chillaton. A rural retreat in their own private valley with over 18 acres of wildlife to explore and get lost in. Elegant and spacious rooms. Outdoor pool. (E6) 01822 860248 torcottage.co.uk

SPECIAL PLACES TO PUBS SERVING FOOD...

Elephant's Nest, Horndon. Always a favourite. Nothing better than sitting out in their garden on a summer's evening with pint in hand. Recently refurbished. Accommodation. (K7) 01822 810273 theelephantsnest.co.uk

Peter Tavy Inn. Popular with all the foodie guides, for you have low beams, slate floors and large cosy fireplaces, plus an ambience conducive to children and dogs. Fine start off point for Dartmoor walks. (J8) 01822 810348 petertavy.co.uk

Royal Inn, Horsebridge. A C15 Inn with Gothic windows, beams and log fires overlooks the Tamar. A no-nonsense attitude to good pub-grub with ingredients sourced locally. Meals 12-2, 7-9. 01822 870214 royalinn.co.uk

The Castle Inn, Lydford. A C16 Inn with an ancient history; Lydford Pennies, Lydford Mint, Ghosts of Sherlock Holmes, all with open fires, settles, pub-grub and beer garden. B&B. Storage for bikes and horse's tack. (J4) 01822 820242 castleinnlydford.com

STAY...TO EAT..TO DRINK...

Arundell Arms, Lifton. One of England's premier fishing hotels for more than a century offering 20-miles

HOTEL ENDSLEIGH, Nr Milton Abbot

If one is allowed a favourite then Olga Polizzi's hotel may be just that. For she blends a fusion of country house style with contemporary boutique and manages to pull it off, magnificently. A former fishing lodge set high above the Tamar Valley of inescapabale beauty. Offset with ornamental gardens; a Fairy Dell, Rock Gardens and Grotto, and an Arboretum. After a long summer lunch there's bound to be a tree to rest under, to dream of Shangri-Las, in this hideaway overlooking the Tamar. 2 rods for hire. Nature Appreciation Weekends. (D8) 01822 870000 hotelendsleigh.com

1698
Samuel Darker sets up first permanent printing press in Exeter.

1698
Thomas Newcomen of Dartmouth invents atmospheric steam pumping engine.

of Salmon, Sea Trout and Brown Trout fishing in a valley with five rivers. Tuition and ghillieing. Comfortable, unpretentious and relaxed. Modern French and English cuisine. (C4) 01566 784666 arundellarms.com

Bedford Hotel, Tavistock. Large, conservative town hotel offers traditional comforts and elegant charm. Quite a pile. It's a former Benedictine Abbey and residence of the Dukes of Bedford. Special Breaks. Serves food all day (the best Minute Steak I have ever tasted!), and if you have been rushed off your feet, a large armchair awaits you. "A Scotch or Pot of Tea, Your Grace…". (H9) 01822 613221 bedford-hotel.co.uk

Dartmoor Inn. More a Restaurant With (3) Rooms than country inn. The beautifully designed pieces of artwork set the scene for great cuisine, a genial atmosphere in the three cosy dining rooms and small bar with log fire. Regular art exhibitions. Classy bedrooms. With being a short distance from the Moor and Gorge, walkers, dogs and their grubby boots (please leave by the front door) are encouraged to venture here. Lunch & dinner served Tu-Sa 12-2.30 & 6.45-9.00, also Su lunch. (K4) 01822 820221 dartmoorinn.com

PERCY'S COUNTRY HOUSE HOTEL & RESTAURANT

Chic, stylish design meets C15 Devon Long Barn. Food of intense quality. Restaurant has won garlands galore. Ingredients from organic producers and their 130 acres. Cookery School. Riding holidays. No children under-12, no dogs in public rooms. (C1) 01409 211236 percys.co.uk

1698
Traveller and chronicler, Celia Fiennes visits Exeter, and marvels at the immense output of serge cloth.
The most commercially productive area of Britain.

115

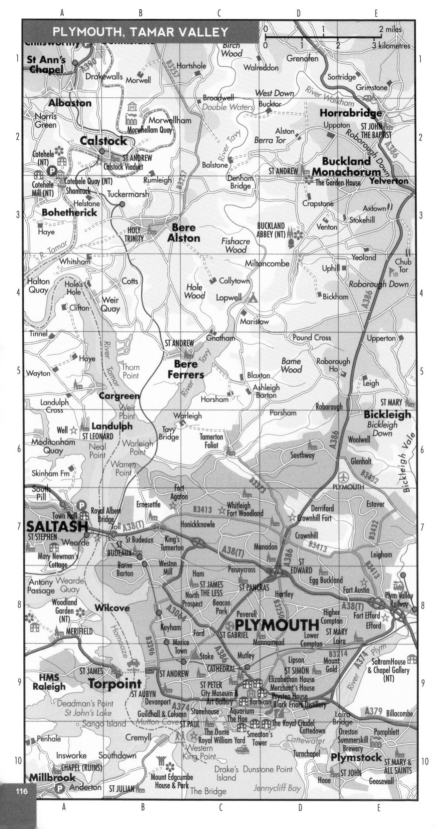

0 1 2 miles
0 1 2 3 kilometres

A B C D E

1
St Ann's Chapel
Chilsworthy
A390
Drakewalls
Morwell
Hartshole
B3257
Birch Wood
Walreddon
Grenofen
Sortridge
Grimstone
River Walkham

2
Albaston
Norris Green
Morwellham
Morwellham Quay
Broadwell
Double Waters
Bucktor
West Down
Uppaton
Horrabridge
ST JOHN THE BAPTIST
A386
Calstock
ST ANDREW
Calstock Viaduct
Rumleigh
B3257
Alston
Berra Tor
ST ANDREW
Buckland Monachorum
The Garden House
Yelverton
Roborough Down
Cotehele (NT)
P
Cotehele Quay (NT)
Cotehele Mill (NT)
Shamrock
Helstone
Tuckermarsh
Balstone
Denham Bridge
Crapstone
Axtown
Stokehill

3
Bohetherick
Haye
R. Tamar
HOLY TRINITY
Bere Alston
BUCKLAND ABBEY (NT)
Venton
Yoland
Uphill
Chub Tor
18
Whitsham
Cotts
Fishacre Wood
Miltoncombe
Roborough Down
A386

4
Halton Quay
Hole's Hole
Weir Quay
Clifton
Hole Wood
Collytown
Lopwell
Maristow
Pound Cross
Bickham
Upperton
Tinnel
Haye
ST ANDREW
Gnatham
Bame Wood
Roborough Ho
Leigh

5
Wayton
Thorn Point
Bere Ferrers
Blaxton
Ashleigh Barton
Horsham
Porsham
Roborough
ST MARY
Bickleigh
Bickleigh Down
Landulph Cross
Cargreen
Weir Point
Warleigh
Tavy Bridge
Tamerton Foliot
Woolwell
Bickleigh Vale

6
Well
ST LEONARD
Landulph
Neal Point
Warleigh Point
Moditonham Quay
Warren Point
Fort Agaton
Southway
Glenholt
B3432
Skinham Fm
South Pill
PLYMOUTH
A386

7
Town Hall
Royal Albert Bridge
Toll
A38(T)
Ernesettle
B3413
Whitleigh
Fort Woodland
Honicknowle
King's Tamerton
Derriford
Crownhill Fort
Crownhill
B3413
Estover
B3432
SALTASH
ST STEPHEN
Wearde
St Budeaux
ST BUDEAUX
Weston Mill
Manadon
A386
ST EDWARD
Leigham
Mary Newman's Cottage
Barne Barton
Ham
Pennycross

8
Antony Passage
Wearde Quay
Woodland Garden (NT)
MERIFIELD
Wilcove
Tamar
A3064
ST JAMES THE LESS
North Prospect
Beacon Park
ST PANCRAS
Peverell
Hartley
Higher Compton
Egg Buckland
Fort Austin
A38(T)
Fort Efford
Efford
Plym Valley Railway
Keyham
Ford
PLYMOUTH
ST GABRIEL
Mannamead
Lower Compton
ST MARY Laira
B3250

9
HMS Raleigh
ST JAMES
Torpoint
ST AUBYN
Devonport
A374
Guildhall & Column
Morice Town
Stoke
B3396
ST ANDREW
Mutley
Lipson
ST SIMON
Mount Gold
B3214
SaltramHouse & Chapel Gallery (NT)
ST PETER
City Museum & Art Gallery
CATHEDRAL
Elizabethan House
Merchant's House
Prysten House
Black Friars Distillery
Barbican
Laira Bridge
A379
Billacombe

10
Penhale
Insworke
Southdown
CHAPEL (RUINS)
Millbrook
Anderton
ST JULIAN
Cremyll
Mutton Cove
ST PAUL
Stonehouse
The Dome
Royal William Yard
Western King Point
Mount Edgcumbe House & Park
The Bridge
Drake's Island
Deadman's Point
St John's Lake
Sango Island
Aquarium
The Hoe
Smeaton's Tower
The Royal Citadel
Cattewater
Dunstone Point
Turnchapel
Jennycliff Bay
Oreston
Summerskill
Brewery
Plymstock
ST JOHN
Pomphlett
ST MARY & ALL SAINTS
Hooe
Goosewell

A B C D E

Sutton Pool, The Barbican

PLYMOUTH

The largest city in Devon, and the most well known, for Plymouth men have exported their birthplace's name to forty other towns and cities across the world. It is the greatest city in the South West, and lies between the rivers Tamar and Plym which form the estuaries of the Hamoaze and Cattewater, making a fine natural harbour. It is a city of its own making with a swashbuckling, seafaring tradition, and although the men who made Plymouth great were Devon men; Drake, Frobisher, Gilbert and Raleigh, their initial loyalty was to their Queen, Elizabeth 1 and to England. They sailed under the Queen's flag, for England, and their own, self-interest, and were party to England's maritime supremacy in the Elizabethan era, and thereafter. In 1585, it became a Naval Base, and at the time of the Armada in 1588, Plymouth had superseded Dartmouth as the principal port of Devon. Sutton Pool was the location for the original port set beside the fishing quays of today's Barbican.

In 1691, William III established the Royal Naval Dockyard at Devonport in five acres, by 1765 it had expanded to a sprawling, 74 acres. Plymouth Dock was renamed Devonport in 1824. Much of the land is today in private hands, the remainder is known as the Plymouth Naval Base where one of their duties is to maintain and refuel the Vanguard Class of nuclear ballistic missile submarines.

The city suffered terrible losses and destruction during the Second World War. The whole centre of the city was virtually obliterated with over 1,200 civilian mortalities, unknown service losses, 10,000 houses destroyed and more damaged. Utter destruction. These lost souls are remembered in the memorial at Charles Church, built 1641-1708 in the Gothic style. It, too, suffered untold destruction, now a mere shell of its former glory. So it is a fitting tribute that the Men of Plymouth saw fit to leave this "much talked about" monument in the centre of the Charles Cross roundabout, in front of the new shopping

development, to be seen by all who drive into the city centre along the A374.

Following the Second World War, the rebuilding of the city centre was not considered a great success from an aesthetic or planning point of view, and the hideous Drake's Circus has been demolished to make way for the new £200 million Drake's Circus Shopping Centre, which opened to much fanfare on the 5th October, 2006. The City fathers and planners have drawn up ambitious plans for regenerating the City; "A Vision for Plymouth." This will be completed by 2020. We are already seeing progress. The Royal William Dockyard at Stonehouse, the former Victualling Yard (storage of food etc) has been developed into £1,000,000 apartments and prestigious offices, attended by art galleries and restaurants - see overleaf.

The Barbican is where most visitors (who are not interested in shops) progress to. It is Plymouth's old harbour area, and luckily avoided the Luftwaffe's bombing raids. A

National Marine Aquarium

place of character and activity, close to the fishing boats of the thriving fishing industry. The fish market trades from 4.00 am and supplies the great wholesale markets of Billingsgate and Birmingham, as well as the countless restaurants of the south-west, and beyond. There are ancient buildings, including Prysten House, the Elizabethan House, and the Merchant's House. Nearby is the Mayflower Stone from where the Pilgrim Fathers set forth aboard the Mayflower. All about you is life and activity, there are coffee shops, pubs and restaurants, and within view, the National Marine Aquarium.

With the sea to your left you ascend to the Hoe passing the Royal Citadel on your right. It is a fine, open space, given to kite flying and dog walking, and memories, dreams, reflections (apologies, dear Carl Jung). There are impressive memorials; Armada Memorial, the Naval War Memorial, Soldiers of Plymouth, Royal Marines Memorial and Smeaton's Tower, which appears to be leaning.

Plymouth is not the city to typify the characteristics of Devon; thatch, cream teas and pastoral bliss. It is out on its own. And like Venice, best approached from the sea. Although, today, most of us arrive by train, or car via unattractive ring roads cutting between dull housing and equally poor industrial estates. Don't let these negatives put you off. One feels tremendous energy emanating from all this activity and new birth. It is a city to explore and grow to like, if not love. It has a future, and if you tire of it, Dartmoor is but a stone's throw away.

SPECIAL PLACES OF INTEREST IN PLYMOUTH…

Black Friars Distillery, 60 Southside St. "Spirit of Plymouth" exhibition - history of the city and its world famous gin. Open daily 10-5, Su 11-5 10:30-4. Party bookings by arrangement. 01752 665292 plymouthdistillery.com

Crownhill Fort. A quite extraordinary building situated on a hill on the northern outskirts of Plymouth, but well worth a visit to see its unique design. It was a Victorian fort built in the 1860s to defend Plymouth, from what one may wonder, given its isolation. Open for visitors to explore the earth ramparts, gun emplacements and tunnels.

Open Apr-Oct 10-5 Su-F. 01752 793754 landmarktrust.org.uk

Drake's Trail. This is a 21-mile cycling and walking route between Plymouth and Tavistock. It is part of the National Cycle Route 27 (Devon Coast-to-Coast). It follows the western edge of Dartmoor beside and through spectacular scenery, passing through tunnels and over bridges. A shared path, ideal for families with pushchairs and dogs, or those in wheelchairs. Marsh Mills and Plymbridge Woods are good start-off points for short excursions. drakestrail.co.uk

National Marine Aquarium, The Barbican. Britain's biggest, Europe's deepest Aquarium; specimens mainly from local waters. Octopi, crabs, lobsters, starfish, conger eels. Open daily 10-6 (-5 in winter). 0844 8937938 national-aquarium.co.uk

PLYMOUTH ARTS & CRAFTS…

Artframe Gallery, 61 Cornwall St. Features include paintings, limited edition prints, hand-made sculptures, ceramics and glass by local and international artists. Open M-Sa 9-5. 01752 227127

1715
Construction of the Exeter Canal completed.

1727
John Gay's Beggar's Opera runs for 62 nights in London – a resounding success.

Barbican Gallery, 15 The Parade. Large selection of original oil and watercolour paintings. Resident artist Nicholas Lewis painting Th & F. Open M-Sa, 11-5, Su 11-4. Closed Tu. 01752 661052 **barbicangallery.com**

New Street Gallery, 38 New Street. Paintings by leading contemporary artists; figurative and abstract work. Agents for the Lenkiewicz Foundation, The Trust dedicated to the work of the late Robert Oscar Lenkiewicz 1941-2002; Artist and Plymouth personality of great verve and renown. Open M 12-4, Tu-Sa 10-4. 01752 221450 robertlenkiewicz.org

Somerville Gallery, 25 Mayflower St. One of the South West's larger galleries promoting original works from local artists especially Robert Lenkiewicz. Open daily. 01752 221600 somervillegallery.co.uk

SPECIAL PLACES TO VISIT…

Antony Woodland Gardens. Privately owned by the Carew Pole Garden Trust has 100 acres of woodland with 300 types of camellias bordering the Lynher River. Open Tu, W, Th & W/Es Mar-Oct 11-5.30. (A8)

Antony House & Gardens (NT). Built for Sir William Carew from 1711-1721 and considered the most distinguished example of early C18 architecture in Cornwall. Colonnades, panelled rooms and family portraits. Open 4 Apr-31 Oct Tu, W, Th & BH M's 12-5 (also Su June-Aug). (A8)

Buckland Abbey (NT). C13 Cistercian abbey bought by the grandfather of Sir Richard Grenville, and later the home of Sir Francis Drake. Now houses period rooms and museum of Drake relics including Drake's Drum, 3 1/2 acre shrub and herb garden and fine tithe barn. Estate walks. Craft workshops. Holiday family activities. Open daily mid-Feb to Dec from 10. Jan to early Feb W/Es. Shop and Refreshments. (D3) 01822 853607

Calstock Viaduct. 12 arch viaduct built to carry railway wagons from local mines to Calstock Quay where the wagons were raised and lowered in a lift. (B3)

Cotehele Gallery, The Quay. Showcasing professional artists and makers from the South West in seven exhibitions annually. Open daily 11-4. (A3)

Cotehele House (NT). Medieval house of grey granite (built 1485-1627) in romantic position overlooking the River Tamar and Devon beyond. For centuries, the Edgcumbe family home containing original furniture, C17 tapestries, armour and needlework. The gardens lie on several levels. Medieval dovecote. Ancient clock in chapel. Refreshment and shop. House open daily mid-Mar to Dec 11-4. Gardens & Estate open all year dawn-dusk. (A2)

Cotehele Mill (NT). Picturesque C18 and C19 buildings beside the River Tamar. A small outstation of the National Maritime Museum and berth for the restored Tamar sailing barge. 'Shamrock'. Museum and the Edgcumbe tea room selling light lunches and cream teas. Open daily from 11. (A3)

Garden House, Buckland Monachorum. Breathtaking terraced walled garden surrounding ruins of medieval vicarage. Innovative with stunning colours. Tearoom and plant sales. Open daily Apr-Oct 10.30-5. 01822 854769 (D3) thegardenhouse.org.uk

Cotehele House nt

Mary Newman's Cottage, 48 Culver St. C15 Cottage of Mary Newman, first wife of Sir Francis Drake. Furniture supplied by the Victoria and Albert Museum. Open Apr-Sept W Th & W/Es 12-4. (A7)

Morwellham Quay. Reconstruction of the busy C19 river port serving copper and arsenic mines, and its associated canals and railways. Workshops, 3 museums. C19 farm with animals, quays, raised railways. People in period costumes. Open daily from 10 Mar-Nov. Tearoom and shop.

(B2) 01822 832766
morwellham-quay.co.uk

Mount Edgcumbe House & Park. Sensitively restored Tudor mansion in beautiful landscaped parkland. Formal English, French and Italian Gardens. National Camellia Collection. Park and gardens open daily all year. House and Earl's Garden open Apr-Sept Tu-Su & BH's 11-4.30. (B10)

Royal Albert Bridge. An iron single-track railway bridge built by I.K. Brunel in 1859, his last great feat of engineering. (B7)

Saltram House (NT). Largest country house in Devon, dating from the mid C18 with Tudor remnants. Mirror Room, Library, Chinese Chippendale bedroom. Furniture, plaster and woodwork. Pictures include 14 Reynolds portraits. Great Kitchen and stables. Garden with Orangery, shrubs and trees. Landscaped park. Open daily Mar-Dec 11-4.30 (winter - 3.30). Garden, Café & Shop open 10-5 all year, Park dawn til dusk. (E9) 01752 336546

Smeaton's Tower, The Hoe

1743
Aug 14. Fire destroys 450 homes in Crediton.

1750
10,000,000 gallons of cider were made for local consumption.

Royal Albert Bridge

Tamar Valley Donkey Park. Donkey sanctuary, Eeyore's Souvenir Store, woodland walk, café. Open daily Apr-Sept 10.30-5, W/Es Feb, Mar, Nov, Dec. (A2) 01822 834072 donkeypark.com

TOWNS OF INTEREST...

Calstock. Attractive old river port on the Tamar. Steep wooded riverbank and the abundance of fruit growing provide a splendid sight in spring, 12 arch viaduct. Numerous disused mining chimneys and engine houses haunt the landscape. (B3)

Devonport. The Royal Naval Dockyard was located here in the late C17. It is now known as HMNB Devonport the largest naval base in Western Europe, and the sole nuclear repair and refuelling facility for the Royal Navy. Home to the Naval barracks, HMS Drake, the Royal Marines base, RM Tamar and the HQ for 1 Assault Group Royal Marines. Within the town, sadly neglected by Devon visitors, you have the Regency Guildhall and Column. Within the Guildhall, the Column Bakehouse, an exceptional café serving fresh bread and cakes M-Sa 10-4 beside a funky art gallery. All visitors must climb the Column. Built between 1821-27 it rises to 124 ft providing panoramic views. Open M-F 9-5, Sa 10-4. devonportguildhall.org

LIGHT BITES...IN THE BARBICAN

You are spoilt for choice. There are a number of street vendors selling food and drinks. **Cap'n Jaspers** is popular with motorcyclists, whilst those on the other two-wheel experience should visit the bike shop and cafe **Rockets & Rascals, 7 The Parade**. A seriously good cafe opening at 8 for breakfast til 12, lunch 12-4. Great atmosphere, great food and great meeting place. 01752 221295 rocketsandrascals.com

For all who love to sew and make stuff walk a hundred yards north towards **Sutton Harbour** to Make at 140 Vauxhall Street. It's a coffee shop and Makery with workshop where you can learn to sew, stitch, cut fabrics, crochet...have lunch. 01752 600130 makeat140.co.uk

Returning to the Barbican, cross into **South Street** to the **Jacka Bakery**. Here since time began. An artisan bakery plus small cafe open daily except Tu 9-4.

For more substantial fare there is: **Monty's Coffee Shop, 13 The Barbican**. All-day breakfasts, and a fine selection of coffees. Burgers and steak sarnis, fishcakes. A comfortable and friendly place to hang out. Open daily 9-7. 01752 252877 montyscafeplymouth.co.uk

Piermasters Seafood Restaurant, 33 Southside Street. The original; the oldest seafood eatery in the City set opposite the old fish market. Full blackboard menu. Open daily for lunch, 12-2, and dinner 7-10. T 01752 229345 piermastersrestaurant.com

Yukisan, 51 Notte Street. The first Japanese restaurant in Devon! You can eat on three floors, on chairs or in the authentic manner, on cushions. Whichever, you choose, you are in for a Sushi feast. Open daily 11.30am-11.30pm. 01752 250240 yukisan.co.uk

1755
Carpet manufacture begun by Thomas Whitty in Axminster at Court House.

1758 Death of Bampfylde Moore Carew at Bickleigh. King of the Gypsies and "Grand Master of the honourable fraternity of beggars".

121

Saltash. Attractive river port with steep streets running down to Tamar estuary. C18 Guildhall. May Fair - 1st week. Regatta - June 3rd week. (A7)

WHERE TO EAT & DRINK IN THE CITY CENTRE...

Chloe's, Princess Street. Gallic and formal with crisp linen provides an air of class. Cuisine inspired by Alain Ducasse and Pierce Gagnaire. Expect the full French experience. Open Tu-Sa lunch 12-2, pre-Theatre 5.30-6.30, Dinner 5.30-9. 01752 201523 chloesrestaurant.co.uk

WHERE TO EAT & DRINK IN THE OUTER REACHES...

Seawings Restaurant, Lawrence Road, Mount Batten Pier, Plymouth. On the Eastern side of the City providing spectacular sea views. Cuisine is Modern English, fish a speciality, of course. Breakfasts from 8 am. Child friendly. Open Tu-Sa 8am-9.30pm, Su 10-5. 01752 402233.

The Brasserie, Mayflower Marina, Richmond Walk. On the Western side of the City overlooking a mass of sail and plastic (hulls). The scallop centre of the south-west. They have compiled 50 scallop dishes. Today, you may choose from 6. Nutritious "Slow Food" menus and light meals. Open daily 11-3, 7-11. 01752 500008

B&BS...UP THE TAMAR...

South Hooe Captain's House, Holes Hole, Nr Bere Alston. Quite a find. A rural idyll set in ten acres of woodland overlooking the Tamar. Free range eggs, home-grown vegetables and your own private jetty, and log fires in winter. Too much. Writers' workshops. 01822 840329. (A4)

The Basket Factory, Weir Quay. A comfortable house proving B&B set within a large garden overlooks the Tamar. Children and dogs by arrangement. 01822 841455 (A4) weir-quay.com

1759
John Smeaton completes the third lighthouse on Eddystone Rock.

1760
Ramillies frigate wrecked off Bolt Head with loss of 500 lives.

Views of Royal William Victualling Yard

1765
Benjamin Donn publishes new Devon map.

1766
Villages and clothiers of the Culm valley riot for better wages.

Winter on Haytor

One of England's greater National Parks; the Forest of Dartmoor covers 365 square miles and contains the highest ground in England south of the Peak District. On its desolate moorland tracks the wanderer can believe they are further from a public road than anywhere in the country, but on the fringes lush valleys lead down on every side to thick woodland, green vegetation and picturesque villages.

Geologically, Dartmoor was formed by the up swelling millions of years ago of a vast mass of molten granite, bursting through the earth and forming a group of colossal and terrifying mountains. Softened and rounded through time, their summits cracked in pieces by the elements of snow and ice. All that remains are the "tors", piles of rock, often in uncanny shapes, which surmount the present day flattened landscape.

The main mass of Dartmoor is to a large extent a desolate peat bog, a challenge to the experienced walker, but to the east, where the rivers Teign and Dart carve their way tortuously through the rocks in deep gorges, is a more friendly landscape of grassy uplands with easily accessible viewpoints - Hound Tor, Haytor and Bonehill Down.

Dartmoor is well known for its attractive herds of ponies with their varied colouring - apparently wild but in fact individually owned. Every year they are rounded up and branded with the owner's mark. Feeding them is strictly prohibited, and in the interest of the animals who have plenty to eat, they must not be tempted to wander towards you across the roads.

Other wildlife includes foxes, badgers and otters - also the occasional adder. Fallow, roe and Sitka deer can often be seen, but the red deer of Exmoor have never penetrated the area. Buzzards, kestrels and various Birds of Prey are frequently seen, as well as the wheatear, while crows, ravens and the skylark are fairly commonplace. A variety of insects inhabit the Moor, and the interesting insect-eating sundew plant can often be identified. Heather, bracken and whortleberries grow in profusion in the drier areas, and in the woodland there is much to interest the student of mosses and lichens. These can often be seen covering the roadside stonewalls.

The Moor abounds in prehistoric remains. There are also many deserted medieval villages with remains of the traditional "longhouse" buildings. For centuries tin mining has been an important activity and there is much to interest the industrial archaeologist, including abandoned tramways and railways of more recent times - notably the Princetown Railway, once the highest railway line in England, now a moderately easy mountain bike track.

Many historic legends surround the Moor. Conan Doyle's "Hound of the Baskervilles" is based reputedly on Fox Tor.

DARTMOOR

TORS

Highest on the Moor are Yes Tor and High Willhays (2038 ft) in the north. To the east, are the fine viewpoints of Kes Tor and Hay Tor, the easily recognised shapes of Hound Tor and Bowerman's Nose, and Buckland Beacon with the Ten Commandments carved in the rock by a religious dissident. Near Tavistock are the westward-looking viewpoints of Pew Tor and Vixen Tor, and the isolated church-crowned summit of Brent Tor.

THE VALLEYS

The River Dart rises in the Moor and crosses its centre. At Postbridge there is a fine clapper bridge, and lower down is Dartmeet, a famous beauty spot. On the eastern fringe the Teign flows for many miles through deep wooded valleys, while on the Tavistock side is the Tavy with its spectacular gorge. Smaller rivers draining the Moor are the Okement, and on the south side the Plym, Avon and Erme, each deeply cleaved into the landscape.

CROCKEN TOR

Once the meeting place of the Stannary Court, arbiters of the tin industry in the Middle Ages. Nearby is Wistman's Wood, a grove of gnarled and twisted trees, the surviving remains of primeval forest. Around here can also be seen parts of the Devonport Leat, an ancient water supply. In the most desolate part of the Moor is Cranmere Pool, a sinister bog and site of the first of the Dartmoor Postboxes (the custom being for visitors to leave a card and note the lapse of time before the next visitor came to collect and post it).

WALKING ON DARTMOOR

Dartmoor offers opportunities for every kind of walker from the easy family stroll through woodland and over grassy hillsides to the long distance endurance test for those who prefer to make their own way across trackless country by map, compass and GPS. Most of the Moor is common land with free access to unfenced

Saddle Tor

country, but there are restricted military training areas in the north-west. These are usually accessible at weekends and school holidays - enquiries should be made locally. A comprehensive programme of guided walks, ranging from 1 1/2 to 6 hours duration is available, through summer starting from a variety of centres. For those who would rather go it alone there are many detailed books available - the following are just a few suggestions. The Ordnance Survey 1:25,000 Explorer series are recommended for use on the Moor.

The Moor is crossed by several ancient trackways which can still be traced. The Lych Way from Bellever to Lydford was used for funeral processions.

Frosty Morning, Drewsteignton

SHORT WALKS UP TO 3 HOURS

1. Sheepstor from Burrator Reservoir.
2. Black Tor & the Meavy Valley from the Princetown-Yelverton road.
3. Birch Tor & Vitifer Mine from Warren House.
4. Dr Blackall's Drive.
5. Vixen, Henwood & Pew Tors from Merrivale.
6. Bench Tor from Venford Reservoir.
7. Grimspound & Hamelton Tor.
8. Great Hound & Grae Tors.
9. Hay Tor & the Granite Tramway.
10. Belstone Tor from Belstone.
11. Bonehill & Honeybag Tors.

Hemsworthy Gate

LONGER WALKS
UP TO 6 HOURS

1. Staldon from Cornwood.
2. Ditsworthy, Eylesburrow & Nuns Cross from Burrator.
3. Duckspool from Whiteworks.
4. Ryders Hill from Holne.
5. Cranmere Pool from Okehampton Military Rd
6. Shiel Top from Cornwood.
7. Doe & Great Links Tor from Lydford.

Spinster's Rock, Nr Sandypark

Walks for the experienced are better left for individual planning, but there are two historic routes which can be traced; the Abbot's Way (Buckfast-Princetown) and the Lych Way (Bellever-Lydford). A complete traverse of the Moor can be made up the Erme Valley from Ivybridge, past Childe's Tomb to Two Bridges, thence north via Cut Hill to Cranmere Pool and down to Okehampton.

The Two Moors Way provides a 100 mile walk from Ivybridge to Lynton, skirting the fringes of Dartmoor and continuing through pastoral mid-Devon, and across Exmoor.

Scorhill Circle

Okehampton Hamlets

Scarey Tor
Belstone Common
Belstone Tor
Foxes' Holt
Hut Circles
East Week
Whiddon D

Black Down
Rough Tor
Winter Tor
Higher Tor
Cawsand Hill
Stone Row
South Tawton Common
Goos

Red-a-ven Brook
West Mill Tor
Beacon
East Okement Fm
Tumuli
White Hill
Cawsand Beacon
Clannaborough
East Ash

Okehampton Common
New Bridge
Hut Circles
Throwleigh
ST MARY

Tumuli
Yes Tor
▲2028
East Mill Tor
1684 Beacon
Danger Area
Taw Marsh
Hut Circles
Raybarrow Pool
Throwleigh Common
Higher Shilstone
Langston
Wonson

Danger Area
Oke Tor
Metherall Hill
1504▲
Tumulus
Little Hound Tor
Kennon Hill
Ensworthy
Moortown
Chapp

High Wilhays
▲2039
White Moor Stone
1570▲
Hut Circles

Fordsland Ledge
Danger Area
Steeperton Tor
1739▲
Hound Tor
Ruelake Pit
Buttern Hill
Gidleigh Castle
HOLY TRINITY

Dinger Tor
OKEHAMPTON RANGE
Knack Mine
Stone Circle
Gidleigh Common
Hut Circles
Gidleigh
Murch
Gidleigh Pa

Lints Tor
Okement Hill
▲1857
Wild Tor
▲1741
Walla Brook
Scorhill Circle
Teigncombe

Kneeset Nose
Danger Area
Watern Tor
Hew Down
Batworthy
Hut Circles
Chagford Common
Waye Barto

Amicombe Hill
Great Kneeset
Tumulus
Taw Head
1984▲
Hangingstone Hill
Tumulus
Triple Circle
Shovel Down
Stone Avenue
Frenchbeer
Hole

Danger Area
Black Ridge
Cranmere Pool
Dart Head
▲1974
Stonetor Hill
Long Stone
Yardworthy

▲1917
Whitehorse Hill
Great Varracombe
Manga Hill
Teignhead Fm
Thornworthy Tor
Hut Circles

Little Kneeset
▲1694
Teign Head
Quintin's Man
Little Varracombe
Teignhead
Stone Circles
Fernworthy Reservoir
Stone Avenue

Hut Circle
Danger Area
Hut Circles
Hemstone Rocks
Metherall Heath Stone

1877▲ Fur Tor
1764▲
Fernworthy Forest
Hut Circles

▲1981
Cut Hill
Sittaford Tor
Grey Wethers
Hut Circles
Chagford Common
Circ

Tavy Head
White Ridge
Stone Row
1654▲
Stone Row
Assycombe Hill
Hurston Ridge
Bush Down
W

D A R T M O O R
Beehive Hut
Hut Circles
Stannon Tor
1517▲
Stone Row
Water Hill
Bennett's Cross

Walkham Head
Dartmoor Forest
Warren House Inn
Merripit Hill
Tumulus

Cowsic Head
Broad Down
Hartland Tor
Hut Circles
Hut Circles

Maiden Hill
Devil's Tor
1791▲ Rough Tor
Hut Circles
Hut Circles
Tumuli
Soussons Down

Conies Down
Beardown Man
Lower White Tor
Cist
ST GABRIEL
Runnage
Stone Circle
Sous

Rich Way
Crow Tor
Hut Circles
Higher White Tor
▲1712
Archerton
Clapper Bridge
Postbridge
Piswell

Hut Circles
Lydford Tor
Stone Row
Longford Tor
Arch Tor
Hut Circles
Lydgate House
Dury
Cator Common

Blackbrook Head
Danger Area
Beardown Tors
1680▲
Hut Circles
Lakehead Hill
Bellever Forest
Bellever
Clapper Bridge
Cator Court

1615▲ Black Dunghill
Cowsic River
Powder Mill Pottery
Clapper Bridge
Hut Circles
Hut Circles
Riddon Ridge
Low Ca

Danger Area
Holming Beam
Wistman's Wood
Beardown Hill
Littaford Tors
Bellever ▲1456 Tor
Hut Circles

Prison Leat
Blackbrook River
Devonport Leat
Beardown
Hut Circles
Crockern Tor
Smith Hill
Cist
Hut Circles
Laughter Tor
Laughter Hole

B3357
Parson's Cottage
Menhir
Babeny
Sha

Rundlestone
Hollow Tor
B3357
Two Bridges
Prince Hall Hotel
Prince Hall
Dunnabridge Pound
Hut Circle
Hut Circles
Huccaby Rings
Hut Circles
Gi
C

High Moorland Visitor Centre
HM Prison
Cist
Princetown
ST MICHAEL
Hut Circles
West Dart River
B3357
Huccaby Tor
Yar Tor

B3212
Tor Royal
Cist
Moorlands
Sherberton
Hut Circle
Huccaby
Dartmeet
Clapper Bridge

Stone Circle

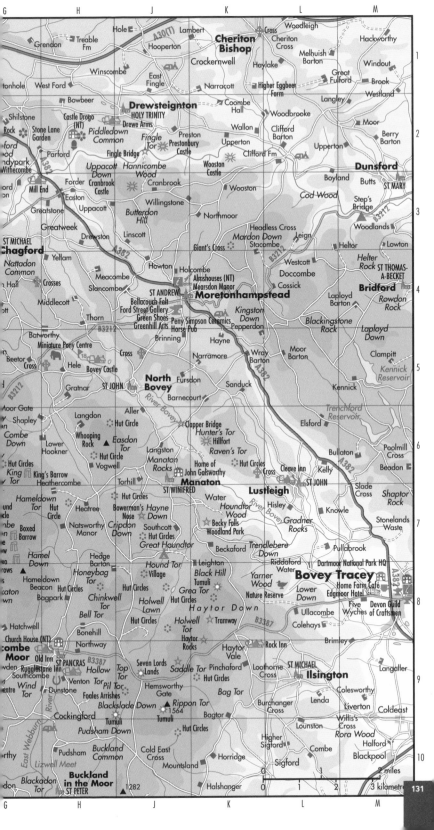

CHAGFORD

One of the four "Stannary Towns" given to manage the medieval tin industry, and thereafter an affluent little town for many years until the Agricultural Depressions of the 1870s and 80s. The far-thinking vicar of the time organised a modern sewage system to encourage tourism. This endeavour moved George Haynes to introduce electric lights, the first town west of London, to do so. The town, and surrounding hamlets are popular with the Retired, although there are always young persons enjoying the health shops and al fresco drinking. Has one of the few ironmongers (stores that sell every device known to man) left in the country. The surrounding hamlets and farms abound with sturdy, Dartmoor architecture, especially those north of Chagford. The Devon Longhouse is much in evidence; the vernacular design, of a long house usually built by a farmer in an L-shape within a courtyard. A comparable design would be a Cotswold house of similar proportions, and magnitude. Chagford is always a pleasant place to visit. Not a happy place in 1642 for the young poet Sydney Godolphin who was shot dead by a jealous suitor besides the church steps, whilst defending the King's name. He returns to curse pub bores. (G3) visitchagford.com

SPECIAL PLACES TO VISIT...

Church of St Michael the Archangel. A stone's throw from the aforementioned inn. For yet another poor soul met a sticky end; Mary Whiddon was shot dead by a jealous suitor beside the church steps, on her Wedding Day in 1641. Some scholars believe her sad end inspired the tale of Lorna Doone. Inside the church, some fine creations; a parclose screen, carved pulpit and roof bosses of rabbits and hares. (G3)

Ludgate Fine Art, 20 The Square. This gallery is a showcase of Eleanor's work; Nature in all its differing forms, from watercolours, to oils and pastels. Open daily except Tu & Su from 10. 01647 433287 devonsnatureinart.com

Monks Withecombe Gallery. An amazing space given to changing exhibitions of contemporary West Country artists in a light and airy studio overlooking the National Park. Open daily 9-6. (G2) 01647 432858 monkswithecombegallery.co.uk

Stone Lane Garden Sculpture Exhibition. 5-acre arboretum presenting an annual sculpture exhibition. National Collections of Birch and Alder trees in a landscaped water and woodland setting. Open daily 10-6. (G2) 01647 231311 stonelandgardens.com

1769
William Cookworthy set up the first British porcelain factory in Plymouth.

1786
Final meeting of the tinners Great Court held at Dunnabridge.

Chagford Landscape

LIGHT BITES...

There is quite a choice; **The Three Crowns** is a comfortable hostelry recently refurbished where you can take morning coffee, lunch and dinner, and or stay the night. 01647 433444 threecrowns-chagford.co.uk. For a relaxed pint and the best Sunday lunch it has to be **The Chagford Inn**, on **Mill Street**. A butchery on hand to supply the finest beef. Scrubbed pine tables, artworks and three bedrooms endears one to rest here, awhile. 01647 433109 thechagfordinn.com If you are self-catering pop across to Jaded Palates for some fine wines. In need of a picnic, sandwich and cheeses, try **Blacks Deli**. Their home-made quiches are yummy. Coffee, a cream tea, down the hill to **The Old Forge**. Serves lunches of Shepherd's Pie, Tuna and mozzarela fishcakes, English Rabbit. 01647 433226 theoldforgechagford.co.uk Across the street for organic fare, a Vegetarian deli/cafe **The Courtyard Cafe & Shop.** Gluten-free cakes, a selection of soups and fresh veg. 01647 432571

For the full Main Course it has to be: **Gidleigh Park**. One could describe this hotel as a Restaurant With Rooms. For it is to the restaurant that the guest is bidden to share an experience to succour and tell tales over the campfire. **Chagford** used to supply the staff; Mothers and daughters, and uncles worked here but now the staff are shipped in from hither and thither. The build is mock Tudor, black and white timber-framed overlooking the river Teign. One wonders if the course of the river has been re-directed. A luxurious double-room and dinner for two will set you back between £500 to £1,000. There will be 8+ courses, and 2-nights might appease your appetite. On the third morning you may well seek a Spa for some colonnic irrigation? Lunch is not so demanding, and is thus, a popular choice for many, to be recommended. 01647 432367 (F3) gidleigh.co.uk

Gidleigh Park ss

Haytor Rock

1787
The ships Friendship and Charlotte depart Plymouth with convicts bound for Australia.

1788 Devonshire ports have 707 registered ships, employing 4,500 men (despite small skiffs and barges not included in register).

133

MORETONHAMPSTEAD

A busy town, beware of the tricky road junction as you enter. Like many a Dartmoor town it profited from the medieval wool industry but has little to show for it save the church and the handsome almshouses built in 1637, for a great fire in 1845 destroyed all but a few of the medieval and Tudor buildings. Today, a centre for many craftsmen, and a convenient place from which to explore the Moor, and to stop for some refreshment, be you walking or on two-wheels. (K4)

ARTS & CRAFTS...

Bellacouch Felt, The Unitarian Chapel. Dartmoor's best wool is used to make felted and hand-made items, all naturally dyed. Open M-F 10-5. (J4) 01647 441404 bellacouche.com

Ford Street Gallery. A poppet of a gallery displaying fine art and sculpture from local artists. Open daily. (J4) 01643 440362 fordstreetgallery.co.uk

Green Shoes, 26A Cross St. Ever hankered for home-made, artisan shoes, sandals and boots. Choose your colour, sole, style, width and Last. Workshops, too. Open M-F 9.15-5. (J4)01647 440735 greenshoes.co.uk

Greenhill Arts, Fore St. Art Gallery with a full-range of arts and crafts. Open daily 10-4 (East-Sept Tu-Su). (J4) 01647 440775 greenhillarts.org

Penny Simpson Ceramics, 44A Court St. Penny makes domestic stoneware for the kitchen in lively colours, and pots for plants and flowers. Open M-Sa. (J4) 01647 440708 pennysimpsonceramics.co.uk

PRINCETOWN

You may wish to visit this isolated village out of curiosity, and wonder at the poor, misguided souls who have thrown their lives away, to be incarcerated in this dark, and dismal place. It is eerie, and is penalised by the full force of weather, from the north and east. And, you may thank god for your good fortune, and freedom, and move on to warmer climes. The prison was built in 1808 by French and American prisoners of war. There are plans to close the prison. What will be done with the building is uncertain. The Officers' Mess is an impressive building, now a Dartmoor National Park Centre. There are tearooms and gift shops. An easy off-road cycling route along the old railway tracks starts from here heading in an easterly direction. (A10)

LIGHT BITES...

On a fine day you will see people (often cyclists) sitting outside the **Central Cafe**, in **The Square**. Here you can order an early breakfast, paninis and toasties, or simple tea and coffees. Opposite, **The Horse Pub & Nosebag** (great name) where you can order fine ales and wine, or sit, in comfort and order a special Pizza, Tapas, fresh fish, all cooked under the eye of Frenchman, Christoff. 01647 440242 thehorsedartmoor.co.uk

If you are a fan of bone china (and old values) try the **Gateway Tea Room** on 17 New Street. 01647 440722 thegatewaytearoom.co.uk

River Teign, Fingle Bridge

1792
Fashionable houses built on the beacon in Exmouth.

1793
Jan 11. The radical Tom Paine's effigy burnt in Exeter.

Widecombe Landscape

WIDECOMBE IN THE MOOR

Set in a bowl of a valley surrounded by rugged country. Journey in from the Haytor road and what impresses is the perfect shape of the church, "The Cathedral of the Moor", and the isolation of the village, originally built by tin miners. The village is famous for the song about Widecombe Fair, held on the second Tuesday of September. Be advised, arrive early. And learn your lines, thus:

Tom Pearce, Tom Pearce, lend me thy grey mare,

All along, down along, out along, lee-

For I want to go to Widecombe Fair,

Wi' Bill Brewer, Jan Stewer, Peter Gurney, Peter Davy,

Dan'l Whiddon, Harry Hawk,

Old Uncle Tom Cobleigh and all,

Chorus - Old Uncle Cobleigh and all.

SPECIAL PLACES TO VISIT...

Parish Church of St Pancras. The striking tower rises to 120 feet. It is a pinnacled battlement design. The interior shows two aisles with 6 bays and a painted screen. In 1638 a thunderstorm struck, killing four of the congregation, an event commemorated by a poem:- "Some had their skin all over scorcht, yet no harm in their cloaths." (H9)

Widecombe Church House (NT). C16 brewhouse, later a village school. Incorporates Sexton's Cottage, now the National Trust shop. Open daily, all year 10.30-4.30 (H9) 01364 621321 nationaltrust.org.uk

LIGHT BITES...

The Old Inn. Cosy and traditional with flagstone floors. Popular so book! Large portions of food. Children and dogs welcomed. B&B. (H9) 01647 281276

Wayside Café. Delicious home-made cakes cooked using traditional family recipes. Look out for the big teapot! (H9) 01364 621313 waysidecafe.co.uk

Ruggelstone Inn. Looking for a jolly country Inn with barrels of beer, open fires, top-notch pub-grub, and all very cosy and intimate? Bingo! (H9) 01364 621327 ruggelstoneinn.co.uk Self-catering at the Rugglestone Cottage, a converted barn nearby.

SPECIAL PLACES TO VISIT...

Becky Falls. 50-acre estate of woodland, rivers and waterfalls plus nature reserve and walking trails with special interest to woodland ecology; mosses and lichens. Visitors in the past have included Bronze Age man, and the writers Rupert Brooke and Virginia Woolf. Café. Open daily Mid-Feb to - end Oct 10-5. (K7) 01647 221259 beckyfalls.com nationaltrust.org.uk

Dartmoor Prison Museum, Princetown. Contains part of the famous prison built between 1805 and 1808. Discover the lives of the French and American prisoners of war held here. Open M-Th & Sa, 9.30-4.30. F & Su 9.30-4. Phone before visiting. (A10) 01822 322130 dartmoor-prison.co.uk

Gidleigh Castle. Ruined Norman keep, with church adjoining. Not open but visible from the road. (E3)

Powder Mill Pottery, Nr Postbridge. Hand-made, glazed pots using the local clays found on Dartmoor. Shop selling Dartmoor arts and crafts. Cream teas. Open daily. (C8) 01822 880263 powdermillspottery.com

The Miniature Pony Stud & Farm. Interact with miniature mares and their foals, tiny

1793
Plymouth Gin is first distilled by Coates.

1796
Bread riots in Exeter.

donkeys and a whole host of other friendly animals. Play areas, miniature farm, shops, restaurants and walks. Open Late Mar to end Oct 10.30-4.30. (H5) 01647 432400 miniatureponycentre.com

DARTMOOR ATTRACTIONS...

Bowerman's Nose. The word is a corruption of bowman, archer or huntsman. So the legend goes that Bowerman was a mighty hunter afraid of no man or beast and dismissive of crones. One day he disturbed a group of witches/crones, and in their disgust they turned him to stone. Access is via a short ascent from the road. Climbing is forbidden. (J7)

Cranbrook Castle, Prestonbury Castle & Wooston Castle. These three Iron Age forts near Drewsteignton were designed to protect families and their livestock from raiding parties. (J3/J4/K2)

Cranmere Pool. The first Letterbox site set up by James Perrott of Chagford in 1854. It can be a bleak, wet and boggy place. Quite a challenge in foul weather. Easier access now the Military road is open. (B4)

Dartmeet Bridge. Remains of C13 clapper bridge. A popular picnic spot, best avoided on bank holidays, and former gathering site for gypsies. Tea rooms at Badgers Holt. (E10)

Fingle Bridge. A popular beauty spot beside the River Teign. Waymarked walks lead off in all directions. There's a pub/tearoom to assuage your thirst, if need be. Steep lane descends from Drewsteignton, so beware of other traffic. (J2)

Haytor Rocks. The most visited rock formation on Dartmoor. It is easily accessed with car parking close to, but best seen at dawn or sunset when the molten granite appears to change colour and shape. At 1,499 feet with two granitee outcrops, it has been classified as an "Avenue Tor" due to the erosion of the central section. (J8)

Hound Tor. Associated with the legend of Bowerman's Nose, for his hounds were too, turned to stone by the witches, and here they lie, scattered and forlorn. It also inspired Conan Doyle's The Hound of the Baskervilles. Some refuse to visit believing it is haunted and a dangerous place. It can be. In 1995, a 500-ton boulder came crashing down. Popular with rock climbers. (J8)

Grey Wethers Stone Circle. Two granite circles excavated in 1898, and restored in 1909.

CASTLE DROGO (NT). Granite castle built by Lutyens between 1910 and 1930 for Julius Drewe, the founder of Home and Colonial Stores. Varied collection of furniture and paintings. Terraced gardens and croquet lawn. Superb views over the Teign Gorge. Castle open daily Early Mar to Oct & Nov to mid-Dec W/Es 11-5.30. Garden, VC Cafe, shop & Estate open all year. (H2) 01647 433306

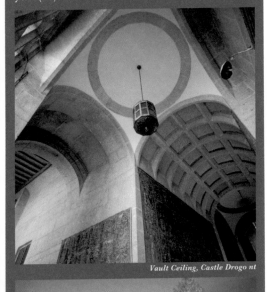

Vault Ceiling, Castle Drogo nt

Drawing Room, Castle Drogo nt

The northern circle has 20 stones and is 107 ft diameter, the southern has 29 with a diameter of approximately 115 feet. All the stones are about 4.5 feet. (D6)

Grimspound. Bronze Age village hut circle overlooked by Hookney Tor. A walled enclosure of about 4-acres, and as its situation is not strategically sound was most probably a farm. (G7)

Postbridge Clapper Bridge. One of Dartmoor's most visited beauty spots built in the C13 and C14. (D8)

Scorhill Circle. A Bronze Age circle with about 35 stones remaining from the original 70. Local legend has it that horses cannot be ridden through the circle. Try it. Waymarked access via Batworthy or Gidleigh. (E3)

Wistman's Wood. According to legend, planted some 600 years ago by Isabella de Fortibus, Countess of Devon.

What remains is a unique collection of stunted, gnarled and weatherbeaten oaks curiously interspersed amongst granite boulders. A sacred place populated by adders. Best advised not to take your dog. A 40-minute walk beside the wall from Two Bridges. Not to be undertaken in mist, or fog. (B9)

PUBS SERVING FOOD...

The Cleave, Lustleigh. C15 thatched pub with inglenook fireplaces and thick cob walls that has had a recent renovation. Cosy and comfortable. Daily specials. Fine ales. Dogs, children, cyclists and walkers made welcome. (L6) 01647 277223 thecleavelustleigh.uk.com

Drewe Arms, Drewsteignton. Lovely old furnishings and photos, simple decor and wholesome food. Formerly run by Mabel Mudge for 75 years, retiring at 99 in 1996. Her memory lives on. Children and dogs welcome.

Accommodation. Bunk Rooms for walkers and families. 01647 281409. (J2) thedrewearmsinn.co.uk

Rock Inn, Haytor Vale. A long-standing favourite of mine. Never know who you might sit next to; Ex-Cabinet Ministers or a UN Ambassador. Friendly atmosphere and good, honest food. Log fires. Large garden. Accommodation. 01364 661305. (K9) rock-inn.co.uk

Warren House Inn, Nr Postbridge. Welcome site on a bleak and blustery day. Third highest Inn in England since 1845. Home cooked fare. Simple decor suits the Dartmoor landscape. (F6) 01822 880208 warrenhouseinn.co.uk

SPECIAL PLACES TO STAY...

Bovey Castle. Perhaps a little over the top, the refurbishment exudes the luxury, elegance and excitement of the 1920s. With castle staterooms, health

and beauty spa, sporting activities including golf and 24-miles of trout and salmon fishing, cocktail bars, Art Deco dining and facilities for children. (H5) 01647 445016 boveycastle.com

Edgemoor Country House Hotel, Haytor Road.
Set in beautiful gardens on the edge of Dartmoor. The owners claim "Elegance without Pretension", and provide clean and neat decor. (M8) 01626 832466 edgemoor.co.uk

Lydgate House, Postbridge.
Set in the heart of Dartmoor. Ideal for walking, pony trekking and golf. Home-cooked evening meal using local produce. Bedrooms have luxurious goose down duvets and pillows. Dogs welcome. No children under 12. (E8) 01822 880209 lydgatehouse.co.uk

Mill End. A small and comfortable hotel with old-style charm and notable restaurant. A fine walking and sportsman's

base from which to explore the National Park. Private salmon and trout fishing. Dogs welcome. (G3) 01647 432282 millendhotel.com

Prince Hall Hotel, Two Bridges. In the heart of

Dartmoor and fine centre for walking, fishing, touring, relaxing. French style cuisine using local produce. Bedrooms with all facilities. Dogs welcome. (C10) 01822 890403 princehall.co.uk

Lustleigh Churchyard

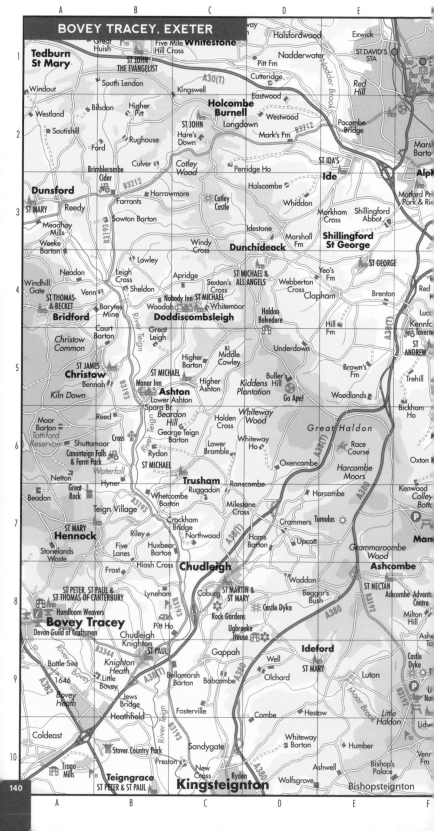

Halsfordwood
Exwick
ST. DAVID'S STA

Way
Great Huish
Five Mile Hill Cross
Whitestone
Nadderwater
Pitt Fm
Cutteridge
Eastwood
Red Hill

Tedburn St Mary
18
ST JOHN THE EVANGELIST
A30(T)
South Lendon
Kingswell
A30(T)

Windout
Holcombe Burnell
Longdown
Westwood
Pocombe Bridge
Mars Barto
Alph

Westland
Bilsdon
Higher Pitt
ST JOHN
Hare's Down
Mark's Fm
B3212

Soutishill
Rughouse
ST IDA'S
Ide
Matford Pri Park & Ri

Ford
Culver
Cotley Wood
Perridge Ho

Brimblecombe Cider
B3212
Horrowmore
Halscombe
Whiddon
Markham Cross
Shillingford Abbot

Dunsford
Reedy
Farrants
Cotley Castle
Shillingford St George

ST MARY
Sowton Barton
Windy Cross
Idestone
Marshall Fm
ST GEORGE

Meadhay Mills
Weeke Barton
Lowley
Apridge
Dunchideock

Neadon
Leigh Cross
Sheldon
ST MICHAEL & ALL ANGELS
Sexton's Cross
Webberton Cross
Yeo's Fm
Clapham
Brenton
Red

Windhill Gate
ST THOMAS-A-BECKET
Venn
Barytes Mine
Nobody Inn
Woodah
ST MICHAEL
Whitemoor
Haldon Belvedere
Hill Fm
Luc
Kennfo Tavern

Bridford
Doddiscombsleigh
ST ANDREW

Christow Common
Court Barton
Great Leigh
Middle Cowley
Underdown

ST JAMES
Christow
Higher Barton
Higher Ashton
Kiddens Plantation
Buller's Hill
Go Ape!
Brown's Fm
Trehill

Bennah
ST MICHAEL
Manor Inn
Kiln Down
B3193
Ashton
Lower Ashton
Woodlands
Bickham Ho

Moor Barton
Tottiford Reservoir
Reed
Spara Br.
Beardon Hill
George Teign Barton
Holden Cross
Whiteway Wood
Great Haldon
Oxton

Shuttamoor
Canonteign Falls & Farm Park
Cross
Rydon
ST MICHAEL
Lower Bramble
Whiteway Ho
Oxencombe
Race Course
Harcombe Moors

Waterfall
Hyner
Trusham
Ruggadon
Ranscombe
Harcombe
Kenwood Colley Botto

Netton
Great Rock
Whetcombe Barton
Milestone Cross
Crammers
Tumulus
P

Beadon
B3193
Teign Village
Crockham Bridge
Northwood
Hams Barton
Upcott
Grammaroombe Wood
Man

ST MARY
Hennock
Riley
Huxbear Barton
Five Lanes
Ashcombe

Stonelands Waste
Hiash Cross
Chudleigh
Waddon
ST NECTAN
Ashcombe Advent Centre

Frost
Lyneham
ST MARTIN & ST MARY
Beggar's Bush
Castle Dyke
Milton Hill

ST PETER, ST PAUL & ST THOMAS OF CANTERBURY
Handloom Weavers
Coburg
Rock Gardens
A380
Ashe To

Bovey Tracey
Devon Guild of Craftsmen
Pitt Ho
Chudleigh Knighton
Ugbrooke House
Castle Dyke

B3344
ST PAUL
Gappah
Well
Ideford
Li Na

Battle Site 1646
Knighton Heath
Little Bovey
Bellamarsh Barton
Babcombe
ST MARY
Olchard
Luton
Little Haldon

A382
Bovey Heath
Jews Bridge
Heathfield
Fosterville
Combe
Hestow
Lidw

Coldeast
Whiteway Barton
Humber
18

Trago Mills
Stover Country Park
Preston
Sandygate
New Cross
Rydon
Ashwell
Bishop's Palace
Venr Fm

8
Teigngrace
ST PETER & ST PAUL
Kingsteignton
A380
Wolfsgrove
Bishopsteignton

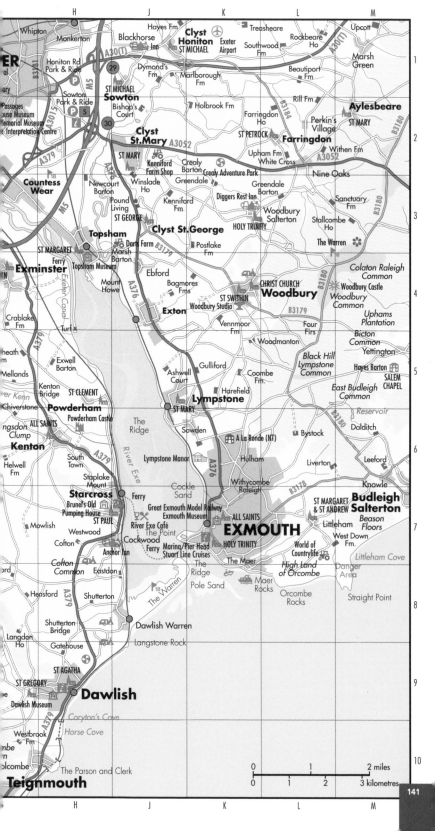

EXETER

The great Cathedral city and county town of Devon, has been a strategic settlement since the Romans came here in 55 AD. Later, developed by Alfred the Great, and followed by the Normans who strengthened the town with City Walls. The magnificent Cathedral can be seen from the M5, where it dominates the view. There are medieval churches and the City Walls to discover, a circuit will take one-and-a-half hours. The City centre was badly damaged during the Second World War but luckily most of the ancient buildings escaped, including the Guildhall, St Nicholas Priory and Tucker's Hall. The city had a busy time of it during the Civil War, changing sides on numerous occasions. Outside the City walls, on the east side, the gracious avenue of C18 buildings, Southernhay, was where hangings took place, and agitators aired their views. John Wesley preached here. It is today the home of lawyers and estate agents, and a convenient place to park if visiting the Cathedral. It is also the address of a fine hotel and restaurant - see below.

When the celebrated traveller Celia Fiennes visited Exeter in 1698 she noted that for twenty miles around, all the villages, farms and country folk were in some way involved in the production of serge cloth. Exeter made more money in a week than any other town in England. This all halted during the Napoleonic Wars, and production moved north to Yorkshire and Lancashire.

The new buildings replacing those destroyed in the Second World War have not had a good press. The High Street has been described as dull. The new Pricesshay Shopping Centre has fine views of the Cathedral from many angles and as part of the City fathers and planners massive reconstruction programme has been an undoubted success amongst the thousands who shop and eat here.

The visitor will naturally first progress to the Cathedral and its spacious Close where there are cafés and smart shops, and the devastation that was once the Royal Clarence Hotel burnt down on 29 October, 2016. Then, onto the Quay, where you can also eat and drink well, and take up some exercise by foot, cycle or paddle, and if this is not to your pleasure, aimlessly visit the many antique and bric-a-brac emporia. For those who seek independent shops head to Fore Street. Here you will discover a rich vein of wacky and creative retailers, as well as some splendid places to Light Bite.

For more retail therapy, a short distance north-west from the Quay you will come to shopping outlets represented by TK Maxx and others.

The Devon County show is in May, and the Exeter Festival in June. (G1)

WHAT TO VISIT IN EXETER; HISTORIC BUILDINGS & MUSEUMS...

Custom House Visitor Centre, Quayside. Earliest surviving brick building in Exeter, used by HM Customs until 1989. Exhibits an audio-visual presentation, "Exeter – 2,000 Years of History", highlighting Exeter, from Roman times to the present day. Open daily Apr-Oct 10-5, Nov-Mar W/Es only 11-4. (F1) 01392 271611 (F2)

Guildhall, High St. One of the oldest municipal buildings in England dating back to 1330. (F1)

Royal Albert Memorial Museum, Queen St. Largest Museum in South West; Prehistory and Roman Gallery, natural history, archaeology, Exeter silver, clocks and watches, pottery, world cultures

1808 Dartmoor Prison founded at Princetown for French and American prisoners of war. Converted to present use in 1850.

1809 First publication of Ordnance Survey's map of Devonshire.

Exeter Canal

and paintings by British artists, especially of Devon. Café. Gift shop. Open Tu-Su 10-5. Free. (F1) 01392 265858 rammuseums.org.uk

The Quayside Exeter. Apart from the Cathedral and its surrounds, this is where the action takes place in Exeter. Wander down from the Cathedral (and car park) and admire the boats and swans, the old warehouse buildings. You have Antique emporia, nightclubs, craft shops, the Custom House Visitor Centre. If you fancy a cycle or a paddle on the river, visit Saddles & Paddles. For food and drink, a varied selection. The **Prospect Inn** serves Devon ales and pub-grub cooked with local produce. Next door, **Mangos** for breakfast, great coffees smoothies, light meals and for people watching. Open 9-6. (F1) cafemangos.co.uk

Underground Passages, c/o Visitor Information Centre, Dix's Field. Guided tours of medieval vaulted passageways from the C14 and C15 stretching under the City's streets. Open daily except M Oct-May. Access on Paris Street between Next and Zara. (F1) 01392 665887

University Gardens. 300-acres of grounds, award winning landscaped gardens, sculptures. Open daily, free admission. (G1) 01392 215566

The House That Moved

West Front, Exeter Cathedral

CATHEDRAL CHURCH OF ST PETER.

One of the finest English cathedrals, and Devon's most magnificent building. Statuesque with twin Norman Towers. Bishop Marshall in the C13 started this great project. However, it was Bishop John Grandisson, 1327-1365, in the C14 who moved the construction forward with greater panache and fortitude, greatly encouraged by Pope John XX11. He organised the construction up to the Nave, largely his own creation. The truly magnificent (and it is difficult not to be over awed by this) rib-vaulting of the Nave extends to over 300 feet, and is quite unique. The carved misericords, 1230-1270, were the first in England. But surely what strikes the visitor, time and again, is the great West Front.

Walter Bronescombe, Exeter

Sit outside in the Close with your coffee and admire the frontage. The large window filled with intricate tracery, Grandisson's work, and the lower wall, filled with sculptured images, eighty-eight in all, of warriors, angels, kings and saints. The effect is unforgettable, truly astounding. In recent years, some have crumbled and have been restored. Defoe claimed it took four hundred years to build, and yet it appears as one whole. No patchwork lines to spy. The interior has more to succour; colourful roof bosses, C14 Choir screen and Bishop's Throne, Lady Chapel, East Window with medieval glass. The C14 Window with modern glass. Sir John Speke's C16 Chantry, The C15 Astronomical Clock and Minstrels' Gallery.

The Nave, Exeter Cathedral

One can't not mention Herbert Read, who did so much to restore the Cathedral following the bombing of 1942. We must give thanks to his memory, for his tireless and patient work. Café/Shop. Open M-Sa 9-5, Su 11.30-5.(F1) 01392 255573 exeter-cathedral.org.uk

1812
Shelley honeymooned in Lynmouth.

1814
The Devon prophetess Joanna Southcott claims to be pregnant with Shiloh, the second Messiah.

Lady Doderidge, Exeter Cathedral

The Resurrection Mural, Exeter Cathedral

Hugh Oldham, Exeter Cathedral

1815
August 7th.Napoleon moored off Berry Head before transportation in the Northumberland to St Helena, exile and death.

WHAT TO SEE IN EXETER; ART, CINEMA, CRAFTS, MUSIC...

Bike Shed Theatre, 162 Fore Street. Calling all Thespians and lovers of the Arts and Theatre. Herewith, an intimate 50+ seat auditorium exuding enthusiasm. One can hear the laughter, the profundity, the farcical and dangerous performances, the excitement. 01392 434169
bikeshedtheatre.co.uk

Bill Douglas Cinema Museum, The Old Library, Prince of Wales Road. Museum housing a unique collection of items relating to cinema history, tracing its roots in earlier forms of entertainment. Explore the Victorian world of animated toys, dioramas, panoramas and magic lanterns, or follow British and Hollywood cinema through the C20. Guided tours. Open daily 10-5. (G1) 01392 724321
bdcmuseum.org.uk

Cygnet Theatre, Friars Gate. A school of drama influenced by their Patron, Peter Brook. There are regular performances by the students, many of whom go on to star on stage and screen, in the 100-seat theatre. 01392 277189
cygnettheatre.co.uk

Exeter Phoenix, Gandy St. Arts and media centre with daily programme of events; music, drama, dance, film, visual arts. A centre of student life in Exeter. Café/Bar. Open M-Sa from 10 til 11 pm. (G1) Box Office: 01392 667080
exeterphoenix.org.uk

Northcott Theatre, Stocker Road. Exeter's premier theatre produces quality plays, opera, dance, comedy and family theatre often before, and after, the West End. 01392 726363
exeternorthcott.co.uk

Polka Dot Gallery, 12 Martins Lane. Attractive gallery just down from the Cathedral brimming with ceramics, glass, jewellery, paintings, photography, sculpture and textiles. Open daily M-Sa. 01392 276500
polkadotgallery.com

Spacex Gallery, Gandy St. Large contemporary gallery devoted to the visual arts, film, phptography, poetry and workshops. Open Tu-Sa 10-5. (F1) 01392 431786
spacex.org.uk

WHAT TO DO IN EXETER; SAIL, TOUR, CANOE, CYCLE...

Exeter Red Coat Guided Tours. Departing from the West Front of the Cathedral these are free entertaining guided walking tours of 90-minutes that reveal Exeter's fascinating history and hidden treasures. No booking required and choice of 17-tours. Open daily, all year. See Notice Board for Start Times. (F1) 01392 265203
exeter.gov.uk/guidedtours

Saddles & Paddles, 4, Kings Wharf, The Quay. Single and double kayaks (with child seats) or Canadian canoes hired out to explore the wildlife beside the River Exe and canal. Drop in on the two pubs en route. Buoyancy aids provided. Or, on bikes explore 7-miles of flat, easy traffic-free routes. Large selection of mountain bikes and hybrids, plus child seats and trailers for under-5s. Open daily 9-6. 01392 424241
sadpad.com

WHERE TO STAY, EAT, DRINK & BE MERRY...

Hotel du Vin, Magdalen St. A feast of chic, spare designs, at times bright and dazzling in this former Eye Hospital. An off-beat venue to meet friends, chat and have coffee, and admire the design features. Cocktail bar, Kino. Restaurant for lunch and dinner. (F1) 01392 790120
hotelduvin.com/locations/exeter

St Olaves Hotel & Treasury Restaurant, Mary Arches St. Set in the heart of the city close to the cathedral. Intimate C19 Georgian house with stunning Spiral Staircase. Walled garden or Conservatory for light lunches and teas. Fine restaurant. 01392 217736. (F1) olaves.co.uk

Mol's Coffee House, Cathedral Close

1816
John Heathcoat, inventor of the bobbin machine, sets up lace manufacture in Twerton.

1817
North Walk cut into cliffs from Lynton to Valley of Rocks.

The Guildhall, High Street

Southernhay House Hotel, 36 Southernhay East. Perhaps, the Exeter Boutique hotel you have been seeking? With 10-bedrooms, all individually created and a spacious bar and al fresco terrace for cocktails, all within a short walk of the Cathedral and City Centre.
01392 439000
southernhayhouse.com

WHERE EAT, DRINK & BE MERRY...

Kupp, The Guildhall, Queen Street. Simple Scandinavian lifestyle and cuisine with food available all day with a cool vibe, healthy and friendly eating. 01392 531777 kupp.co

Michael Caines Academy @34 Restaurant, Laurence Building, Exeter College. The students will cook you lunch daily (M-F 12-2) and supper two evenings (W & Th 7-9) per week. A 5-course table d'hote menu. Their passion and expertise will surprise you, and it's great value, too.
01392 400334 exe-coll.ac.uk

Plant Café, 1 Cathedral Yard. Child friendly café-deli has a full range of organic, free trade, vegetarian and children's food. Sit inside or out overlooking Cathedral Green, now a sad sight. Open daily 9-6. (F1) 01392 428144

Rendezvous Wine Bar & Restaurant, 38 Southernhay East. This venue is smart, casual and friendly. The wines are extensive and the food is classic English fare from Devon's rich larder of fresh seafood and pastoral meadows. Two-course set lunch. Open M-Sa 12pm - 12am.
01392 270222
rendezvous-winebar.co.uk

Steaks n Sushi, 23 North Street. Their imaginative cuisine has got Exeter folk rushing to their doors. Traditional Japanese food, all freshly made to order. Takeaways, too. Open M-Sa 12-3.30, 5.30-9. 01392 250414 steaksnsushi-exeter.co.uk

The Hour Glass, 21 Melbourne Street. Just up from the Quay. This is a proper pub since 1848 with atmosphere and fine ales, an assortment of old chairs, newspapers, books, wooden panelling and dark red paintwork. The food is good, pub grub. Basement restaurant. Open 12-3, 5-11. (F1) 01392 258722 hourglassexeter.co.uk

The Old Firehouse, 50 New North Road. This is a popular haunt of students and locals keen to hear live music, enjoy real ales

and start a romance on their candlelit tables. 01392 277279 oldforehouseexeter.co.uk

Rood Screen, Parish Church, Bovey Tracey

BOVEY TRACEY

A quiet, elongated town noted for its exquisite church (and Beckett associations) and the Devon Guild of Craftsmen, the finest craft gallery in Devon (and the South-West). The town's wealth was built from china clay deposits, or Bovey Clay, established in 1772. The results can be seen on Bottle Road, statuesque, old kilns. In the C18 and C19, Haytor quarries carried granite on tramways to Bovey for onward transport to the Dart Valley. These were used in the construction of London Bridge and the pillars for the British Museum. In the Second World War lignite (peat and coal mix) was mined for a short time. Park beside the bridge and the Information Centre (hut), following the road over the bridge takes you to the little High Street. The magnificent C12 Church is at the top of the town where there is parking available. (A8)

SPECIAL PLACES TO VISIT...

The Devon Guild of Craftsmen. The largest contemporary craft centre in the South West exhibiting work by artists of national and international renown, in the converted grade 11 listed Riverside Mill, in a beautiful location. Refurbished with new Jubilee Gallery, extended Craft Shop and The Terrace Café with rooftop seating. Open daily 10-5.30. (A8) 01626 832223 crafts.org.uk

Handloom Weavers, 1 Station Road. For 70 years, and two generations, they have produced tweeds, ties, scarves and throws from soft, pure new wool, in exclusive designs. View the production process in the workshop. Shop stocks sheepskin products and classic knitwear. Shop opens M-Sa 9-5. (EC W). Workshop mid-May to Oct, times vary. (A8) 01626 833424 boveyweavers.co.uk

Bovey Tracey Heritage Trust, The Old Railway Station. The Trust is a registered charity which researches and preserves the history of the town and area. Open East-Oct M-F 10-4, Sa 10-12. (A8) TIC 01626 832047 devonhistorysociety.org.uk

Parish Church of St Peter, St Paul & Thomas of Canterbury. Catholic guilt hath no bounds with William de Tracey, one of the four knights who carried out Henry 11's dastardly command "Who will rid me of this meddlesome priest"? Hacking to death Thomas a Beckett on the High Altar of Canterbury Cathedral, in 1170. For his penance, he built this church. Later additions in the C14, and a C15 Tower with pinnacled battlements and the C15 rood screen, considered the town's greatest treasure, and one of Devon's finest, has an exquisite panel of carved sculptures of the 31 apostles. And a medieval stone, carved pulpit and old wood bosses. (A8)

House of Marbles, Pottery Rd. Museum of glass, games, marbles, and Bovey Pottery. Coffee shop. Open M-Sa 9-5, Su 10-5. (A8) 01626 835285 houseofmarbles.com

1823
Jul 19. The first cholera case reported in Exeter in an epidemic in which 440 were to die.

1824
Jan 1. Plymouth Dock renamed Devonport.

DAWLISH

A modest resort compared to its neighbours. Yet recognised in literature as the birthplace of Dickens' Nicholas Nickleby, and as a pleasing place in Jane Austen's Sense and Sensibility. IK Brunel's railway cut a swathe through the red cliffs, a brilliant feat of Victorian engineering. Troubled today by heavy seas and an eroding coastline. To the north of the town, a row of pretty cottages, then onto Dawlish Warren, a naturalist's feast. (H9)

PLACES TO VISIT...

Dawlish Museum, The Knowle. Victorian rooms, military and railway with unique collection of photos of Dawlish. Open daily May-Sept W-F 10.30-5, W/E 2-5. (H9) 01626 888557 dawlishmuseum.co.uk

Dawlish Warren. A spit of land at the mouth of the Exe Estuary, its shape, best appreciated from a bird's eye. On the seaward side, an extensive beach noted for shells. Inland, the mudflats are teeming with birdlife, especially autumn and winter migrants. The botanist will be excited with the Rare Crocus in spring, and the Ladies Tresses Orchid, in summer. Guided walks. No dogs. (J8) 01392 279244 devonwildlifetrust.org

SPECIAL PLACES TO VISIT...

Canonteign Falls. Dramatic waterfalls, featuring the highest (manmade waterfall) in England, lakes and ancient woodland, in private 100-acre park. Assault course, children's play areas. Restaurant/Tea room. Open daily East to Nov 10-dusk. (B6) 01647 252434 canonteignfalls.com

Exe Estuary. You can pick up leaflets that describe the cycleways, ferries, history, walkways, watersports, wildlife and all manner of activities associated with this little corner of Devon. The Estuary invites a multitude of fun-packed days. exe-estuary.org

Go Ape, Haldon Forest Park. Treetop adventures via two zip wires that fly you from hilltop to hilltop. Awesome fun! Book at: 0333 3315995 or online goape.co.uk

Haldon Belvedere. A monument to Major General Stringer Lawrence, built in 1788 by Sir Robert Park. Restored in 1994. Superb viewpoint. Also called Lawrence Castle. Open East-Sept Su 2-5. (D4) haldonbelvedere.co.uk

Powderham Castle. Built in 1390 by Sir Philip Courtenay whose descendants, the Earls of Devon, have lived here ever since. Restored and altered in C18 and C19. Fine interiors including music room by Wyatt. Furniture, paintings, tapestries, china and plasterwork. Newly restored C18 Woodland Garden. Formal garden and well stocked deer park with fine views. Diary of Events. Open daily Apr-Oct 10-5.30. (H6) 01626 890243 powderham.co.uk

Powderham Country Store. Produce from the estate; with butchery, bakery, delicatessen and food hall. A great day out. Open M-F 9.30-5.30, Sa 9-5, Su 10-5. (H6) 01626 891883 powderhamfoodhall.co.uk

Rock Gardens, Station Hill. 8 acres of wild garden with ponds, rare trees and shrubs set in the old Palace Quarry. Plant sales. Open daily 9-5. (C8) 01626 852134 therockgardens.co.uk

Taverner's Farm. The 5th generation of a 500-acre farm are the makers of Orange Elephant ice cream named after the herds of Devon cattle (of long ago) because of their enormous size. 18-different flavours to savour. Open in season. (F4) 01392 833766 tavernersfarm.co.uk

Ugbrooke House & Gardens. Medieval House redesigned by Robert Adam. Home of the Clifford family. Fine furniture and paintings, embroideries, uniforms and costumes. Library. Marble St Cyprian's Chapel, of 1830, the oldest Catholic Parish Church in the south-west. Cardinal's 4-poster bed. Gardens and grounds by Capability Brown. Open early July to late Sept Tu, W, Th & Su & Aug BHMs 12-5.30. Guided tours 12.30, 2 & 3.30pm. Orangery Tearooms 12-4.45. (D8) 01626 852179 ugbrooke.co.uk

PUBS SERVING FOOD

Anchor Inn, Cockwood. C16 Inn with superb estuary views and an enthusiastic nautical flavour, as well as a fine range of beers. Bar and restaurant menu. Dog/child friendly. (J7) 01626 890203 anchorinncockwood.com

Manor Inn, Lower Ashton. Fine country pub loaded with ambience. Range of fine ales. Large portions. Open Tu-Su. (B5) 01647 252304 manorinn.co.uk

Nobody Inn, Doddiscombsleigh. C17 Inn provides jolly atmosphere and supreme service. Serious wine and whisky list. Local ales. Lunch M-Sa 12-2.30, dinner Su-Th 6-9.30. 5-luxury bedrooms. (C4) 01647 252394 nobodyinn.co.uk

Powderham Castle ss

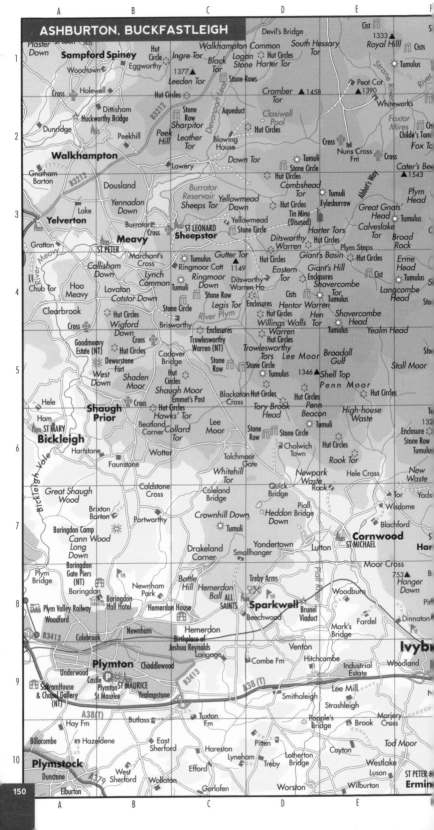

Plaster Down
Sampford Spiney
Woodtown
Holewell
Cross
Dittisham
Huckworthy Bridge
Dunridge
Peekhill
Walkhampton
Gnatham Barton
Dousland
Yelverton
Gratton
Meavy
Burrator Cross
ST PETER
Callisham Down
Marchant's Cross
Lynch Common
Hoo Meavy
Lovaton
Catstor Down
Clearbrook
Cross
Wigford Down
Goodmeavy Estate (NT)
Dewerstone Fort
West Down
Shaden Moor
Shaugh Moor
Cross
Hele
Ham
ST MARY
Bickleigh
Shaugh Prior
Hartstone
Faunstone
Beatland Corner
Collard Tor
Wotter
Great Shaugh Wood
Coldstone Cross
Brixton Barton
Portworthy
Boringdon Camp
Cann Wood
Long Down
Boringdon Gate Piers (NT)
Plym Bridge
Boringdon
Plym Valley Railway
Woodford
Colebrook
Newnham Park
Newnham
Hemerdon House
Hemerdon Birthplace of Joshua Reynolds
Langage
Saltram House & Chapel Gallery (NT)
Underwood
Plympton
Castle
Plympton ST MAURICE
St Maurice
Chaddlewood
Yealmpstone
Hay Fm
Butlass
Hazeldene
Billacombe
Plymstock
Dunstone
West Sherford
East Sherford
Elburton
Wollaton
Efford
Hareston
Lyneham
Treby
Gorlofen
Devil's Bridge
Walkhampton Common
Ingre Tor
Black Tor
Logan Stone
Hut Circles
Eggworthy
Hut Circle
Leeden Tor
1377
Stone Rows
Harter Tor
South Hessary Tor
Royal Hill
1333
Cists
Tumulus
Cist
B3212
Hut Circles
Stone Row Sharpitor
Leather Tor
Peek Hill
Aqueduct
Blowing House
Clasiwell Pool
Hut Circles
Cramber Tor
1458
Peat Cot
1390
Whiteworks
Strane River
River
Foxtor Mires
Child's Tomb
Fox Ta
Lowery
Down Tor
Tumuli
Stone Circle
Hut Circles
Cross
Nuns Cross Fm
Cross
Cater's Bee
1543
Plym Head
Burrator Reservoir
Sheeps Tor
Yennadon Down
ST LEONARD
Sheepstor
Yellowmead Down
Yellowmead
Stone Circle
Combeshead Tor
Tin Mine (Disused)
Tumuli
Eylesburrow
Hut Circles
Great Gnats' Head
Calveslake Tor
Tumulus
Broad Rock
Ditsworthy Warren
Harter Tors
Hut Circles
Plym Steps
Gutter Tor
1149
Hut Circles
Giant's Basin
Hut Circles
Erme Head
Tumulus
Tumulus
Ringmoor Cott
Ringmoor Down
Ditsworthy Warren Ho
Eastern Tor
Giant's Hill
Endosures
Cist
Shavercombe Tor
Tumulus
Langcombe Head
Sto
Lynch Common
Tumuli
Stone Row
Legis Tor
Cists
Hentor Warren
Shavercombe Head
Yealm Head
Stone Circle
Brisworthy
River Plym
Enclosures
Hut Circles
Hen Tor
Sto
Wigford Down
Cross
Cadover Bridge
Enclosures
Hut Circles
Trowlesworthy Warren (NT)
Willings Walls Warren
Hut Circles
Trowlesworthy Tors
Lee Moor
Broadall Gulf
Stone Row
Hut Circles
Shaugh Moor
Emmet's Post
Stone Circle
Tumulus
1346
Shell Top
Penn Moor
Stall Moor
Hawks' Tor
Blackaton Cross
Hut Circles
Tory Brook Head
Penn Beacon
High-house Waste
Hut Circles
Lee Moor
Stone Row
Stone Circle
Cholwich Town
Hut Circles
Rook Tor
Tumuli
Tu
132
Enclosure
Stone Row
Tumulus
Tolchmoor Gate
Whitehill Tor
Coleland Bridge
Newpark Waste
Rook
Hele Cross
New Waste
Crownhill Down
Quick Bridge
Heddon Bridge Down
Piall Bridge
Tor
Wisdome
Yads
Tumuli
Blachford
Cornwood
ST MICHAEL
Har
Drakeland Corner
Smallhanger
Yondertown
Lutton
Moor Cross
753
Hanger Down
B
Pit
Bottle Hill
Hemerdon Ball
ALL SAINTS
Treby Arms
Sparkwell
Beechwood
Brunel Viaduct
Woodburn
Mark's Bridge
Fardel
Dinnaton
Combe Fm
Venton
Hitchcombe
Woodland
Ivybri
Chaddlewood
A3413
Industrial Estate
Lee Mill
Smithaleigh
Strashleigh
N
A38(T)
Tuxton Fm
Popple's Bridge
Brook
Mariery Cross
Tod Moor
Pitten
Lotherton Bridge
Coyton
Westlake
Luson
ST PETER &
Ermin
Worston
Wilburton

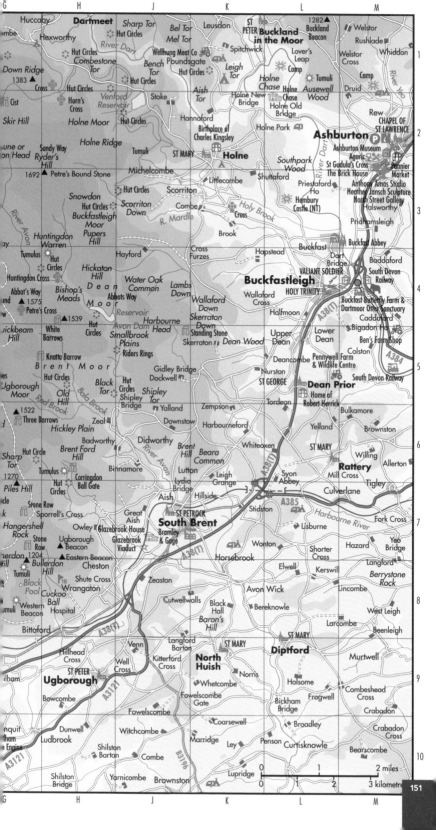

ASHBURTON

A charming town just off the A38, and well placed to explore Dartmoor and the South Hams. An ancient borough and "Stannary Town" considered by Anthony Trollope, to be the fairest corner of England. There is a gracious air and steady civility here, and pleasing architecture of slate carved roofs and oriel windows. Now a centre for good eating. It also has everything an outdoors person requires; an outdoor equipment retailer, deli, and just outside town on the industrial estate, Big Peaks, bike shop. The Post Office is the first in the UK to house a Public Library. Brilliant! (M2)

SPECIAL PLACES OF INTEREST...

Anthony Amos Studio, 8 West Street. Devoted to the late artist who specialised in architectural and marine paintings, and drawings, now widely shown in West Country galleries. Open F & Sa 12-3. (M2) 07792 624206 anthonyamos.com

Ashburton Museum, The Bull Ring. History and geology of Dartmoor. Tin and woollen industries. Red Indian collection. Open May-Sept Tu Th & F 2-4, Sa 10-12. (M2) 01364 653595 ashburton.org

Heather Jansch Sculpture, East Street. Heather creates life-size sculptures and horses heads out of driftwood, and bronze castings of horses. The gallery is a showcase, rarely open. (M2) For appointments call: 07775 840513 heatherjansch.com

North Street Gallery, 22 Fore Street. A new venture for a co-operative of 5-artists; sculpture, landscape paintings and ceramics. Open Tu-Sa 10-4.30. (M2) 01364 653334

Parish Church of St Andrew. C15 creation with cradle roof and fine bosses. Herbert Read's sculptures fill three niches over the west door. (M2)

Buckfast Abbey. Benedictine Abbey church built by personal labour of the community of monks during the years 1903-38, on site of the former medieval Cistercian abbey. Finely decorated interior. Chapel of the Blessed Sacrament added in 1966 with the colourful mosaic window. Exhibition of monastic history, vestments and plate in C15 Guest Hall. The community produce honey, wine and other artefacts for sale. These, they sell onto the visitors who come in charabancs and coaches, in their teeming hundreds. Their commercial acumen has had the locals decrying the place as "Fastbuckleigh." Bookshop. Grange Restaurant. Open daily; church and grounds 5.30-19.00. Visitors from 9 (9.30 in winter). (L3) buckfast.org.uk

Buckfast Butterfly Farm & Dartmoor Otter Sanctuary. Butterflies from all over the world in tropical landscaped garden. Otters in underwater viewing areas. Open daily Mar-Oct 10-5 (dusk). 01364 642916 ottersandbutterflies.co.uk

South Devon Railway, The Station. The SDR is a 7-mile Great Western heritage steam railway (built in 1872) from Buckfastleigh to Totnes beside the picturesque River Dart. Buckfastleigh Station, with free car parking, beside the A38 Devon Expressway. Totnes Station beside Mainline Station. (M4) 01364 644370 southdevonrailway.org

BUCKFASTLEIGH

Worth a detour to visit this pretty, well-groomed village with a one-way High Street. Swimming pool and museum, below. (L4)

The Valiant Soldier, 80 Fore Street. A village inn for two centuries where time was never called, and now a museum showing furniture, pub artefacts of the 40s and 50s. Open East-Oct M-Sa 10.30-4.30. (Tu Th & Su from 12.30) (L4) 01364 644522

SPECIAL PLACES TO VISIT...

Ben's Farm Shop, Wash Barn. Home to their award-winning organic restaurant, the Riverford Kitchen, and where they organize organic vegetables from the farm to table. Their vegetable box scheme allows you to choose from a range of box sizes, the contents of the box will be different each week. Open M-Sa 9-6, Su 10-5. (M5) 01803 762851 bensfarmshop.co.uk

LIGHT BITES...

Towards the top of **North Street** is the **Agaric Rooms B&B, 30 North St**. Former restaurateurs now provide luxurious B&B, parallel with their on-line shop selling quality cookware, frozen meals annd preserves. (M2) 01364 654478 agaricrestaurant. co.uk. Further down the street, the **Asburton Delicatessen**. I always visit this store for their amazing sausage rolls and Bakewell tarts, and cheeses for filling rolls. Across the street for a conventional tea drinking experience amongst period antiques and soft furishings, **Tea at Taylors** open from 9.30. Perhaps you require a more substantial repast then cross the road into **East Street: The Brick House, 26 East St**. A real find; spacious elegant rooms to enjoy home produced food, all day from 9; Soups, light lunches, cream teas, cocktails after 5 and suppers. Garden. (M2) 01364 653939 thebrickhouseashburton.co.uk

In need of seafood? **The Fish Deli, 7 East Street**. Fresh fish sourced from local boats, and Isles of Scilly lobster. Fish cooked on premises for home consumption. Deli for olive oils and tapas. Books and organic wines. Open M-Sa 9-5. (M2) 01364 654833 thefishdeli.co.uk And finally, should you wish for a mediterranean cuisine, walk into **West Street** to **Moorish** for tapas, grilled lamb with spinach and wondrous oils and balsamic vinegars. 01364 654011 moorishrestaurant.co.uk

1830
Plymouth Brethren formed.

1839
Fire destroyed 260 homes in Cullompton.

Buckfast Abbey

Dean Prior, Church of St George. For all lovers of English poetry, and considered by some scholars to be our finest poet, the home of Robert Herrick, Cavalier Poet and acolyte to Ben Johnson. It was here he wrote his great Hesperides, a lengthy manuscript on Celibacy, Marriage, Ritual and Sexual Politics. Appointed vicar by Charles 1 in 1629, he took a long, long time to understand his flock, eventually to be driven out by Puritans, to return fifteen years later after the Restoration. It is a little church, on a fast road, with parking. The east window is his Memorial. He lies outside in an unmarked grave. (L5)

Hemerdon House. Georgian family house. Collection of West Country paintings and prints, furniture and library. Open May & Aug BHs 2.15-5.30 and occasional days May-Aug. (B8) 01752 337350 hemerdonhouse.co.uk

Lukesland Gardens, Harford Road. 24-acres of flowering shrubs, trees and wild flowers by a Dartmoor stream. Open late Mar to mid-June Su W & BH Ms 11-5. In the Autumn Su & W early Oct to mid-Nov. Special Events - see website. (F8) 01752 691749 lukesland.co.uk

Pennywell Farm & Wildlife Centre. 80-acres to roam, with activities every half-hour. Farm & British wild animals. Owl and Falconry Centre. Pets corners. Special Events. Open Feb half-term for lambing special, to end Oct 10-5. (L5) 01364 642023 pennywellfarm.co.uk

Rattery. Village with one of the oldest inns in Christendom, and Devon, if you believe the tall stories told here in the Church House Inn. C13-C15 church beside the village green with Norman font and C15 oak screen restored in the C20. Rambling old mill with leaded windows. (L6)

Treby Arms, Sparkwell. For that Special Occasion unless your pockets are lined with gold. A rustic country pub that serves Michelin starred, style of cuisine. So in short, it's more of a precious restaurant within a pub build. (D8) 01752 837363 thetrebyarms.co.uk

Well Hung Meat Company, Cordonford Farm. A wonderful selection of pork sausages, from the garlicky Toulouse taster to the softer Breakfast type, also with organic apples. Lamb, chicken and beef, too. 8-holiday lets to rent, from a romantic cottage for 2, to a 14-bed residence. Open M-F 9-5 01364 643087 wellhungmeat.com

DARTMOOR SPECIAL PLACES OF INTEREST...

Childe's Tomb. A stone cross marks the site of the tragedy of the Lord of the Manor of Plymstock. Caught in a blizzard, he killed his horse and climbed inside to keep warm but still froze to death. He left a Will leaving his estate to those who would find and bury him. The monks of Tavistock did so, and thus, claimed his land. (F2)

Dewerstone Rocks. Granite outcrop 300 feet high, packed with legend and known as the Devil's stone. Fine views to be had over Goodameavy, the River Meavy and beyond. (B5)

Holne Bridge. A beauty spot, especially colourful in Spring and late Autumn on either side of this fine old bridge. (L2)

SPECIAL PLACES TO STAY...

Boringdon Hall Hotel & Spa. An Elizabethan manor house, formerly a National Trust property, combines antique furnishings, superb fireplaces and 4-poster bedrooms coupled with jacuzzis, spa treatments and mod-cons on tape to usher you to a stress-free weekend. Yoga Breaks. (B8) 01752 344455 boringdonhall.co.uk

Glazebrook House, South Brent. This boutique-style hotel with 9-bedrooms is bold, brash and has style in bucket loads. Open for breakfast, lunch and dinner to non-residents, and the perfect location from which to explore Dartmoor, Exeter, Plymouth and South Hams. No dogs or children u-16. (J7) 01364 73322 glazebrookhouse.com

Holne Chase Holiday Cottages. A former hunting lodge for the Abbots of Buckfast Abbey set amidst a nature reserve. A centre that specialises in fly fishing, riding and shooting. There is the Carriage House that sleeps 8, the Grooms Cottage sleeps 5 and the Fishermans Flat for 2. Dogs welcome. (L2) 01364 631471 holne-chase.co.uk

To the east of the Exe is a stretch of coastline where for the most part sand gives place to shingle interspersed with high cliffs; Devon Red to start with, but changing to White Chalk towards the Dorset border.

Along the coast, the busy port of Exmouth, the genteel town of Budleigh Salterton, the elegant Regency buildings of Sidmouth, and Seaton with its attractive neighbouring village of Beer. Inland, the market town of Honiton, renowned for lace, and Ottery St Mary, with its magnificent church. All around is a beautiful landscape of patchwork fields and rolling hills, where Devon meets Somerset. It is a countryside worthy of exploration and best suited to those with time on their hands. Best to leave the A-roads and to wander aimlessly from village to village.

Explore the Farway Valley and you may imagine you are lost in time, or if you are lost on a foreign shore, dreaming of England's green pastures and smooth hillsides, it is this valley that may come to mind; a bowl of aching beauty, bidden with villages of thatch and little churches. Climb out of this valley, and you will find yourself on a plateau with stupendous views, to west and east.

But if architecture, or to be more specific, church art and craftsmanship, interests you, then this corner of England will hold your attention for hours. You will be entranced by the magnificent churches of Broadclyst, Colyton, Cullompton and Ottery St Mary, and the smaller, no less charming ones, of Branscombe, East Budleigh, Northleigh, Shute, Southleigh and Uplyme … the list goes on.

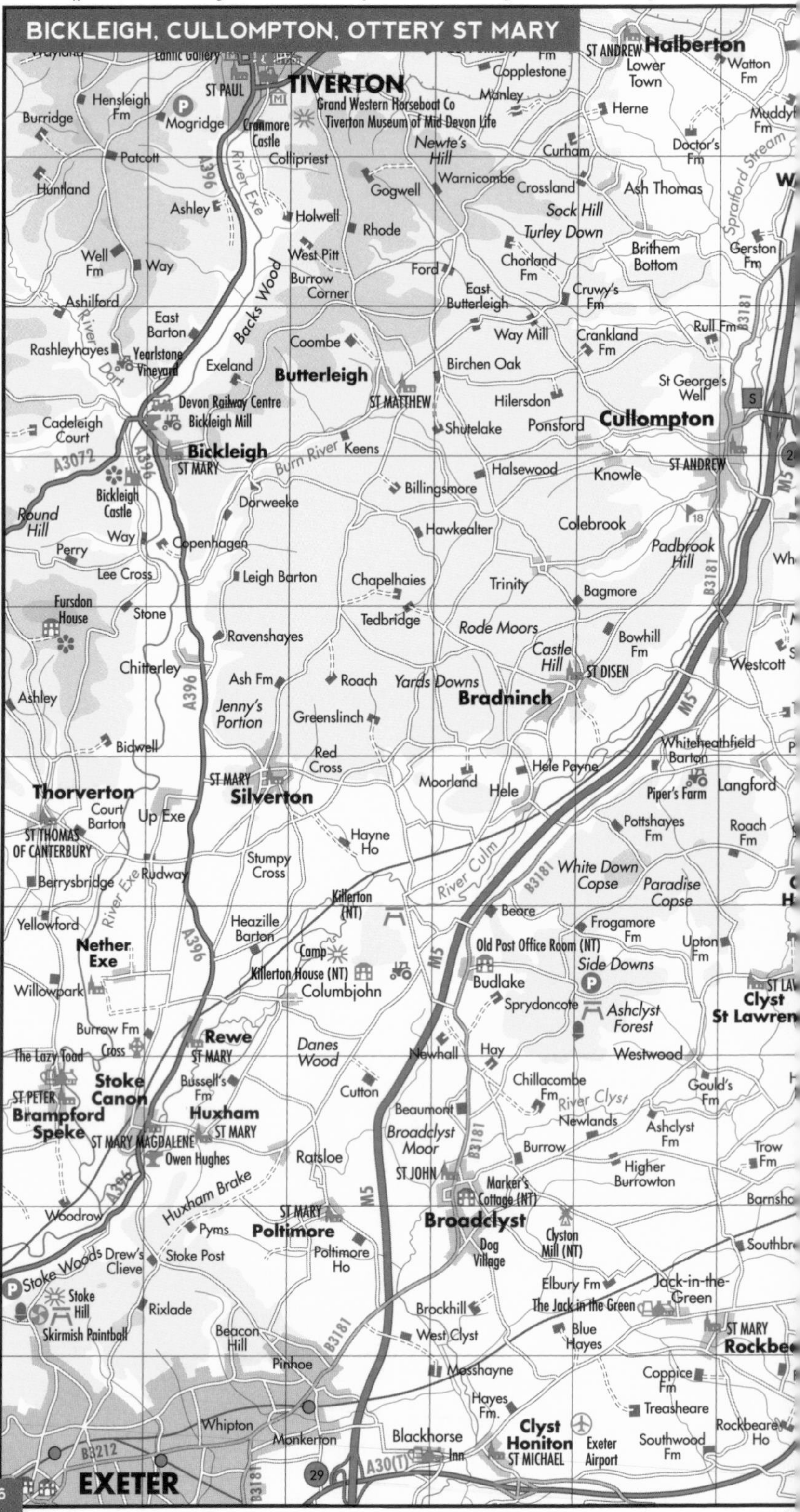

TIVERTON
ST PAUL
Grand Western Horseboat Co
Tiverton Museum of Mid Devon Life
Cranmore Castle
Collipriest
Hensleigh Fm
Mogridge
Burridge
Patcott
Huntland
Ashley
River Exe
A396
Holwell
Rhode
Gogwell
Newte's Hill
Copplestone
Manley
Warnicombe
Crossland
Curham
Halberton
ST ANDREW
Lower Town
Watton Fm
Herne
Doctor's Fm
Ash Thomas
Spratford Stream
Sock Hill
Turley Down
Brithem Bottom
Gerston Fm
Chorland Fm
Cruwy's Fm
Well Fm
Way
West Pitt
Burrow Corner
Ford
East Butterleigh
Backs Wood
Ashilford
River Dart
East Barton
Rashleyhayes
Yearlstone Vineyard
Exeland
Coombe
Butterleigh
ST MATTHEW
Way Mill
Crankland Fm
Rull Fm
B3181
Birchen Oak
Hilersdon
St George's Well
Devon Railway Centre
Bickleigh Mill
Cadeleigh Court
Shutelake
Ponsford
Cullompton
ST ANDREW
A3072
Bickleigh
ST MARY
Burn River
Keens
Halsewood
Knowle
Billingsmore
Bickleigh Castle
Round Hill
Dorweeke
Hawkealter
Colebrook
Padbrook Hill
M5
Way
Copenhagen
Perry
Lee Cross
Leigh Barton
Chapelhaies
Trinity
Bagmore
Fursdon House
Stone
Tedbridge
Rode Moors
Ravenshayes
Castle Hill
Bowhill Fm
Westcott
Chitterley
ST DISEN
Ash Fm
Roach
Yards Downs
Bradninch
Ashley
Jenny's Portion
Greenslinch
Bidwell
Red Cross
Whiteheathfield Barton
Thorverton
ST MARY
Silverton
Moorland
Hele
Hele Payne
Piper's Farm
Langford
Court Barton
Up Exe
ST THOMAS OF CANTERBURY
Hayne Ho
Pottshayes Fm
Roach Fm
Stumpy Cross
Rudway
Berrysbridge
River Exe
River Culm
White Down Copse
Paradise Copse
Killerton (NT)
Yellowford
Heazille Barton
Beare
Frogamore Fm
Upton Fm
Nether Exe
Camp
Old Post Office Room (NT)
Side Downs
Killerton House (NT)
Columbjohn
Willowpark
Budlake
Spyrdoncote
Ashclyst Forest
Clyst St Lawrence
Burrow Fm
Rewe
ST MARY
Danes Wood
Cross
The Lazy Toad
Newhall
Hay
Westwood
Stoke Canon
ST PETER
Brampford Speke
Bussell's Fm
Cutton
Chillacombe Fm
River Clyst
Gould's Fm
Huxham
ST MARY
ST MARY MAGDALENE
Beaumont
Newlands
Ashclyst Fm
Owen Hughes
Broadclyst Moor
Ratsloe
Burrow
Higher Burrowton
Trow Fm
ST JOHN
Marker's Cottage (NT)
Huxham Brake
Woodrow
ST MARY
Poltimore
Broadclyst
Clyston Mill (NT)
Pyms
Dog Village
Stoke Woods
Drew's Clieve
Stoke Post
Poltimore Ho
Stoke Hill
Elbury Fm
Jack-in-the-Green
The Jack in the Green
Rixlade
Brockhill
Skirmish Paintball
Beacon Hill
B3181
West Clyst
Blue Hayes
ST MARY
Rockbeare
Pinhoe
Mosshayne
Coppice Fm
Hayes Fm.
Treasheare
Whipton
Clyst Honiton
ST MICHAEL
Exeter Airport
Rockbeare Ho
Southwood Fm
Monkerton
Blackhorse Inn
A30(T)
B3212
EXETER
29

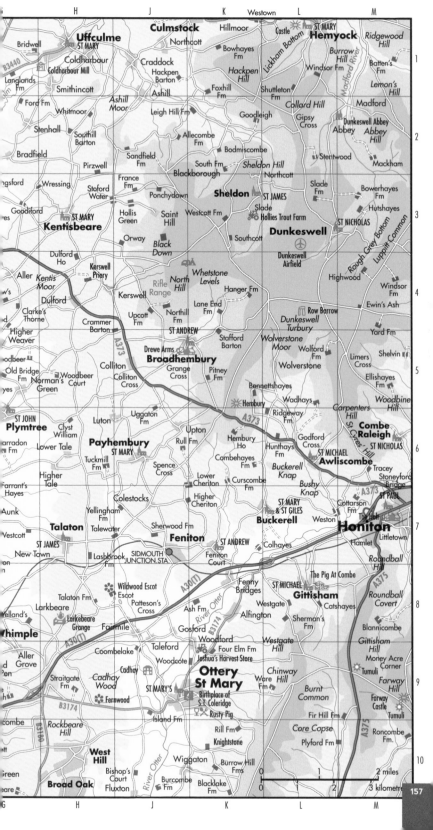

Cadhay

BICKLEIGH

A pretty village beside the River Exe with fine bridge and fisherman's cottages. You can sit in the garden of the Inn and admire the pastoral scene. (B3)

SPECIAL PLACES TO VISIT...

Bickleigh Castle. Royalist stronghold spanning 900 years of history. C11 Chapel, Armoury, Guardroom, Great Hall and Tudor bedroom. Picturesque moated garden. Now a Wedding Venue with a number of B&B options. B&B line on 01884 855796. Tours of the Castle by appoinment. (A4) 01884 855363
bickleighcastle.com

Bickleigh Mill. Extensive shopping with crafts, gallery, ladies' & gentlemen's fashions, interiors, furnishings and the Bistro Restaurant and Bar which is open from 10. Riverside walks in 10-acres of land. Open daily 9.30-5. (B3) 01884 855419
bickleighmill.com

Devon Railway Centre. Train rides on two lines with 10 working model layouts and over 30 trains in motion. Museum. Shop. Café. Open East-Sept & Oct W/Es & half-term 10.30-5. (B3) 01884 855671
devonrailwaycentre.co.uk

Yearlstone Vineyard. Devon's oldest vineyard producing wines for almost thirty years. This year, due to major renovation work the vineyard is closed. To buy wines, by appointment only. (A3) 01884 855700
yearlstone.co.uk

OTTERY ST MARY

Famous as the birthplace in 1772 of Samuel Taylor Coleridge; poet, philosopher, naturalist, and son to the Vicar of the parish. Set in the valley of the River Otter, the town is a friendly and pleasing place to visit. The surrounding, pastoral landscape, is distinguished by a web of narrow lanes, these join little farms and hamlets. Map reading requires concentration, or you can just let the road take you hither and thither, and explore the rich, red earthy lanes. The Blackdown Hills rise to the north, and to the East, the Jurassic Coast of East Devon. The church is not to be overlooked, and is plainly, a feast for the churchophile. (K9) St Mary's, Ottery St Mary. One of the great churches of Devon. Largely built in the C14 but later modelled on Exeter Cathedral with its fine transeptal towers. The Dorset Aisle from 1520, is an exquisite example of fan faulting perhaps

only matched by Gloucester Cathedral. Fine Grandisson tomb. Unusual 600-year old clock. The father of the great Romantic poet, Samuel Taylor Coleridge was vicar here from 1760-81. A studious and simple man, he read the bible in Hebrew to his parishioners; country folk and farm workers! (J9)

SPECIAL PACES TO VISIT...

Broadclyst – Marker's Cottage (NT). A thatched medieval cob house with an interesting interior containing a screen decorated with "grotesque" work, and a landscape scene of St Andrew. Cob summerhouse in garden. Open Apr-Oct Sa-W, 1-5. (D8)

Budlake – Old Post Office (NT). A charming thatched cottage in 1950s style that housed the village post office. Outside the washhouse, double-seated privy, pigsty and chicken house. Half an acre of vegetable garden. Open Apr-Oct Sa-W, 1-5. (D7)

Cadhay. Built in 1550 on the site of an earlier house to incorporate its Great Hall with a fine, timbered roof. Elizabethan Long Gallery and some Georgian work. Splendid Courtyard with statues of Henry V111 and his children.

*1840
Braunton Great Field is recorded as having 448 strips, 46 landowners and 62 cultivators.*

1841   Construction of Plymouth Breakwater to protect the Fleet from the south-westerlies. Before they would seek safety in Torbay.

Ottery St Mary New cob house

Maritime paintings and ancient fishponds. House is available to rent for house parties, sleeping up to 22 persons. Tea room. House and gardens open F May-Sept, also Spring & Aug Su & M BHs 2-5. (J9)
cadhay.org.uk

Clyston Mill (NT). C19 water powered grain mill lovingly restored to its former glory, and now producing top quality flour. Set beside the River Clyst surrounded by farmland and orchards, an idyllic spot. Open Apr-Oct, Sa-W 1-5. (D9)

Coldharbour Mill. 200-year old working woollen mill in continuous production since 1797. You can relive the sights and sounds of the Industrial Revolution and witness the creation of textiles, knitting yarn and hand-woven rugs. Giant water wheel. Special Events; Steam Up Days and Autumn Country Fair. Mill shop and waterside gardens. Picnics. Open daily Apr-Xmas 10-5. (H1)
01884 840960
coldharbourmill.org.uk

Diggerland. Children (and adults) can drive real JCBs and construction machinery. Fully trained instructors on hand. Open daily from 10. (F2)
0871 2277007
diggerland.com

Fursdon House. The Fursdons have lived here since 1259. The guided tour takes you through the medieval, Jacobean, Georgian and Regency periods. Family portraits, furniture and paintings to view. Costume Museum featuring C18 and C19 clothes. House open June-Aug W Th & BH Ms from 2-5, tours at 2.30 & 3.30 pm. Gardens and Tea Room open East M-Sept W Th & BH Ms 2-5. You can stay in one of their holiday cottages or an apartment within the manor house. (A5) 01392 860860
fursdon.co.uk

Coldfharbour Mill, Uffculme

Killerton House & Garden (NT). Home of the Acland Family for over three hundred years, and rebuilt in 1778. Downstairs rooms furnished in different periods. Upstairs the Pauline de Bush Costume Collection. 15 acres of superb gardens developed through many generations. Victorian laundry. Ice House. Garden, Park, shop, stables café, plant centre open all year from 10-5.30 House & Restaurant open from early Feb-29 Oct, 25 Nov-31 Dec. Park open all year 8-7. 01392 881345 (C7)

Skirmish Paintball. Set in 120 acres of Stoke Woods, close to Exeter city centre. Trenches, bridges, ravines, jungles and swamps. Catering & sheltered rest areas. (A9) 01548 580025 paintballskirmish.co.uk

St Andrew's Church, Cullompton. The great West Tower added in 1545-1549 dominates the town's skyline, and is exceptional. It measures 100 feet and the pinnacles are nearly 20 feet higher. One of the great wagon roof and rood screens of Devon. Fan vaulting in the Lane Aisle with stained glass window by Burne-Jones on south side. Carved heraldic shields of the Moore family on the parclose screen. C15 Golgotha carving on west side. (F3)

COUNTRYSIDE INTERESTS...

Joshua's Harvest Store, Gosford Road. One of the leading specialist food shops

*1846
Braunton Tower built to commemorate the abolition of the Corn Laws.*

*1848
The railway reaches Torquay.*

St Mary's, Ottery St Mary

in Devon. It celebrates local, fresh, organic and specialist food and drink, and sells gifts and greeting cards. The café serves beautifully presented platters allowing you to sample the food sold in store. Open M-Sa 9-6, Su 10.30-4.30. (K9) 01404 815473 joshuasltd.co.uk

Pipers Farm. They support a community of local family farms producing red meats, poultry, and sausages and burgers of the highest quality. Visit their shop in Exeter at

Killerton Garden

the Magdelan Road shopping parade. (E6) 01392 881380
pipersfarm.com

Hollies Trout Farm, Slade Lane. Supplies many local pubs and restaurants with their award-winning fish. Try catching your own with rod and line.Fly fishing tuition. Log cabins to hire. (K3)
01404 841428
holliestroutfarm.co.uk

CHURCHES OF INTEREST...

St John the Baptist, Broadclyst. A magnificent church in the Perpendicular style; the tower is 100 feet and decorated in the style of Somerset tracery with eight pinnacles of Beer stone. This is the fourth church on this site, and forms the second largest parish in Devonshire. The roof was restored with iron tiles by I K Brunel. There are four elaborate tombs and some beautiful, and sad stained glass; the Ellen Acland window commemorates

the ten year old killed in a cycling accident. Up high, some fine bosses, the Green Man and the Three Rabbits. In the churchyard, a board remembers the Veitch family of gardeners, of Killerton. (D8)

WHERE TO EAT, DRINK & BE MERRY...

The Lazy Toad, Brampford Speke. Centre of village facing a cobbled courtyard. Log fires in winter. Specially brewed Speakeasy Ale and Adnams. Good honest food; casseroles, fillet of Devon beef, confit neckfillet of lamb or seared corn fed chicken breast. (A8)
01392 841591
thelazytoad.co.uk

Drewe Arms, Broadhembury. A thatched hostelry with a warm atmosphere ; open fires for winter night, fresh fish, quality wines and real ale (loved by CAMRA) Put simply- Your hosts, Kate, Dan and Viv are true exponents of their craft

and proud of their hostelry. (K5) 01404 841267
drewearmsinn.co.uk

The Jack in the Green, Rockbeare. One of the first dining-pubs in Devon started 20+ years ago that has become more a restaurant than a pub. It has won countless awards and accolades from food writers and built up a loyal clientele. Seasonal menus. The one drawback, the large, open space lacks intimacy. (E9)
01404 822240
jackinthegreen.uk.com

The Rusty Pig, Yonder Street, Ottery St Mary. If you seek a 'pig out' - yes, their expression. Thses guys are specialist charcuteries, and are passionate about pigs and they source the pork from their smallholding. Open for breakfast Th, F & Sa 10-12, lunch 12-2 is the plat du jour, pizzas for Th & F evenings. Sa evenings require a booking. (K9) 01404 815580
rustypig.co.uk

1855
Charles Kingsley's novel Westward Ho! Published.

1855
Oct 20. The North Devon Railway opened from Bideford to Barnstaple.

THE PIG AT COMBE, Gittisham, Nr Honiton. This is one of the great Country House Hotels and Restaurants of England. A Grade 1 Elizabethan manor surrounded by 3,500 acres of parkland has been fully modernised with large sofas, old carpets have been removed to reveal stripped floors. The conversion of the stables into a bedroom is a masterstoke of pragmatic design. Gone is the formality but the old style elegance remains. They provide contemporary luxuries and an ambience where you can relax and feel totally at ease. This could indeed be your Country Retreat, for you will have the tranquillity, the blissful comfort and Master chefs on hand to create superb cuisine from your massive Kitchen Garden. You, too, can walk in the surrounding parkland and join footpaths, or explore Gittisham with its pretty thatched cottages. Non-residents are welcome here and it is a wonderful place to stop for lunch and coffee. The Pig at Combe, Gittisham, Nr Honiton. (L8) 01404 540400 thepighotel.com

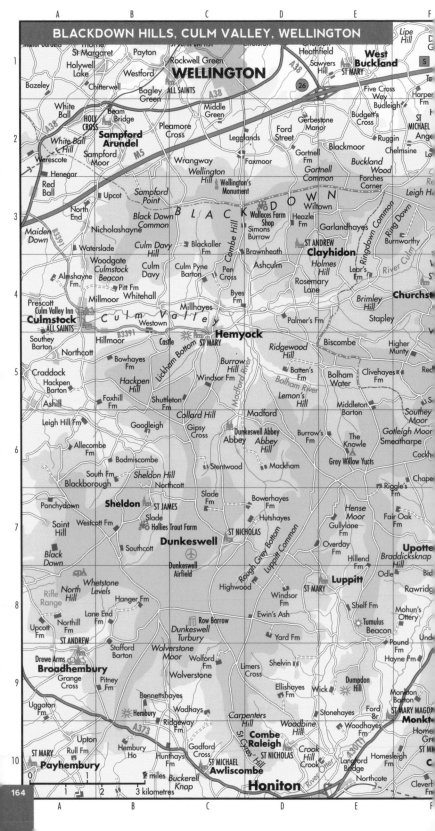

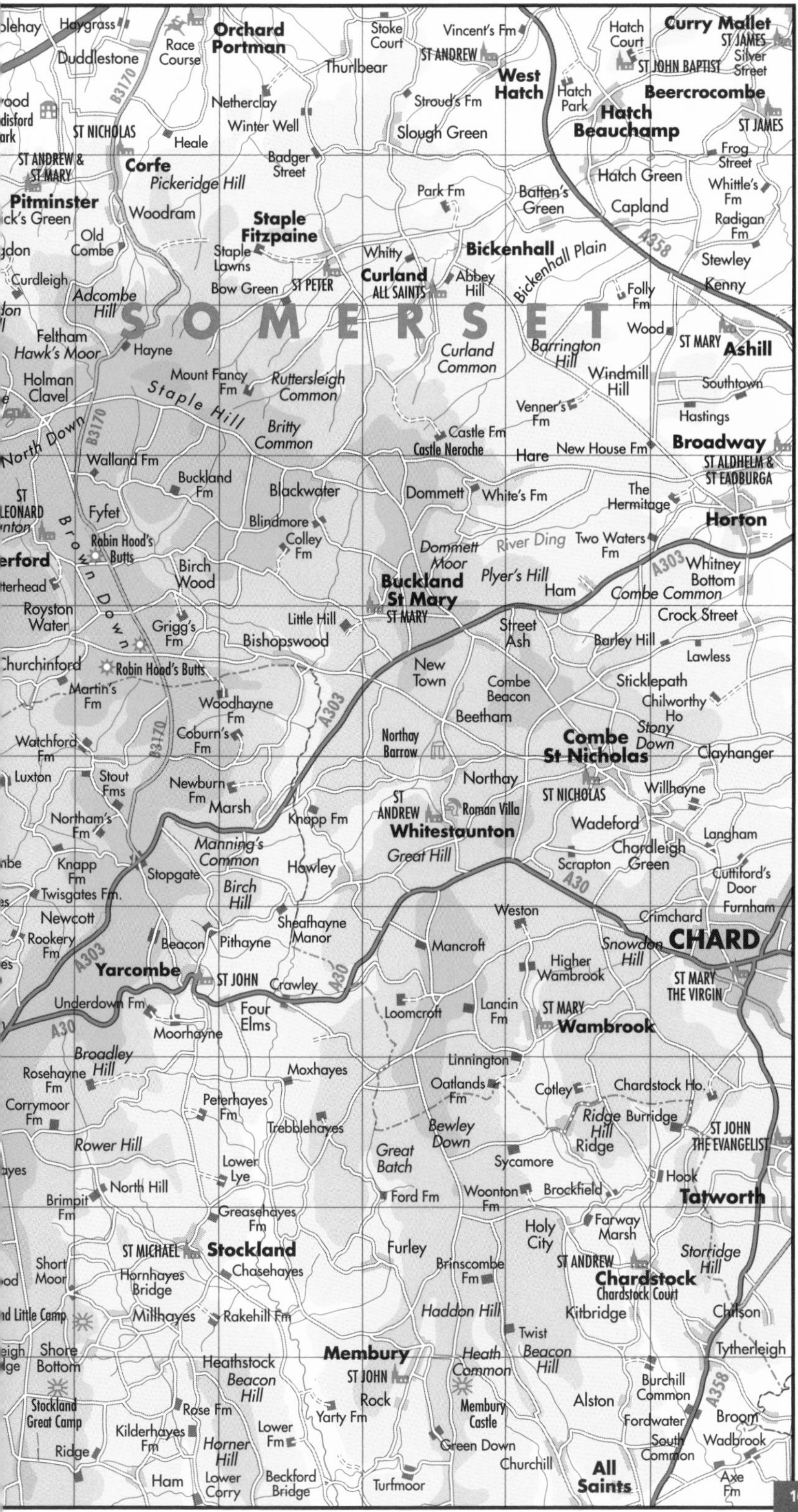

G
H
J
K
L
M
Haygrass
Duddlestone
Race Course
Orchard Portman
Stoke Court
Vincent's Fm
ST ANDREW
Thurlbear
West Hatch
Hatch Court
Curry Mallet
ST JAMES
Silver Street
ST JOHN BAPTIST
B3170
Netherclay
Stroud's Fm
Hatch Park
Beercrocombe
ST NICHOLAS
Winter Well
Slough Green
Hatch Beauchamp
ST JAMES
Heale
Badger Street
Frog Street
ST ANDREW & ST MARY
Corfe
Pickeridge Hill
Hatch Green
Whittle's Fm
Pitminster
Woodram
Park Fm
Batten's Green
Capland
Radigan Fm
Old Combe
Staple Fitzpaine
Staple Lawns
Whitty
Bickenhall
Bickenhall Plain
A358
Stewley
Curdleigh
Curland
Abbey Hill
Kenny
Adcombe Hill
Bow Green
ST PETER
ALL SAINTS
Folly Fm
SOMERSET
Wood
ST MARY
Ashill
Feltham
Hawk's Moor
Hayne
Curland Common
Barrington Hill
Mount Fancy Fm
Ruttersleigh Common
Windmill Hill
Southtown
Holman Clavel
Staple Hill
Venner's Fm
Hastings
B3170
Britty Common
Castle Fm
Castle Neroche
Broadway
North Down
Hare
New House Fm
ST ALDHELM & ST EADBURGA
Walland Fm
Buckland Fm
Blackwater
Dommett
White's Fm
The Hermitage
ST LEONARD
Fyfet
Blindmore
Horton
Brown Down
Robin Hood's Butts
Colley Fm
Dommett Moor
River Ding
Two Waters Fm
Birch Wood
Buckland St Mary
Plyer's Hill
A303
Whitney Bottom
Ham
Combe Common
Royston Water
Grigg's Fm
Little Hill
ST MARY
Street Ash
Crock Street
Bishopswood
Barley Hill
Lawless
Churchinford
Robin Hood's Butts
New Town
Combe Beacon
Sticklepath
Martin's Fm
A303
Chilworthy Ho
Woodhayne Fm
Beetham
Stony Down
Watchford Fm
B3170
Coburn's Fm
Northay Barrow
Combe St Nicholas
Clayhanger
Luxton
Stout Fms
Northay
Newburn Fm
ST ANDREW
Roman Villa
ST NICHOLAS
Willhayne
Marsh
Knapp Fm
Northam's Fm
Whitestaunton
Wadeford
Langham
Manning's Common
Chardleigh Green
Knapp Fm
Great Hill
Howley
Scrapton
Cuttiford's Door
Stopgate
Twisgates Fm.
Birch Hill
A30
Furnham
Crimchard
Newcott
Sheafhayne Manor
Weston
Rookery Fm
Beacon
Pithayne
Mancroft
Snowdon Hill
CHARD
A303
Yarcombe
Higher Wambrook
ST MARY THE VIRGIN
ST JOHN
Crawley
A30
Underdown Fm
Four Elms
Loomcroft
Lancin Fm
ST MARY
Wambrook
A30
Moorhayne
Broadley Hill
Linnington
Rosehayne Fm
Moxhayes
Oatlands Fm
Cotley
Chardstock Ho.
Corrymoor Fm
Peterhayes Fm
Ridge Hill
Burridge
Trebblehayes
Bewley Down
ST JOHN THE EVANGELIST
Rower Hill
Great Batch
Ridge
Sycamore
Lower Lye
Hook
North Hill
Woonton Fm
Brockfield
Tatworth
Brimpit Fm
Ford Fm
Greasehayes Fm
Holy City
Farway Marsh
ST MICHAEL
Stockland
Furley
Storridge Hill
Short Moor
Hornhayes Bridge
Chasehayes
Brinscombe Fm
ST ANDREW
Chardstock
Chardstock Court
Little Camp
Millhayes
Rakehill Fm
Haddon Hill
Kitbridge
Chilson
Shore Bottom
Heathstock Beacon Hill
Membury
Heath Common
Twist
Beacon Hill
Tytherleigh
ST JOHN
Rock
Burchill Common
Stockland Great Camp
Rose Fm
Yarty Fm
Membury Castle
Alston
A358
Broom
Kilderhayes Fm
Lower Fm
Fordwater
Wadbrook
Ridge
Horner Hill
Green Down
South Common
Churchill
All Saints
Ham
Lower Corry
Beckford Bridge
Turfmoor
Axe Fm
G
H
J
K
L
M
1
2
3
4
5
6
7
8
9
10

Wellington Monument

BLACKDOWN HILLS

Fine bit of country on the Somerset/Devon border. Get off the A303 and turn right following the B3170, after three miles, take a left at the North Down junction to follow a straight road beneath a tree lined avenue, towards Clayhidon. Follow to Culmstock turn off. Wonderful. (D3)

CULM VALLEY

An enchanting valley fed by the rivers Culm, Bolham and Madford. Culmstock has a fine pub (described) and Hemyock is an ancient village with castle and church. (C4)

WELLINGTON

Old established centre of the woollen trade. Fine Georgian houses. The Duke of Wellington took his title from here, and is commemorated in monument on the hilltop three miles south. Small museum. E/C W. (C1)

Wellington Monument. A notable landmark, 175 feet high on the Blackdown Hills. The first stone was laid in 1817, and completed in 1892. Arthur Wellesley took his title from Wellington, although it is claimed he only visited the area once in 1819. He did own land hereabouts. Popular dog walking spot. (C3)

WHERE TO EAT & DRINK...

Wallace's Farm Shop, Hill Farm. Breeds Highland cattle, Red Deer and Bison. Sells Giant Pork Pies, venison and dry cured bacon. Open daily 9.30-5. (D3) 01823 680307 wallacesfarm.co.uk

WHERE TO SLEEP & STARGAZE...

Grey Willow Yurts, Knowle Farm. They call them Yabins. Three solitary Yurts within a 3-acre field that sleep 5-persons. Comfy with wood burner. Dog/family/Environmentally friendly. You share a loo and shower. (E6) 079666 17488 greywillowyurts.co.uk

Culm Valley Inn. If one has to have favourites then this has been one of mine for many years. When you enter you are rewarded with a warm welcome and a proper old fashioned bar leading off to a chic restaurant with artworks hanging from the walls. Now under new ownership, it is their purpose to maintain the high standards of food and good living. 5-bedrooms to slumber and rest. (A4)
01884 840354
theculmvalleyinn.co.uk

Culm Valley Inn ss

1857
June. School Examination system set up in Exeter by Sir Thomas Acland.

1858
Philp's prehistoric cave discovered on Windmill Hill, Brixham.

1859
Brunel's Royal Albert Bridge carries the railway over the Tamar to Cornwall.

1860   Great Consols mine above the Tamar is the largest copper mine in the world, and by 1869, half the world's output.

167

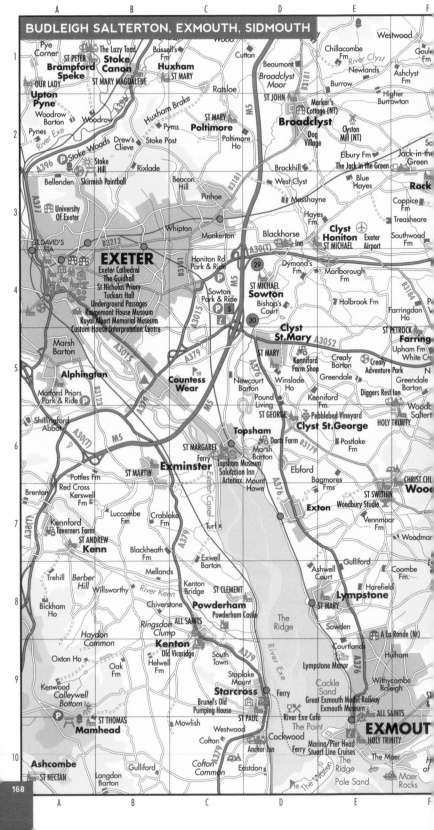

Map Labels

Pye Corner
The Lazy Toad
Bussell's
Cutton
Wood
Westwood
ST PETER
Stoke Canon
Huxham
Chillacombe Fm
River Clyst
Goul...
Fm
Brampford Speke
ST MARY MAGDALENE
ST MARY
Beaumont
Newlands
Ashclyst Fm
OUR LADY
Ratsloe
Broadclyst Moor
Burrow
Higher Burrowton
Upton Pyne
Woodrow
ST JOHN
Marker's Cottage (NT)
Woodrow Barton
ST MARY
Poltimore
Broadclyst
Pynes
River Exe
Drew's Clieve
Pyms
Poltimore Ho
Dog Village
Clyston Mill (NT)
Stoke Post
Stoke Woods
Elbury Fm
Jack-in-the Green
Rixlade
Brockhill
The Jack in the Green
So...
Stoke Hill
Beacon Hill
West Clyst
Blue Hayes
Rock
Bellenden
Skirmish Paintball
Pinhoe
Messhayne
Coppice Fm
University Of Exeter
Whipton
Monkerton
Hayes Fm.
Treasheare
ST DAVID'S STA
Blackhorse
Clyst Honiton
ST MICHAEL
Exeter Airport
Southwood Fm
EXETER
Honiton Rd Park & Ride
Dymond's Fm
Marlborough Fm
Farringdon Fm
Ho
Exeter Cathedral
The Guildhall
St Nicholas Priory
Tuckers Hall
Underground Passages
Rougemont House Museum
Royal Albert Memorial Museum
Custom House Interpretation Centre
Sowton Park & Ride
ST MICHAEL
Sowton
Bishop's Court
Holbrook Fm
ST PETROCK
Farring...
Upham Fm
White Cr...
Marsh Barton
Clyst St.Mary
ST MARY
Kennford Farm Shop
Crealy Barton
Crealy Adventure Park
N...
Greendale Barton
Alphington
Countess Wear
Newcourt Barton
Winslade Ho
Greendale
Diggers Rest Inn
Matford Priors Park & Ride
Pound Living
Kennford Fm.
Woodb...
Salter...
Shillingford Abbot
ST GEORGE
Pebblebed Vineyard
HOLY TRINITY
Clyst St.George
Topsham
Darts Farm
Postlake Fm
Pottles Fm
ST MARGARET
Marsh Barton
Bagmores Fms
CHRIST CHL
Red Cross
Kerswell Fm
ST MARTIN
Exminster
Ferry
Topsham Museum
Salutation Inn
Artenax
Mount Howe
Ebford
ST SWITHIN
Woodbury Studio
Woo...
Brentan...
Luccombe Fm
Crablake Fm
Exton
Kennford
Taverners Farm
ST ANDREW
Kenn
Turf
Vennmoor
Woodmar...
Blackheath Fm
Exwell Barton
Mellands
Gulliford
Coombe Fm.
Trehill
Berber Hill
Willsworthy
River Kenn
Kenton Bridge
ST CLEMENT
Ashwell Court
Harefield Fm
Lympstone
Bickham Ho
Chiverstone
Powderham
Powderham Castle
ST MARY
Sowden
A La Ronde (NT)
Haydon Common
Ringsdon Clump
ALL SAINTS
Kenton
Old Vicaridge
The Ridge
Courtlands
Hulham
Oxton Ho
Oak Fm
Helwell Fm
South Town
Lympstone Manor
Withycombe Raleigh
Kenwood
Colleywell Bottom
Staplake Mount
Starcross
River Exe
Cockle Sand
Great Exmouth Model Railway
Exmouth Museum
St...
&...
ALL SAINTS
ST THOMAS
Mamhead
Brunel's Old Pumping House
ST PAUL
Ferry
River Exe Cafe
The Point
EXMOUT...
HOLY TRINITY
Mowlish
Westwood
Cockwood
Marina/Pier Head
Stuart Line Cruises
The Maer
Ashcombe
ST NECTAN
Cofton
Anchor Inn
Ferry
The Ridge
Pole Sand
Maer Rocks
Langdon Barton
Gulliford
Cofton Common
Eastdon
The Warren

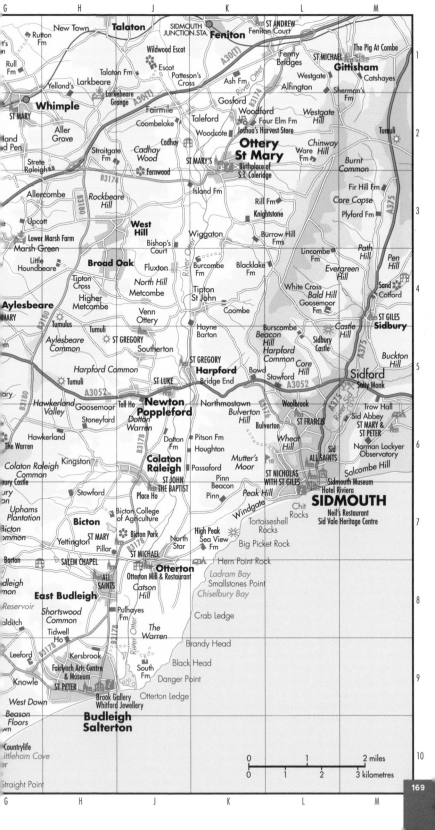

Fairlynch Arts Centre

BUDLEIGH SALTERTON

A genteel town favoured by the retired, especially elderly Ladies of Means. The shelving, oval pebbled beach festooned with fishermen's boats used not to attract day visitors or families, like nearby Exmouth and Sidmouth. But, today those "In The Know" realize it to be a heaven-sent suntrap. The High Street has greatly improved of late wth new cafés, delis, galleries and restaurants. The climate, mild, sheltered and well suited for the frail and weary. The high point of one's visit may be the conversation. The wisdom gained from meeting a lonely soul. It is possible to strike up an easy conversation with the residents who are often over-blessed with charm and manners, but they will frankly inform you that they would prefer to keep the town to themselves, than be overrun by outsiders. But, things are a changing. Late April invites the Jazz Festival for 3-days, budleighjazzfestival.org, and when the sun shines, come summer, Naturists are to be found desporting their hides on the western fringes of the beach!

If you seek fresh seafood look for the Skull & Crossbones flag on the beach.

There are some attractive, little Regency and Georgian houses. Sir John Millais lived here and painted "The Boyhood of Raleigh". The Fairlynch Museum is an interesting building. Of more interest, East Budleigh to the north with its fine church, and monuments to Sir Walter Raleigh. Also, Otterton Mill and the gardens of Bicton. (H9)

SPECIAL PLACES TO VISIT...

Brook Gallery, Fore Street. This is an energetic space given over to West Country artists, ceramicists and sculptors. Open daily. Associated with Brook Contemporary Art, a fine art consultancy. 01395 443003 brookgallery.co.uk

Fairlynch Arts Centre & Museum, 27 Fore Street. Interestingly shaped building designed in 1811 with costumes, geology and lace making exhibits plus demonstrations. Open Tu-Su East-Oct 2-4.30 (H9) 01395 442666 fairlynchmuseum.uk

Whitford Jewellery, 4 High Street. Steve's journey into jewellery making started with swashbuckling adventures in the Eastern Bloc and a passion for 18-carat gold brought him here. Open daily. 07939 057297 whitfordjewellery.co.uk

1860s.
Farm rents are high and farm workers wages are 70% of the national average resulting in a mass exodus of 126,000 folk leaving England.

Exmouth Lifeboat Station

EXMOUTH

The oldest seaside resort in Devon, and the fourth largest town, in population, in Devon. It is a town with two sides; on the one, the commercial port and new marina development, and on the other eastern side, the sweeping sands of the seaside resort meet the cliff wall of the World Heritage Site.

The town's beaches developed as a recreation area for Exeter folk in the early C18 before the upper classes came here during the Napoleonic Wars barred from Continental travel. Thus, the demand for civilised housing was acute which prompted the building of The Beacon in 1792, a fine Regency Terrace and the finest piece of architecture in the town. The numbers 6 and 19, were to become homes for the widows of Nelson and Byron. There are a multitude of recreational activities to be gained from visiting Exmouth;

deep sea fishing, watersports, donkey rides, and a fine cricket ground used for Minor County and Devon Youth Cricket. The new Marina and Pier Head are interesting spots to while away the time. Just to the north of the town, the fascinating property, A La Ronde, and across the road the new Michael Caines creation, Lympstone Manor. More recently, new eating-out places have sprung up, and will soon (perhaps) rival the best of Exeter - see below. (E10)

LIGHT BITES...

We now come down to earth...On the **Exeter Road** at **No. 57** is **Krispies Fish and Chips**. Tim and Kelly Barnes have won garlands galore for their fry ups, and raised hundreds of pounds for charities. Open daily 12-10. 01395 278823 krispies.co.uk Moving into town heading toward the **Pier/Quay** you must drop in to the **Grapevine Brew House** on **2 Victoria Road** for one of Ruby's burgers and their home brewed beer. My children cried when they closed in Exeter! Succuluent burgers that drip down your chin with delight. Yum yum. 01395 222208 rubyburgers. com To the **Pier and Quay** we must go! A delight is in store....splice the main brace...prepare yourself for a seaward passage, to the **River Exe Café**. How did they do it? It's a custom built barge that floats in the centre of the channel. Access is via a Puffin Water Taxi from **Exmouth Pier Head/Marina**. Tricky to concentrate on your food when the views are 180 degrees. You have 3-hours to enjoy your booking on this floating gastro shed. 07761 116103 riverexecafe.com

Returning to terra firma, there is **The Point** for grilled steaks and ciabatta sarnis, and shelter. 01395 227145 the pointbarandgrill.com Now if you are still are in need of fresh fish you will be able to spy **The Rockfish** on your right. therockfish.co.uk

WHERE TO STAY...TO TREAT YOURSELF..

Lympstone Manor (formerly Courtlands).
The realisation of Michael Caines dream: to create an English Country House hotel for the twenty-first century. Two-and-a-half years in the making. The exterior is white and formal, the landscaped gardens are sparse, a sward of English turf soon to be planted with vines, and all sweep down to the glittering Exe Estuary. The sumptuous bedrooms are named after the indigenous birds and the walls are beautifully painted by local artist Rachel Troll. The bar is very swanky and the parallel lounge is comfortable. The ambience is relaxed and informal and most visitors wore denim jeans. But, it is for the cuisine that the visitor has made the journey. Caines, the patron/chef has his many disciples, far and wide, and you know the cuisine will be exceptional, and expensive. Dinner recently cost 4-couples a mere £800.00. This is a very special Restaurant With Rooms. 01395 202040 lympstonemanor.co.uk

SPECIAL PLACES OF INTEREST...

A La Ronde (NT), Summer Lane. Unique 16-sided house designed in 1795 by two ladies on returning from the 'Grand Tour' combining the features of a rustic cottage with the style of the Basilica at Ravenna. Inside are Gothic grottoes, the Shell Gallery, and the Feather Frieze and Dado. 12 acres of parkland with fine views. Shop & tea room. Open daily Feb-Oct from 10.30 (E8) 01395 265514

Bicton College Gardens, via Sidmouth Lodge. Monkey puzzle avenue, walled garden, herbaceous borders, rock garden and arboretum. Open Daily, 10-4.30. (H7) 01395 562353 bicton.ac.uk

Bicton Park. 60-acres of glorious gardens and parkland spanning 300-years of horticultural history. Specialist greenhouses. Tropical & Palm House. Bird Garden, children's fun world, 'Fabulous Forest'indoor activity for under teens. Restaurant, gift and plant shop. Disabled facilities. Open daily 10-6 (-5 winter). (J7) 01395 568465 bictongardens.co.uk

Crealy Adventure Park, Sidmouth Road. Animal and working dairy farm in 100-acres to explore with viewing galleries, milk a cow - hands on adventures for children, and over 60 rides and attractions. Accommodation in glamping tents and hot tub lodges. Restaurant. Open daily from 10. (E5) 01395 233200 crealy.co.uk

Darts Farm. Award-winning farm shop and independent gift retailer with food hall, restaurant (child friendly), bakers/deli, fish shed, plant centre, Aga, Fired Earth, Cotswold Outdoor, contemporary art and much, much more. Open daily from 8. (D6) 01392 878200 dartsfarm.co.uk

Jurassic Coast. This is a Natural World Heritage Site, and the only one in England. It runs from Exmouth along the coast to Swanage in Dorset. From Exmouth to Lyme Regis the rock is of the Triassic Period - 250 and 230 million years ago. Red rocks formed in a Triassic desert, would you believe in the time of dinosaurs and giant marine reptiles? The local Information Centres have details of the guided walks. jurassiccoast.org

Stuart Line Cruises, Exmouth Pier. Boat trips to cruise the River Exe, Jurassic Coast, a day cruise to Brixham/Torquay, or Sidmouth, all year in all weathers. 01395 222144 stuartlinecruises.co.uk

Wildwood Escot. East Devon's conservation and wildlife branch of the Wildwood Trust. In 200+acres of parkland; Birds of Prey, otters, red squirrels, wild boar and lynx. Coach House restaurant, arts & crafts, and a Saxon Village. Open daily Apr-Sept from 10.(J1) 01404 822188 wildwooodescot.org
Also, wildcamping - see: escotcampwild.co.uk

1864
Vitifer Mine, near Warren House produces 154 tons of tin, reducing to 22 tons in 1907.

1864
Kents Cavern systematically explored.

Twin Thatch, Sidmouth

World of Country Life.
All-weather family attraction
with falconry displays
(except Sa), farm museum,
playgrounds and petting farm,
vintage cars - Hall of Transport
'Victorian' street, lots of stuff
to exhaust kids. Open daily
mid-Mar to Oct 10-5 & half-
terms. (G10) 01395 274533
worldofcountrylife.co.uk

**Kenniford Farm Shop,
Clyst St Mary**. Succulent
produce from their free range
herd of pigs; ideal for hog roast
baps, bacon and pork joints.
Holiday cottage to let. Shop &
Café open daily M-Sa 9.30-5,
Su 10-4. (D5) 01395 273004
kennifordfarm.com

Otterton Mill. 1,000 years
of baking on this site! There's
a working water mill, bakery
and shop selling local produce,
restaurant, and art and crafts
gallery. Live music most Th
eves. Award-winning café-
restaurant. Open daily 10-5.
(J8) 01395 568521
ottertonmill.com

Woodbury Studio Gallery.
Tim Andrew's raku ceramics,
and pieces by other well-known
contemporary ceramicists.
Summmer Garden exhibition
in May/June and Annual
Ceramics Exhibition in mid

September. Open M-F 10-6, Sa
10-1. (F7) Please phone out of
season to check times.
01395 233475
timandrewsceramics.co.uk

**SPECIAL PLACES TO
STAY...**

Larkbeare Grange. A large
house set in idyllic country
close to Exeter and the
Jurassic Coast. The beds are
Vi-Spring, the bathrooms are
luxurious, the breakfast will
set you up for the day, and
you have all the mod-cons
available to deal with this
crazy world. Also, on site
luxury self-catering in The
Granary. (H2) 01404 822069
larkbeare.net

SIDMOUTH
One of Devon's earliest, and
most elegant, of seaside resorts
developed in the late C18 and
C19s. First patronised by the
Prince of Wales (later George
111) who came here to escape
his creditors, and childhood
home of Queen Victoria, who
narrowly escaped being shot by
a neighbouring child.

The town is positioned within
a narrow valley beset by high,
sandstone cliffs, and bisected
by the River Sid rising from

the hills to the north. A town
of distinction and character,
with no less than 484 "Listed"
buildings. Many of whom
belong to the Blue Plaque
Scheme.

The town has an open and
relaxed air about it. The sun
reflects brilliantly on many
of the Regency buildings
painted in their creams and
whites. Often mirrored by the
cricketers standing about on
the turf laid down in 1820.

Surely one of the country's
most attractive town grounds,
where I have had the good
fortune to play, for The Boffins,
these past 30-years.

There are energetic coastal
walks to be had, to the west
and east, but if architecture
holds your attention, then
spend a few hours wandering
around with the Blue Plaque
Guide. I was at a loss to find a
guide detailing the entire, 484
"listed" buildings. You may
have more luck.

The town comes alive during
the Folk Festival in August, and
while I was there in November
surfers were riding a Slow
Break. It has youth in numbers,
and unlike nearby Budleigh, it
likes to party. (L7)

1866
Thurlestone Sands – a submerged forest discovered.
(re-exposed in 1923).

1872
Kelly College, Tavistock founded by Admiral Kelly.

173

LIGHT BITES...

You will most probably enter via the **High Street** which then runs into **Fore Street**, then onto the **Seafront**. For that extra special coffee and pastry, **Coffee 1 at 36 Fore Street**. 01395 514371 coffee1.co.uk Around the corner is **The Loft, 4-6 The Parade**. A glamorous, Mediterranean-inspired cafe specialising in seafood; lemon sole, platters and gourmet burgers. The best **Devon** cream teas. Open daily. (L6) 01395 489681 theloftsidmouth.co.uk Now back to the **Seafront**. **Dukes** has a loyal, local following and entertains Al fresco wining and dining. A seaside cafe/restaurant with rooms. 01395 513321 dukessidmouth.co.uk Going west you will soon come to **Pea Green Boat**. A rustic-style cafe offering imaginative med-style cuisine. Opens M-Sa 9.30-11.30 coffee/ brunch, lunch 12-2.30, dinner 5-9, Su 12-3.30. 01395 514152 thepeagreenboat.com Perhaps, you seek a no fancy tea and cake, or English breakfast with a view, then stroll along to the **Promenade** to **The Clock Tower Cafe**, Jacob's Ladder, **Seafront**. 01395 515319 clocktowercafesidmouth.co.uk

SPECIAL PLACES TO VISIT...

Sid Vale Heritage Centre, Church St. Local lace, costumes, geology, archaeology, prints, photographs etc. Open Apr-Oct M 1-4, Tu-Sa 10-4(L6) 01395 516139

FINE DINING...

Neil's Restaurant, Radway Place. Chef Neil Harding has 30+ years experience, so be prepared to be spoilt and indulge yourself in the English Channel's rich larder, for fish is his speciality. Booking advised. Open Tu-Sa from 6.30 pm. Lunch and business parties by arrangement. (L6) 01395 519494 neilsrestaurant.com

Salty Monk, Church Street, Sidford. Annett and Andy Witheridge have been running this Restaurant With Rooms for an age where they delight in Devon's propitious source of goodies. All the food is prepared on the premises. The accommodation includes mini-spa baths, hydro massage showers and King-size beds. (M5) 01395 513174 saltymonk.co.uk

TO STAY...THAT SPECIAL OCCASION...

Hotel Riviera, The Esplanade.One of the great architectural sights of Sidmouth's seafront. The bow fronted windows hide a hotel that determines convention and old-fashioned hospitality. There is a solid formality that is loved by a diminishing, some might argue discerning market. (L7) 01395 515201 hotelriviera.co.uk

TOPSHAM

One of South Devon's most attractive little towns, and a popular "Eating Out" destination for Exeter folk. The nearby Darts Farm has multiplied the visitors of late. The long, narrow High Street is fronted with many old houses in the "Dutch" style dating from the C17 and C18. Take a stroll along the High Street and admire the many Lifestyle shops, the view from the Churchyard, take some refreshment in one or more of the hostelries and you will soon come to the small harbour and antique emporium. The former port of Exeter, hence its evident heritage of past wealth. (C6)

WHERE TO STAY, EAT & DREAM...

The Salutation Inn, 68 Fore Street. Unless you are already (wisely) staying here, and are in dire need of refreshment, best to stop here awhile for breakfast, brunch or lunch and head for The Glasshouse Café. Dinner is slightly more formal and extravagant with three menus on offer. Your Patron has worked with Caines, Ramsey...This is the hostelry to eat, sleep and head to in Topsham. (C6) 01392 873060 salutationtopsham.co.uk

SPECIAL PLACES TO VISIT...

Artenax, 32 Fore Street. Nikki, your hostess, has over 100 British designers/makers

Beach House

Stacks, Ladram Bay

...upplying her with original works, all with a splash of colour. A visit will brighten your day and bring a smile to ...ll. Open daily. 01392 874172 ...rtenax.co.uk

...ebblebed Vineyard. Vineyard and wine tastings ...ours of producers of Sparkling ...ose from May-Sept on Th, F ...& Sa. See web for details. (D6) ...ebblebed.co.uk

...opsham Museum, 25 The ...trand. Late C17 merchant's ...ouse with attractive period ...ooms, sail loft, gardens. ...hipbuilding, maritime trade, ...he Exe Estuary. Honiton Lace ...nd Vivien Leigh. Teas. Shop. ...pen Apr-Oct M W Th & W/ ...s (Tu in Aug), 2-5. (C6) ...1392 873244 ...evonmuseums.net

...OUNTRY PUBS SERVING ...OOD...

...lack Horse, Old Honiton ...oad, Sowton. Large inn ...erving all manner of food. ...ery popular with local ...usinessmen, and the Retired ...ith time on their hands. (D3) ...lackhorseinnexeter.co.uk

...iggers Rest Inn. Child ...riendly pub serves pasta ...nd fishnchips, and free ice ...ream. Beer garden. Food ...rom 12-2, 7-9.30 pm. (F5) ...1395 232375

BEACHES...

Exmouth. Wide sandy beach with rocks. Water sports. D/LG/R/WC. Also, a sandy beach at the east end beneath Orcombe Cliffs. (E10)

Budleigh Salterton. Steeply shelving with oval pebbles. D/R/WC. (H9)

Ladram Bay. Pebble beach with high cliffs. Short walk from P. Café/D/R/WC. (K8)

Sidmouth. Sand at low tide. "Jacobs Ladder" leads down to western beach with rock pools, pebbles and shingle. Main beach below promenade has pebbles. Water sports. Surfing is unusual. D/R/WC. (L7)

COASTAL FOOTPATH...

Exmouth to Budleigh Salterton; 6 miles. The first 2 miles are along Exmouth Promenade, followed by an ascent to the 'High Land of Orcombe' (NT). Then a descent to Littleham Cove and a steep climb to 'The Floors', where the undercliff is noted for birdlife, and a gradual descent into the town.

Budleigh Salterton to Sidmouth; 8 miles. A detour is needed to cross the Otter a mile upstream. Returning to the coast the path ascends the red sandstone cliffs and provides a fairly level walk with fine views. Ladram Bay is noted for its curious rock formations and bird life. The final section involves a steep climb over Peak Hill.

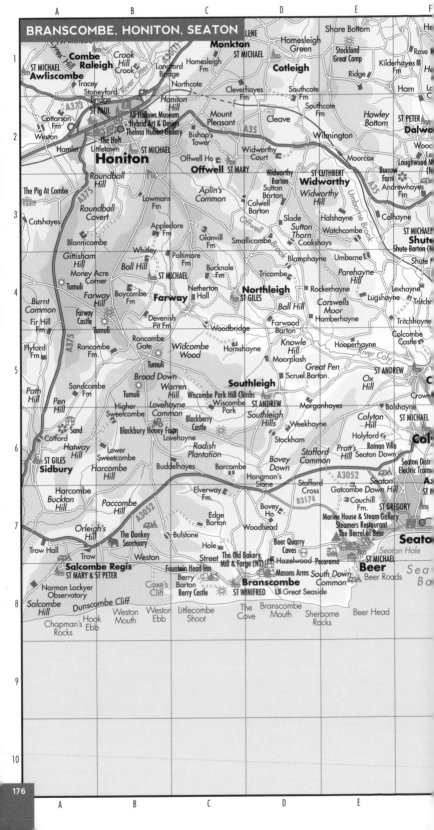

Map labels

ST MICHAEL

Combe
Raleigh

Awliscombe

Tracey

Stoneyford
Bridge

Crook
Hill
Crook

Langford
Bridge

Northcote

Homesleigh
Fm

Monkton
ST MICHAEL

Homesleigh
Green

Shore Bottom

Stockland
Great Camp

Ridge

Kilderhayes
Fm

Cotleigh

Rose

Ham

Cleverhayes
Fm

Southcote
Fm

Southcote
Fm

Cottarson
Fm

Weston

Hamlet

ST PAUL

Honiton
Hill

All Hallows Museum
Hybrid Art & Design
Thelma Hulbert Gallery

The Holt

Littletown

Mount
Pleasant

Bishop's
Tower

Cleave

A35

Wilmington

Hawley
Bottom

ST PETER

Dalwo

Honiton

ST MICHAEL

Offwell Ho

Offwell

Widworthy
Court

ST MARY

Widworthy
Barton

Sutton
Barton

Moorcox

Wood

Loughwood M
(N

Burrow
Farm

Andrewhayes
Fm

The Pig At Combe

Roundball
Hill

Catshayes

Roundball
Covert

Lowmans
Fm

Aplin's
Common

Colwell
Barton

Widworthy
Hill

ST CUTHBERT

Widworthy

Slade
Sutton
Thorn

Cookshays

Halshayne

Watchcombe

Calhayne

ST MICHAEL

Shute

Shute Barton (N

Blannicombe

Appledore
Fm

Whitley

Glanvill
Fm

Smallicombe

Cookshays

Blamphayne

Umborne

Shute

Gittisham
Hill

Money Acre
Corner

Ball Hill

Poltimore
Fm

Bucknole
Fm

Tricombe

Parehayne
Hill

Tumuli

Farway
Hill

Boycombe
Fm

ST MICHAEL

Farway

Netherton
Hall

Northleigh
ST GILES

Rockerhayne

Carswells
Moor

Hamberhayne

Lexhayne

Lugshayne

Tritchr

Burnt
Common

Fir Hill
Fm

Farway
Castle

Tumuli

Devenish
Pit Fm

Woodbridge

Ball Hill

Farwood
Barton

Tritchhayne

Plyford
Fm

Roncombe
Fm.

Roncombe
Gate

Widcombe
Wood

Hornshayne

Knowle
Hill

Moorplash

Hooperhayne

Colcombe
Castle

River Coly

Path
Hill

Sandcombe
Fm

Tumuli

Broad Down

Warren
Hill

Wiscombe Park Hill Climbs

Southleigh

Scruel Barton

Great Pen

ST ANDREW

Ox
Hill

Crown

Pen
Hill

Higher
Sweetcombe

Lovehayne
Common

Wiscombe
Park

ST ANDREW

Southleigh
Hills

Morganhayes

Bolshayne

ST MICHAEL

Cotford

Sand

Blackbury Honey Farm

Blackberry
Castle

Weekhayne

Colyton
Hill

Holyford

Col

ST GILES

Hatway
Hill

Sidbury

Lower
Sweetcombe

Harcombe
Hill

Lovehayne

Radish
Plantation

Stockham

Bovey
Down

Stafford
Common

Pratt's
Hill

Roman Villa

Seaton Down

Seaton Distr
Electric Tram

Harcombe
Buckton
Hill

Paccombe
Hill

A3052

Buddelhayes

Borcombe

Hangman's
Stone

Stafford
Cross

A3052

Gatcombe

Seaton

Down Hill

A

ST

Orleigh's
Hill

The Donkey
Sanctuary

Bulstone

Elverway
Fm.

Edge
Barton

Woodhead

Bovey
Ho

Couchill
Fm.

B3174

ST GREGORY

Seato

Trow Hall

Trow

Weston

Hole

Street

The Old Bakery,
Mill & Forge (NT)

Beer Quarry
Caves

Hazelwood

Pecorama

Marine House & Steam Gallery
Steamers Restaurant
The Barrel of Beer

Sea

Salcombe Regis
ST MARY & ST PETER

Fountain Head Inn

Berry
Barton

Caxe's
Cliff

Berry Castle

Masons Arms

Branscombe
ST WINIFRED

Great Seaside

South Down
Common

ST MICHAEL

Beer

Beer Roads

Sea
Ba

Norman Lockyer
Observatory

Salcombe
Hill

Dunscombe Cliff

Chapman's
Rocks

Hook
Ebb

Weston
Mouth

Weston
Ebb

Littlecombe
Shoot

The
Cove

Branscombe
Mouth

Sherborne
Rocks

Beer Head

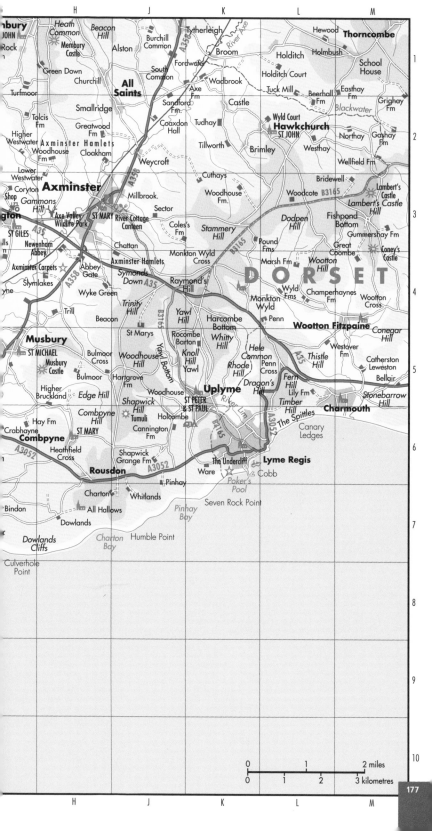

AXMINSTER

Well situated to be an ancient and quiet market town on a slight contour above the River Axe. The Roman Fosse Way passed close by. King Athelstan, the first King of All England fought a victorious battle against the Danes in 937 nearby on Brunanburgh field, and in celebration he founded a College, now completely vanished. The Royalist troops occupied in 1644 during the Siege of Lyme Regis. Later, Axminster Carpets were in business from 1755-1835, later to be revived in 1937 by Harry Dutfield.

Just off the central square, there is a little Bookshop and The Arts Café, a crafts shop, open M-F 10-3 and weekends displaying outdoor sculpture. Next door, the little museum opens from May to September, from 10. For a traditional pint of ale there is the George Hotel, a friendly local and host to Oliver Cromwell during his siege of Lyme Regis. (H3)

SPECIAL PLACES TO VISIT…

Axe Valley Wildlife Park. A small zoo home to zebras, antelopes, wallabies, flamingos, owls, otters, snakes, and creepy crawlers. Daily feeding times. Childrens play areas. Open daily mid-Feb to Oct from 10. 01297 34472 (H3) axevalleypark.co.uk

Axminster Carpets, Musbury Road. Factory showroom with small museum and video of production,from fleece to floor. Seconds, remnants and perfects available here. Open M-F 9-5.30, Sa 10-5. 01297 33993 (H4) axminstershop.co.uk

White Space Gallery, West St. Co-operative of 4 artists selling and displaying their work; paintings, mixed media, sculptured ceramics. Open M-Sa 10-5. 01297 35807 (H3) whitespaceart.com

Axminster Church, St Mary. Cruciform in shape with Norman doorway. Fine E window in Chancel, exceptional N & S windows, sedilia and piscina. Effigy of headless priest. Finely carved C17 pulpit. On his travels in 1740 Daniel Defoe saw the Monuments of the Saxon Bishop of Sherburne and two Dukes slain at the Battle of Brunanburgh, yet nothing in evidence today. (H3)

LIGHT BITES…

Axminster Inn, Silver Street. If you are in dire need of some ale you could do worse. It's a friendly ale house serving fresh seafood. 01297 34947 (H3) axminsterinn.pub If perhaps a coffee, a pizza or some pasta is to your liking then just opposite the **Churchyard** is **Le Pisani**. A charming building of style and comfort. You get the full med experience (Devon style). 01297 631697 lepisani.com

And, finally…your reason for being in **Axminster** is to visit **River Cottage Canteen & Deli, Trinity Square**. The space is quite stark and spare, modest in style, for the emphasis is on seasonal food; rustic fare and seafood in all its glory. The staff are friendly and knowledgeable Opens at 9 for breakfast, lunch and dinner. 01297 631715 rivercottage.net

---

AXMOUTH

Before this village silted up in the C17 it held a large harbour. Now the silted mud flats are a haven for birdlife, an ornithologist's delight. Large campsite. Two fine inns, the Harbour Inn is a popular dining pub, authentic in design and purpose. (F7)

Axmouth Church, St Michael. Norman c. 1140 with additions in 1330. A perpendicular stair-turret tower. Three Italianate wall paintings. (F7)

BEER

The major coastal attraction in this part of East Devon. An old fishing and smuggling village made notorious by the published diaries of one Jack Rattenbury in 1837 who later lived the life of a gentleman. Lace making was a major occupation; Queen Victoria's wedding dress was woven here, and Beer Stone was quarried here, first in Long Galleries, then as open cast supplying the stone for Exeter Cathedral.

The fishing boats are shelved on the beach and you can buy fresh fish (usually sole or flounders) from the fishermen's hut above the beach. A dashing stream runs beside the high street and plunges over a cliff into the pebbles. Gift and craft shops, tearooms and inns aplenty all serving freshly caught fish.

The coastal path rises 400 feet to Beer Head, the most southerly chalk cliffs in England that run down from Flamborough Head in Yorkshire. Below are cliffs, "riddled with caverns and rent with spires", made useful by smugglers past. (E7)

SPECIAL PLACES TO VISIT…

Beer Quarry Caves. A 2,000-year old history of quarrying stone from the Romans until the last century. Tour of awe-inspiring caves like a vast underground cathedral. Also formerly used to hide persecuted Catholics and for storing the contraband of notable smuggler, Jack Rattenbury. Open daily Apr-Oct 10-5. (D7) 01297 680282 beerquarrycaves.co.uk

Marine House & Steam Gallery, Fore Street. Established gallery representing a fine collection of painters, sculptors, ceramicists and jewellers. One of Devon's best. (E7) 01297 625257 marinehouseatbeer.co.uk

Pecorama. The Beer Heights Light Railway, PECO model railway exhibition, children's safety surfaced activity area, all surrounded by manicured gardens with fine sea views. Restaurant. Open daily 10-5. (E7) 01297 21542 peco-uk.com

1872
Devon County Agricultural Association formed.

1874 United Services College founded at Westward Ho! Alma Mater to Rudyard Kipling (and appears in Stalky & Co).

WHERE TO EAT, DRINK & BE MERRY...

Steamers Restaurant, Fore Street. Bright and colourful eatery serving local fish, duck and pasta dishes. Sunday lunch specials. Open Tu-Sa 10-12, 12-1.45 & 6.45-9. (E7) 01297 22922 steamersrestaurant.co.uk

The Barrel O' Beer, Fore Street. Dining pub specialises in seafood dishes where your chef has earned his stripes in some top class restaurants across the globe. Real ales. (E7) 01297 20099 barrelobeer.co.uk

BRANSCOMBE

One of the most romantic and picturesque villages in Devon set amidst a series of deep, narrow, tortuous combes. Three hamlets, or nests of houses make up the village. Notable church, forge (NT) and baker. Many of the cottages (some thatch) and houses are built of local Beer stone. Legend has it that a Spanish galleon foundered here in the C17, whence the sailors wed the local girls, and dark haired and brown eyed folk have "melted into the flaxen-haired Saxon fold". The ladies would sit at their cottage doors with cushion and bobbin darning the lace.

At Branscombe Mouth (parking charge) there is a fine stretch of chalk cliff, broken by landslips and noted for fossils. There's also a café/beach restaurant serving locally caught fish. Shingle beach. (D8)

SPECIAL PLACES TO VISIT...

Branscombe Church, St Winifred. Magnificent and stately for a small, isolated village with Norman tower, gallery, 3-decker pulpit and tomb of Joan Tregarthen d. 1583, mother of twenty children, fathered by her two husbands who stand opposite each other. Turn R out of the entrance descending to a footpath that leads along the valley, zig-zagging to Branscombe Mouth. (C8)

Branscombe Cottages

The Old Bakery, Manor Mill & Forge (NT). Now thankfully restored to working order after the closure of the business in 1987. The baking equipment has been preserved and the building is used as a tearoom. The Manor Mill supplied the flour for the bakery, and the forge is open daily, all year, where the blacksmith sells the ironwork he produces, and takes commissions. Old Bakery Open in season. Manor Mill open Su Apr-Oct, 2-5. (D8)

WHERE TO EAT, DRINK & BE MERRY...

Masons Arms. "Here Ye Toil Not" but enjoy the fine ales and food; lobster and crab dishes, a speciality. Fireplaces and exposed walls. Summer beer festival. Restaurant. Bar food. Sit outside and idly watch passes-by. Accommodation. Sadly, it's all gone rather corporate and lacks character. (D8) 01297 680300 masonsarms.co.uk

Fountain Head Inn. On the western (top end) edge of the village. An intimate, popular little C14 pub serving fresh meals (12-2 & 6.30-9) and real ales (from the local Branscombe Vale Brewery). Popular with CAMRA afficionados. Small seating area outside. 01297 680359 (C8) fountainheadinn.com

COLYFORD

Former site of Roman villa on the western edge of the **River Axe**, and probable fort beside the **Fosse Way**. Wide water meadows beside the river strike northwards towards **Colyton**. (F6)

COLYTON

A pretty village noted for its sumptuous church, village square and highly rated Grammar School. In the C15 one of the wealthiest wool towns in Devon that took advantage of exporting

Day's Catch, Bee

its goods through nearby Seaton. Saxon traditions still prevail in the town, for the Town Councillors are still known as Feoffes. Move off in a north west direction and you'll experience the beautiful Umborne Valley with its grassy water meadows and wild flowers. (F5)

SPECIAL PLACES TO VISIT...

Colyton Church, St Andrew.
Fine, impressive building with central tower. Memorials to Margaret, Countess of Devon, granddaughter of John of Gaunt. Her tomb was smashed up by the Parliamentarian troops in Civil War. Also monuments to Sir John Pole and his wife Elizabeth who lived at nearby, Shute. (F5)

HONITON

One gets the feeling that Honiton is undergoing a revival of good fortune. New restaurants, new coffee shops and galleries...there's a buzz about the place. The long, wide High Street with Georgian buildings is always busy and bustling. I counted half a dozen antique-bric-a-brac-emporia shops at the west end, and more

at the top, east end. At the east end, the earthy Honeybee coffee shop, and at the west end, next to a wine bar, the Boston Tea Party with art gallery and garden.

A deep connection with lace and glove making, as illustrated in the little museum. The almshouse was the former leper hospital, St Margaret's. July Fair, Agricultural show in August, Carnival in September. (B2)

SPECIAL PLACES TO VISIT...

All Hallows Museum of Lace & Antiquities, High Street. Local history and world famous lace with demos in Honiton's oldest building. Open East-Oct M-F 9.30-4.30, Sa 9.30-1. (B2) 01404 44966 honitonmuseum.co.uk

Hybrid Gallery, 51 High Street. An attractive and lively art gallery, and shop, selling original and hand-crafted work. Also, a Design Consultancy. Open Tu-Sa 10-5. (B2) 01404 43201 hybrid-devon.co.uk

Thelma Hulbert Gallery, Dowell Street. East Devon's only public art gallery shows an exciting programme of contemporary art and craft

exhibitions. Open Tu-Sa 10-5. (B2) 01404 45006 thelmahulbert.com

1884
John Babbacombe Lee unsuccessfully hanged three times for the murder of Mrs Keyes.

1887
Sep 5. Theatre Royal, Exeter, destroyed by fire with loss of 160 lives.

SEATON

A small resort with pebble beach not noted for its architecture like nearby Sidmouth but there are attractive Georgian buildings in the centre of town. The small harbour is of interest, also the coastal path to Downland Cliffs. The cliffs rise to either side of the town affording sweeping views from the coastal footpath. There are precious stones to be found on the beach; jaspers and garnets.

In former times the Romans used the Fosse Way and the harbour here as a conduit to ship out Cotswold and Mendip wool back to their Republic. A Roman pavement was found here in 1921 measuring 16 feet square with a twisted pattern, now in Exeter Museum. Much later in the C19 coal was exported off the beach, sometimes beside patients seeking the calm waters of Seaton Spa! A fact noted in Francis Kilvert's diaries, the Worcester parson. The bridge crossing the Rive Axe was opened in April 1877 and became the first concrete toll in England, until September 1907. Bass are caught off the bridge. The Axe is also known to favour salmon and sea trout. (F7)

SPECIAL PLACES OF INTEREST...

Seaton Tramway Co., Harbour Road. An unforgettable 3-mile ride; Seaton-Colyford-Colyton. Unique open top and enclosed single deck trams giving superb views of the beautiful Axe valley, noted for its wading river birds. Open daily East-Oct. (F6) 01297 20375 tram.co.uk

SPECIAL PLACES TO VISIT...

Blackbury Camp (Castle) (EH). When the bluebells are in bloom this is a magical place. An Iron Age hillfort dating back to the C4. Impressive ramparts and ancient tracks excavated in the 1950s. (C6)

Blackbury Honey Farm. Butterflies and bees flourish here, amongst the wild flowers. The Basterfield family have been beekeeping since 1972.

They hold courses and display the art of pollination and have a shop selling honey and beeswax products. Open early Mar to Dec Th-Su 10-5. (B5) 01404 871600 blackburyfarm.co.uk

Burrow Farm Gardens. Just celebrated 50-years of colour and form, all within a 13-acre woodland garden; rhododendrons, azaleas, primulas. Planned for a foliage effect. Bog garden. Open daily Apr-Oct 10-6. Cream teas. (F3 01404 831285 burrowfarmgardens.co.uk

Church of St Giles, Northleigh. A fine Norman doorway with intricate carvings of animal heads. C16 fan-vaulted screen with colourful vine leaves, and so it is claimed, the oldest stained glass in Devon; figures of St Peter and St Paul. (C4)

Hawkesdown Camp. An oblong earthwork consisting of two banks with a fosse between. (G6)

Lyme Bay Winery. A specialist producer of English Wines, Country Wines, ciders, meads and liqueurs, all on sale from M-F 9.30-5, Sa 10-3, Su 11-3 (F4) 01297 551355 lymebaywinery.co.uk

Miller's Farm Shop, Kilmington. Established 30+-years ago, it's a successful combination of a French deli (with imports from Miller's Normandy farm) and an English farm shop. Open M-Sa 7-6, Su 8-1. (G3) 01297 35390 millersfarmshop.com

Musical Woods & Wild School. Chris Holland's forest school has a musical and wild twist. Helping children to connect with nature and each other through music. All set in a magical wood with a shallow stream and heathland. (C6) 07980 601830 wholand.org.uk

Sand. An Elizabethan manor house in the Huyshe family for over 50 years set in 6-acres of varied gardens. Medieval hall and period features in Guided Tour by members of the Huyshe-Shires family. Teas. House open East, Spring & Aug BHs, and Su & M & June & Aug, 2-6 (A6) 01395 597230 sandsidbury.co.uk

Shute Barton (NT). Impressive entrance to medieval manor house built in 1380 with later additions in the C18. The Pole family lived here until the fire, leaving just the gatehouse and one wing. Open some W/Es May-Nov. Details: 01752 346585

The C13 **Church of St Michael**, just up the hill, is cruciform, and has fine memorials of William Pole d.1741, Master of Queen Anne's household. (F3)

Wiscombe Park Hill Climbs. Hill climbs have been staged here since 1958. All started over a glass or two of Malt. The two Majors, Richard Chichester and Charles Lambton thought the terrain suitable for such goings-on. The parkland is of great beauty and a wonderful backdrop for racing vintage cars and motorcycles, some reaching speeds of 125mph on what is considered a demanding 'drivers' hill. Events take place from April to September. (C5) 01258 861030 wiscombepark.co.uk

Wiscombe Park Hill Climbs ss

VILLAGES OF INTEREST...

LYME REGIS

Although just over the border in Dorset, if you are touring this area you can't exclude this fascinating little town from your itinerary. Its literary and film connections are endless; from Jane Austen to John Fowles. Who can forget the French Lieutenant's Woman (Meryl Streep) standing isolated on the Cobb, almost being swept away by the crashing waves until rescued by the dashing Jeremy Irons in the film of the same name? There are two parts of the village, the High Street area, and the Cobb (harbour). The High Street has a number of galleries, fossil emporia and places to eat plus the excellent local museum, to visit. A walk along the promenade connects to the Cobb where you can watch the fishing boats come and go, and sit on the little beach. A small aquarium is open in season, and there are a number of pubs, cafés and gift shops. (L6)

MUSBURY

Birthplace in 1650 of John Churchill, the first Duke of Marlborough. The Musbury

Ammonite, Lyme Regis Fossil Shop ss

Monument erected in 1611 commemorates the Drake family. A pleasant walk is to be had leading away from the Musbury Castle earthwork, an Iron Age hillfort along the old packhorse route to Combpyne via Higher Bruckland farm. (G5)

UPLYME

Attractive village to the north west of Lyme Regis just across from the Dorset border. Set amidst quaint, sheltered valleys. An early Saxon and Roman settlement connected to the fort at Seaton. (K5)

CHURCHES...

Uplyme Church, St Peter & St Paul. Pretty little church with Gallery and wagon roof painted with clear blue and embellished with gold stars. (K5)

COASTAL FOOTPATH...

Sidmouth to Seaton
11 miles. One of the toughest sections of the path with cliffs up to 450 ft and intervening valleys. Much of this stretch is National Trust land. The red sandstone gradually changes to chalk and there is some difficult going in places. The path descends to sea level at Branscombe Mouth, and again at Beer.

Seaton to Lyme Regis
8 miles. After crossing the Axe there is a steep climb and the path enters the 'Landslip', an area of broken ground caused by a major earth movement in 1839. Here again there is some difficult ground but there is much to interest the naturalist and geologist. Shortly before reaching Lyme, the path crosses into Dorset.

BEACHES...

Branscombe. Steep pebble beach. Interesting rocks at LT. 45-minute walk to Sherborne Rocks. P Charge. R/WC. (D8)

Beer. Steep shingle and pebble beach with rocks. Boating pool. Short walk from P. D/R/WC. (E7)

Seaton. Shelving pebbles. Sand at LT. D/R/WC. (F7)

Sherborne Rocks, Branscombe

*1892
May 20. The final broad gauge railways in Devon converted to standard gauge over this weekend.*

*1892
Aug 15. Torquay granted royal charter for incorporation as a municipal borough.*

This is the "Glorious Devon" of the old railway posters. Centred on the wide bay made popular in Napoleonic times as an important naval base. The mild climate and fine coastal scenery attracted the naval officers to set up their domestic quarters, the foundation of present-day Torquay.

Around the Bay, the three contrasting towns of Torquay, Paignton and Brixham, providing amenities for differing tastes; Torquay with its fine situation, imposing buildings and lush semi-tropical vegetation, the wide beaches and traditional seaside diversions of Paignton, and the old-world charm of the fishing port of Brixham.

To the north, beside the beautiful Teign Estuary lie the smaller resorts of Shaldon and Teignmouth, set just to the south of the bright red sandstone cliffs so characteristic of this part of Devon. Brunel's Great Western Railway hugs the coast, perhaps forming a barrier to local visitors but providing a magnificent introduction to Devon for generations of rail travellers.

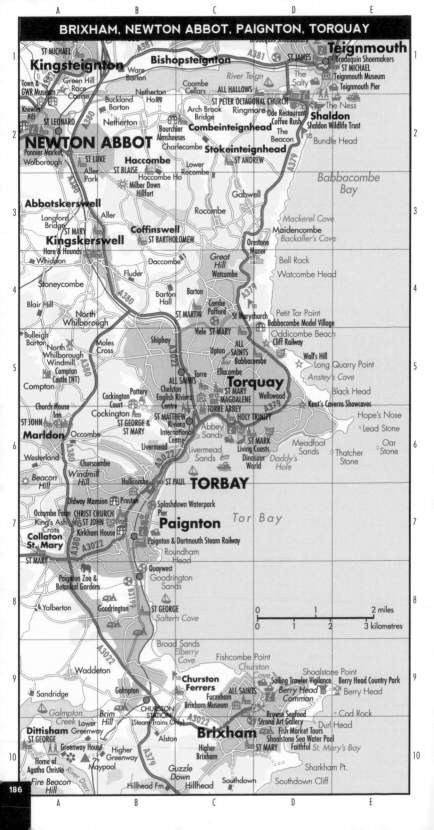

BRIXHAM, NEWTON ABBOT, PAIGNTON, TORQUAY

Brixham Fleet

BRIXHAM

One of the oldest fishing ports in Britain manages to combine the balance of a busy fishing industry with the demands of modern tourism. In the last few years new builds are aplenty: note the Marina and the Fish Market. Colour-washed cottages on the hillside front narrow, winding streets that overlook the harbour and rows of colourful craft. The prettiest of the three Torbay towns, popular with artists and writers. Robert Graves, Flora Thompson and Francis Brett Young, all made Brixham their home, for a short while. Prominent in the war against the Spanish Armada, and later, the landing place of William of Orange, for his rebellion to rid England of the Stuart dynasty and Catholicism, although he had the indignity of being piggy-backed off his stranded ship by a local fisherman. Church of All Saints' vicar Henry Lyte wrote the hymn "Abide With Me' which rings out daily at 18.00 hours. An oasis for all lovers of seafood. You may need to book a full 2-days sojourn to take full advantage of the food on offer. Annual Trawler Race in June. (D9)

SPECIAL PLACES TO VISIT...

Berry Head National Nature Reserve. Within a half-hour walk of Brixham; an old Napoleonic fort on the headland with lighthouse, Café and Visitor Centre open Apr-Sept. Live TV link to bird colonies all year. (E9) 01803 882619 countryside-trust.org.uk/berryhead

Browse Seafood, The Quay. Wholesale crab business with wet fish shop, crab sandwiches and café. Supplies top hotels in Devon. (D9)

Brixham Heritage Museum, The Old Police Station. Local maritime and social history, boat building and navigation. Scale model of Brixham Station as in 1947. Open Apr-Oct Tu-F 10-4, Sa 10-1 (C9) 01803 856267 brixhamheritage.org.uk

Fish Market Tours, Brixham Fish Market. £25 million of fish is annually landed at Brixham to provide local fishmongers and restaurants. 50% is exported worldwide. Book a tour to start at 6.00am and you can view 40 species of fish auctioned to be followed by a hearty breakfast. Book early: bfmt2014@gmail.com (D9) 07973 297620

Shoalstone Sea Water Pool. This is a stunning 'Art Deco" icon of the south-west's coastline. Originally buiilt in 1896, with alterations in 1926, 1946, storm damage in 1979, Torbay Council involvement in 2004, and finally in 2012 some action to restore it. The fund raising goes on, and on... the Friends work tirelessly to make it live for another day, season...to wild swim. shoalstoneseawaterpool.co.uk

Strand Art Gallery, 2 The Strand. Working studio and large gallery of original paintings. Open daily 10-5. 2 The Strand 01803 854762 strandartgallery.com

Vigilance of Brixham. One of the last four restored 78-foot sailing ketches in existence available for charter and afternoon/evening trips. Built for strength and speed they were unique in British waters and they were able to tow heavy trawl gear and capable of getting fish to market on time. Sailings from Easter. (E9) 07764 845353 vigilanceofbrixham.co.uk

Brixham Nets

LIGHT BITES...

If you seek seafood in all its simple and Arthropodic (crustacean) forms you have come to the right place. Beside the quay are huts selling whelks and mussels, and to reach the harbour you will have passed by many an emporium selling fishn'chips, too. You can also sit in a comfortable restaurant, order a cool glass of Chablis or Meursault and partake of a glorified feast of fresh fish, dining. For better or worse, try **Rockfish, Harbourside** for freshly caught cod, haddock and hake. 01803 850872 therock fish.co.uk

Robert's Fisheries (Merchants) own **Simply Fish**
01803 883858
robertsfisheries.com

WHERE TO STAY AFLOAT...

Faithful, Brixham Marina. Ideal for 2-Romantics who seek a retreat afloat. The double-cabin has a King-size bed and a fully equipped galley. To be welcomed by fresh flowers and delish pastries. (D9)
07939 850680

NEWTON ABBOT

A busy market town dating back to Roman times. The Great Western Railway moved their locomotive and carriage repairs here in the 1800s, and this made it a centre of rail transportation. In the 1960's the specialist Canal and Rail publisher David & Charles opened their offices bringing succour to all transport enthusiasts with their range of books. C17 Forde House, now Council Offices, and one-mile to the south, Bradley Manor. Racecourse open from April to early September for Flat racing. Air Fusion Festival. Merrymaker's Day in May. Cheese and Onion Fair in September. E/C Th. (A2)

SPECIAL PLACES TO VISIT...

Burnham Nurseries Orchid Paradise, Forches Cross. Herwith a rare and exotic orchid specialist for 60-years. Mail order. Open daily 10-4. (A1) 01626 352233
orchids.org.uk

Plant World, St Marychurch Rd. Outstanding collection of rare and exotic plants from around the world. 4-acres of landscaped gardens. Large cottage garden. Mediterranean garden. Seeds from rare plants are offered for sale through mail order catalogue. Open daily, Apr-Oct 9.30-5. (A2) 01803 872939
plant-world-seeds.com

Newton Abbot Town & GWR Museum, 2a St Paul's Road. History of the GWR and the people who operated it. Working signal box, Aller Vale Art Pottery Collection, John Lethbridge's diving machine automaton, and the magnificent Sandford Orleigh Overmantle, a highly carved 1534 floor to ceiling fire surround. Open Apr-Oct M-Th 10-4, F 10-12, (Town Museum Sa 2-4). (A2) 01626 201121
museum-newtonabbot.co.uk

PAIGNTON

Often overlooked given its proximity to Torquay, and as a family resort has had to struggle against the cheap Mediterranean and Far Eastern resorts. It has a little harbour, a flat, extensive beach and a number of interesting attractions described below. An affordable place to live for those who work and socialise in nearby Totnes and Torquay. Theatre and cinema. June carnival. E/C W. (B7)

1901
Devon population recorded at 660,000.

1904
Motor cars first registered in Exeter.

SPECIAL PLACES TO VISIT...

Kirkham House (EH), Kirkham St. Small C14 merchant's house somewhat hidden among back streets. Display of furniture, pottery, and fabrics. Open BHs Good F-Aug, & all Su July/Aug 2-5. (B7) 0370 3331181

Occombe Farm, Preston Down Rd. Here you are invited to engage in the whole organic process; the food, farming and wildlife (as well as butchers and bakers). Cookery School & café. Open 9-5.30. (B6) 01803 520022
occombe.org.uk

Oldway Mansion, Torquay Rd. Building planned by Isaac Merritt Singer, 1811-1875 (of Singer sewing machines) in 1873 in the style of the Palace of Versailles. Remodelled 1904. Marble staircase, ballroom, ornamented painted ceilings and extensive gardens. Open M-Sa 9-5, also Su in summer 2-5. Grounds open daily. No charge. Café open in summer. (B6) 01803 207933
torquay.com/listings/oldway-mansion

Dart Valley Railway. Relive the 'Great Age of Steam' on the Nations Holiday Line along the spectacular Torbay coastline to Kingswear for Dartmouth and the fascinating River Dart Estuary. Steam trains run East BH, selected days in Apr, May & Oct. Daily June-Sept. The Timetable is complex and I can't get it. Santa Specials in Dec. 01803 555872
dartmouthrailriver.co.uk

Paignton Pier. All visitors to this town must, just must visit this iconic build. A few years ago there was a £1,000,000 rebuild to part of the pier. Pier head includes trampolines, mega slide & kiddies cars, all in wonderful colour and razzamatazz. Open Mar-Oct 9-late. Nov-Feb 10-6/8. (C6) 01803 522139
paigntonpier.co.uk

Paignton Zoo, Totnes Road. Whatever your reserves about zoos this one's raison d'etre is about conservation and education. In 80-acres there are 2,000 animals: Elephants, giraffes, Gorillas, lions, tigers, gibbon islands. Birds flying freely. Tropical plants. Rhino

House. Family activity centre. Miniature railway (East-Sept). Open daily summer 10-6, winter 10-5. (B7) 01803 697500
paigntonzoo.org.uk

Splashdown Waterpark, Goodrington Sands. Outdoor waterpark with 8-slides and pool, go-karts, bumper boats, shops etc. Open daily from 10. (B7) 01803 555550
splashdownquaywest.co.uk

SHALDON

A seafaring community of long standing that has made its livelihood from fishing, boat trips and water sports. Connected since the C13 by foot ferry to Teignmouth. A thriving village with an immaculate village green used for the game of Bowls. Georgian and earlier buildings. Five pubs. June Festival attracts world-class musicians. (D2)

SPECIAL PLACES TO VISIT...

Shaldon Wildlife Trust, Ness Drive. Collection of small, rare, and unusual mammals, birds reptiles and invertebrates born here in a woodland setting. Open daily East-Sept 10-5, winter 10-4. (D2) 01626 872234
shaldonwildlifetrust.org.uk

WHERE TO EAT, DRINK & BE MERRY...

Ode Dining, 21 Fore Street. World-travelled Tim Bouget brings his vast experience of working at Michelin Star restaurants to this Georgian house. Open for a Tasting Menu F & Sa 7-10.30 pm. (D2) 01626 873977
odetruefood.com

The Coffee Rush Café, 27 Fore Street. Friendly, comfortable café sells home made cakes, pastries and delish hot chocs and coffees. The "Cream Tea", oh my God!. Open daily. (D2) 01626 873922
thecoffeerush.co.uk

Dart Valley Railway ss

Torquay Marina

TEIGNMOUTH

A seaside resort of long standing that is in the process of reinventing itself, big time. There are new restaurants and cafés springing up, and folk are realizing it's a cheaper place to live than Exeter, and not so far away, either. The band Muse were brought up here, and every so often they play to the town's rock lovers. The harbour and estuary side is always a busy and attractive sight with fine views across to Shaldon. The town centre still needs a lot of paint and tlc. The Den, an area of open space and early C19 buildings overlooks the sea front. Sea and river excursions. August carnival and regatta. (E1)

SPECIAL PLACES TO VISIT....

Brodequin Shoemakers, 42 Teign Street. Handmade colourful shoes, boots and sandals for men and women, plus satchels, bags & other leather goods. Open M-Sa 10.30-4. (D1)
01626 776341
handcraftedshoes.co.uk

Teignmouth & Shaldon Museum, 27 French Street. The story of sea and land, war and peace, of interactions with far off places and developments of domestic industries. Open all year Tu-Sa from 10. (E1)
01626 777041
teignheritage.org.uk

WHERE TO EAT, DRINK & BE MERRY...

The Owl and Pussycat Restaurant, 3 Teign Street. You will dance to the light of the moon after sampling this fine Devon cuisine and friendly service. Live Jazz on Mondays. Open M-F 6-9, Sa 12-2, 5.30-9.30. (D1) 01626 775321
theowlandthepussycat.co.uk

LIGHT BITES...

For breakfast head down to the Seafront where you can spy the Beachcomber Café. It opens at 8am till 9pm. Family and rockn'roll friendly. You may just see Matt Bellamy and his Muse friends sipping coffee and cakes whilst taking the sea air. Bumper breakfasts, burgers, toasties, fajitas, salads and licensed.
01626 778909
beachcomber-cafe.com

Now if you fancy some shellfish for lunch or dinner move along the beach to **Crabshack On The Beach** where you can start with Crab soup or parfait, or oysters followed by Seafood Platter, a whole lobster or crab or simple fish and chips. Child's portions available. 01626 777956
crabshackonthebeach.co.uk

1914
The three towns amalgamated into Plymouth.

1917
During the U-boat blockade, 100 merchant ships were sunk around the coasts of Devon and Cornwall.

TORQUAY

Devon's "Queen of Resorts" occupying a magnificent natural setting on the north side of Tor Bay where the mild climate encourages sub-tropical vegetation and all-year-round visitors. There are twenty-two miles of attractive cliff paths stretching around to Babbacombe, and beyond. Well provided with a comprehensive shopping centre, numerous hotels, entertainments and a thriving nightlife.

There was an early Premonstra-tension house at Torre Abbey in the C12 but it was not until the Napoleonic Wars that Torquay expanded so. During the C17 and C18s the Navy would seek shelter here from all but the East and South Easterly winds. More often in preference to Plymouth Sound. The Napoleonic Wars attracted the wives and families of the Naval officers to Torquay, to be near their loved ones. The difficulties of travel on the Continent also brought new visitors, and physicians would recommend their consumptive patients to come here for the clear skies and sea air for towns and cities

were often ridden with smog and damp conditions. The C19 saw an explosion of new villas and terraces set amidst woodland drives. Much in evidence today. It can best be described as a genteel resort that has had to change some of its old-fashioned ways to meet the demands of today. Some of the larger hotels have realised they must improve their interior design, service and cuisine, and to go upmarket, returning to their origins. One wonders who fills all the beds in the other mediocre hotels and guesthouses. It can't all be coach parties and businessmen attending the numerous conferences held in the Riviera Centre. A name taken from the marketing men's slogan, "The English Riviera". A poor cousin when compared to the original, and a misleading description. Better to wax lyrical about the mild, temperate climate, the shimmering sea, the miles of footpaths leading up and down to numerous beaches, the English civility, the fine terraces and tree-lined avenues. And, if you should tire of this oasis, and wish for action and company, strike to the harbour, a haven of coffee shops, bars and restaurants, and if you still have your sea legs, take a boat

trip to Brixham, or further afield, to Dartmouth and Totnes, pleasing towns very different from your hostess. (C5)

SPECIAL PLACES TO VISIT...

Dinosaur World, 3 Victoria Parade. For those rainy days when your children need some Jurassic excitement, and you wish they were fossilised. Open daily East to mid-Sept 11-3, winter Tu W & W/Es 11-3. (C6)

Kents Caverns, Ilsham Road. Two million years in the making. Let your imagination and senses be challenged as you travel back to the realm of bears, cavemen and beyond. Visitor Centre, Rock & Fossil shop. Café. Open all year from 10. Cave tours from 11, 12.30, 2 & 3.30. (D5) 01803 215136 kents-cavern.co.uk

Living Coasts Zoo & Aquarium, Beacon Quay. Aquatic visitor attraction; penguins, seals, puffins. Reconstructed beaches, cliff-faces and an estuary. Gift shop. Café with panoramic sun terrace serving child-size portions. Open daily 10-dusk. (D6) 01803 202470 livingcoasts.org.uk

Hesketh Crescent, Torquay

Greenway Boat & Bath House ss

Torbay Quad Centre, Moles Lane. Bikes for all ages 5yrs+, beginners welcome, supervised instruction track. Open 9.30-5.30 W/Es & Schl Hols. (C5) 01803 615660 torbayquadcentre.co.uk

Torquay Museum, Babbacombe Rd. Animal remains from Kent's Cavern. Fairytale Exhibition, Pictorial records, Victoriana, rural Devon, pottery, archaeology, Agatha Christie Gallery, world jewellery and adornment. Gift shop & Tea room. Open M-Sa 10-4 all year (Su in school hols). (C5) 01803 293975 torquaymuseum.org

Torre Abbey & Gallery, Kings Drive. Torquay's oldest historic building. Art gallery specialising in maritime paintings and landscapes by local artists. Devon miniatures, antiques, Torquay terracotta & sculpture. Open W-Sa 10-4. (C5) 01803 293593 torre-abbey.org.uk

Waves Leisure Pool, Riviera Centre. Giant inflatable, paddling pool, sloping beach, indoor soft play area, gym, sun beds, sauna, steam room & jacuzzi, beauty suite & aerobics. Café diner. (C5) 01803 299992 rivieracentre.co.uk

LIGHT BITES...

Calypso Coffee Co, 45 Fleet Street. It's chic and urban, and homemade drinks are a speciality of the house. It's a cool place to hang out, and breakfast and croissant will set you up for a day of plentiful adventures. 01803 213728

WHERE TO EAT, DRINK & BE MERRY...

Elephant Bar & Restaurant, 3-4 Beacon Terrace. Award-winning restaurant considered one of the most stylish places to eat in the South West sources their pork, lamb, chicken, turkeys and vegetables from their South Devon farm. Michelin Star in 2016. Open M-Sa for lunch and dinner. (C5) 01803 200044 elephantrestaurant.co.uk

No 7 Fish Bistro, 7 Beacon Terrace. Simply cooked fish just off the boats. Specials; lobster, Dover sole, oysters. Warm and efficient service. (C5) 01803 295055 no7-fish.com

SPECIAL PLACES TO VISIT...

Babbacombe Model Village, Hampton Avenue. 4-acres of gardens with miniature landscapes and 413 buildings to scale of 1 inch to 1 foot. Model railway. Open daily. (D4) 01803 315315

Bishopsteignton Museum of Rural Life, Shute Hill. Displays ranging through geology, occupations, dress, village and school life. Open East-Sept Su & BHs 2.30-4.30. (C1) 01626 775308 devonmuseums.net

Bygones, St Marychurch. Nostalgic look at a life-size Victorian Street of shops. Giant Model Railway and Railwayana Collection. Militaria from Waterloo to WW1, WW11 & The Gulf War. Open daily all year. (C4) 01803 326108 bygones.co.uk

Cockington Court. Set amidst a traditional Devon material village there are 20+ Craft studios which makes this a destination for all creatives. Café. Wedding Venue. Open daily from 10. (B5) 01803 607230 cockingtoncourt.org

Compton Castle (NT). C14 manor. Great hall, Solar, Chapel, Rose Garden and kitchen. Open Apr-Oct Tu W & Th 10.30-4.30. 01803 661906 nationaltrust.org

Greenway (NT). Birthplace of Sir Humphrey Gilbert in 1539. The beautiful woodland garden

*1921
March. Henry Williamson moves to live in Georgeham, arriving on his 499 cc long-stroke Norton motorcycle and rents Skirr Cottage for £5 a year.*

slopes down to the River Dart. Now famous as the former home of Agatha Christie with new features about her life. Unique bath and boathouse. Café. Try visiting by river transport aboard the Greenway ferry from Dartmouth. The NT operates a traffic management system. Open daily mid-Feb to Dec 10.30-5, W/Es 11-4 Nov/Dec.(A9) 01803 842382 nationaltrust.org.uk

SPECIAL PLACES TO STAY...

Orestone Manor, Rockhouse Lane. A mix of the Mediterranean and English Country House/boutique style pervades this well appointed, small manor overlooking Lyme Bay, and beyond (on a clear day). 14 Spacious bedrooms. Fine cuisine. Non-residents are welcome to try their cream teas. You may then decide to stay further. 01803 897511 (D3) orestonemanor.com

INNS SERVING FOOD...

Church House Inn, Village Road, Marldon. A large C14 inn with stunning Gothic-style windows and steps leading up to the front door, no doubt originally designed for horsemen. A popular inn noted for fine ales, and honest-good fare. Flagstone floors and fireplaces add to the rustic scene. Pretty garden. Dogs and children welcome. Two cottages to let. (A5) 01803 558279 churchhousemarldon.com

BEACHES

St Mary's Bay, Brixham. Sand and shingle. Safe bathing. Access tricky at the bottom of cliffs. Panoramic views from the coast path above. Dogs permitted. P. (D9)

Churston Cove, Brixham. Sand and shingle. Safe bathing. Dogs permitted. P. (D8)

Fishcombe Cove, Churston Ferrers. Sand and shingle. Safe bathing. Dogs permitted. P/R/WC. (C8)

Elberry Cove, Churston Ferrers. Shingle. Safe bathing. Dogs permitted. P. (C8)

Preston, Paignton. Popular sandy beach lined with colourful beach huts. Restricted parking. Deckchairs. (B6)

Goodrington Sands, Paignton. Expansive, wide beach with red sand. Safe bathing. Rock pools at LT. Deckchairs. Disabled access. Dogs permitted in restricted areas. P/R/WC. (B7)

Central Paignton, Paignton. Extensive, flat sands attract young families wishing to paddle, and water sports. Pedaloes/boats for hire. D/R/WC. (B6)

Corbyn Head Beach, Torquay. Shingly sand and rocky pools. Beach huts. Disabled facilities. Boating pool. No dogs in summer. D/R. (C6)

Torre Abbey Sands, Torquay. Main beach for Torquay and traditional family beach with flat sand. No dogs in summer. D/R. (C5)

Beacon Cove, Torquay. Sheltered position makes for a warm, sunny spot. Pebbles and rocks. Short walk from the harbour. D/R/WC. (C5)

Meadfoot, Torquay. Shingle. Safe bathing. Beach huts. Paddle boats. Café. Dogs permitted in restrictive areas. P/R/WC. (D6)

Ansteys Cove, Torquay. Shingle and rocks. Set between high cliffs and wooded hillside. Steep path leads down from P. D/R/WC. (D5)

Babbacombe, Babbacombe Bay. Sand and shingle with safe bathing. Local sailing club. Steep walk down, or take the short railway ride. Spectacular views from above. Dogs permitted. P/R/WC. (D4)

Oddicombe, Babbacombe Bay. Shingly sand. Steep path descends to beach or take the cliff lift. Café. Paddle boats. Disabled facilities. D/R/WC. (D4)

Watcombe, Babbacombe Bay. Sand. Short, difficult access from parking down steep path. Café. D/WC. (D4)

Maidencombe, Babbacombe Bay. Sand and rocks. Short hike from parking, steep in places. Café. D/R/WC. (D3)

Shaldon, Babbacombe Bay. Sand and cliffs. Cliff access. D/WC. (D2)

COASTAL FOOTPATH...

Kingswear to Brixham; 10 miles. A fairly arduous stretch with some fine scenery. The first few miles traverse National Trust land. The path gives access to sandy beaches at Scabbacombe and Man Sands, later rounding Sharkham Point and Berry Head.

Brixham to Godrington Sands; 5 Miles. An easy semi-urbanised stretch passing some pleasant beaches. From Godrington the route passes through Paignton and Torquay, and there is no path as such.

Meadfoot Beach to Teignmouth; 10 miles. The route follows the Marine Drive past Thatcher Point and round Hope Nose. The path branches off at Hope Cove and runs for the most part close to the cliff edge with a series of ups and downs. Beyond Maidencombe, sea views tend to be obstructed by thick hedges. After passing Ness Headland, Teignmouth is reached by ferry from Shaldon.

Cockington Village

1921
Sir Ernest Shackleton's ship, Quest, bound for the south seas on her final voyage, puts in at Plymouth.

1927
October. Henry Williamson's "Tarka the Otter" is published.

193

Stretching from Plymouth to Salcombe and Start Point, and up the eastern coastline to Dartmouth. This curiously named area, based on the old English name "Hamme" meaning enclosed or sheltered place, is one of rocky coasts and beaches broken up by the tidal estuaries of the Yealm, Erme and Avon, and the lovely stretch of water below Kingsbridge with its quiet creeks delving far inland.

High cliffs mostly dominate the coastline, but here and there are attractive little villages of thatched cottages; Wembury, Bigbury, Inner and Outer Hope. Inland is a pastoral landscape of rolling hills and red-earthed fields bisected by twisty roads beneath high hedges - not a place for the traveller in a hurry.

Arriving from the north of the county one first descends on Totnes, the Jewel of the South Hams, which is bordered to the north eastern edge by the enchanting Dart Estuary and the well-tended villages on its shoreline; Cornworthy, Dittisham and Tuckenhay, all are worth a leisurely visit.

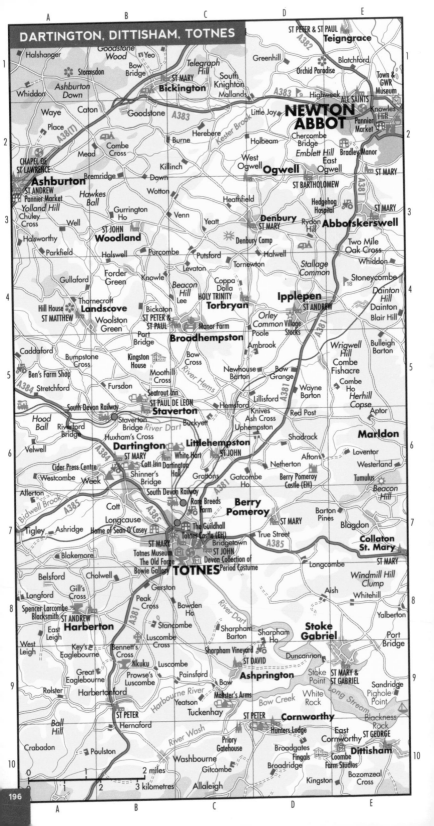

DARTINGTON, DITTISHAM, TOTNES

Halshanger
Goodstone Wood
Stormsdon
Yeo
Bow Bridge
Telegraph Hill
ST MARY
Bickington
Greenhill
South Knighton
Mallands
ST PETER & ST PAUL
Teigngrace
Blatchford
Orchid Paradise
Town & GWR Museum

Whiddon
Ashburton Down
Caton
A383
Knowles Hill
ALL SAINTS

Waye
Place
Goodstone
Burne
Little Joy
Highweek
NEWTON ABBOT
Pannier Market

Mead
Combe Cross
Killinch
Herebere
Holbeam
Chercombe Bridge
Emblett Hill
Bradley Manor

CHAPEL OF ST LAWRENCE
Ashburton
ST ANDREW
Pannier Market
Bremridge
Down
West Ogwell
East Ogwell
Ogwell
ST MARY

Yolland Hill
Chuley Cross
Well
Hawkes Ball
Wotton
Heathfield
ST BARTHOLOMEW
ST MARY

Halsworthy
Parkfield
ST JOHN
Woodland
Gurrington Ho
Venn
Yeatt
Denbury
ST MARY
Rydon Hill
Hedgehog Hospital
Abbotskerswell

Halswell
Purcombe
Putsford
Denbury Camp
Halwell
Tornewton
Two Mile Oak Cross
Whiddon

Gullaford
Forder Green
Knowle
Beacon Hill
Lee
Levaton
Stallage Common
18
Stoneycombe

Hill House
ST MATTHEW
Thornecroft
Landscove
Bickaton
ST PETER & ST PAUL
HOLY TRINITY
Torbryan
Coppa Dolla
Ipplepen
ST ANDREW
Dainton Hill
Dainton
Blair Hill

Caddaford
Woolston Green
Port Bridge
Manor Farm
Broadhempston
Orley Common
Village Stocks
Poole
Wrigwell Hill
Combe Fishacre
Bulleigh Barton

Bumpstone Cross
Kingston House
Moothill Cross
Bow Cross
Ambrook
Combe Ho
Herhill Copse

Ben's Farm Shop
A384
Stretchford
Fursdon
Seatrout Inn
ST PAUL DE LEON
Staverton
Hemsford
Newhouse Barton
River Hems
Bow Grange
Wayne Barton
Aptor

Hood Ball
Riverford Bridge
South Devon Railway
Staverton Bridge
River Dart
Buckyett
Knives Ash Cross
Uphempston
Lillisford
Red Post
Marldon

Velwell
Huxham's Cross
Dartington
ST MARY
Littlehempston
ST JOHN
Shadrack
Loventor
Westerland
Tumulus

Cider Press Centre
Westcombe
Week
Cott Inn
Shinner's Bridge
White Hart
Dartington Hall
Grattons
Gatcombe Ho
Netherton
Afton
Berry Pomeroy Castle (EH)
Beacon Hill

Allerton
Bidwell Brook
A385
Cott
Longcause
Home of Sean O'Casey
South Devon Railway
Rare Breeds Farm
Berry Pomeroy
ST MARY
Barton Pines
Blagdon

Tigley
Ashridge
The Guildhall
Totnes Castle (EH)
ST JOHN
True Street
A385
Longcombe
Collaton St. Mary
ST MARY

Blakemore
ST MARY
Totnes Museum
The Old Forge
Bowie Gallery
TOTNES
Bridgetown
Devon Collection of Period Costume
Windmill Hill Clump
Whitehill

Belsford
Langford
Gill's Cross
Cholwell
Gerston
Peak Cross
Bowden Ho
Aish
Yalberton

Spencer Larcombe Blacksmith
ST ANDREW
Harberton
Stancombe
Sharpham Barton
Stoke Gabriel
Port Bridge

West Leigh
East Leigh
Key's Cross
Bennett's Cross
Luscombe Cross
Sharpham Ho
Duncannon
Stoke Point

Great Eaglebourne
Nkuku
Prowse's Luscombe
Luscombe
Painsford
Sharpham Vineyard
ST DAVID
Ashprington
ST MARY & ST GABRIEL

Rolster
Harbertonford
ST PETER
Hernaford
Harbourne River
Bow
Malster's Arms
Yeatson
Tuckenhay
Bow Creek
White Rock
Long Stream
Sandridge
Pighole Point
Blackness Rock
ST GEORGE

Ball Hill
Crabadon
Poulston
River Wash
ST PETER
Cornworthy
Hunters Lodge
East Cornworthy
Coombe Farm Studios
Dittisham
Bozomzeal Cross

Washbourne
Gitcombe
Allaleigh
Priory Gatehouse
Broadgates
Broadridge
Fingals
Kingston

0 1 2 miles
0 1 2 3 kilometres

TOTNES

"The Jewel of the South Hams", so they say, and who would argue with them. If music be the food of your love, and art your divine mistress, then Totnes is the town for you. The close proximity to Dartington and the well-heeled villages of the Dart Estuary has given Totnes an artiness and comfort level rarely seen outside London. It is the "Boho" Look, mix of bohemian and affluence, you see here. The many health shops, cafés and restaurants, busy all year, lend the town an affluence unique to Devon. It is a colourful place to people watch, best seated from the many cafés above East Gate, the medieval arch. The shops are unusual and independent, festooned with colour, a welcome relief from the samey, dull, dreariness of many British High Streets.

The town is split into two parts connected by the ascending Fore Street. The lower end, beside the River Dart, has open spaces and riverside walks overlooked by yacht marinas and former warehouses converted into prestigious flats. It is here you can hop on a boat to Dartmouth. The ascending Fore Street which becomes the High Street above the medieval arch is one of Devon's and England's most historic and interesting thoroughfares leading to the Castle and Guildhall, passing by Elizabethan and Jacobean houses fronted by more modern exteriors.

According to legend, Totnes was discovered by Aeneas (Brutus), who had left Troy encouraged by a prophecy from the Goddess Diana. He sailed up the Dart, landing here, to discover Albion. He rid the land of giants and serpents, and created The Britons. The Brutus stone on Fore Street commemorates this unlikely tale.

Totnes is the second oldest borough in England, minted coins in 979, and was granted a Charter by King John in 1206, authorising the Merchant's Guild. The export of tin and wool enriched the town's medieval merchants who also imported wines from France. Defoe noted that in 1740 "the town has more gentlemen in it than tradesmen of note". A truism of today? The history of the town can be discovered in the castle, church and museums.

And when next you climb the draughty High Street think of William Wills, born 1834 in Totnes, the first white man to cross Australia, south to north (Melbourne to the Gulf of Carpentaria), who finally succumbed to starvation at Cooper's Creek in 1861, missing out on the £2,000 prize money. (C7)

SPECIAL PLACES TO VISIT...

Bowie Gallery, 54b Fore Street. Contemporary art in all its finery and creativity; paintings, sculptures and ceramics. Open daily. (C7) 01803 865779 thebowiegallery.co.uk

Dart Valley Cycleway (NCN2). Totnes lies in the middle of this route and you can cycle/walk north to Hood Manor via Dartington (7km/4miles), or south to Ashprington via Sharpham (8km/5miles). Terrain is mostly off-road except through Totnes and near Sharpham. Park in Totnes Station or Dartington. (C7)

Fashion & Textiles Museum, 43 High St. A Tudor merchant's house hpuses the Devonshire Collection of Period Costume. Costumes from the mid-C18, onwards. New themed exhibition each year. Open Spring BH-Sept Tu-F 11-5. (Oct by appoint). 01803 862857 devonmuseums.net/Totnes

Sharpham Vineyard ss

The Guildhall, 5 Ramparts Walk. Originally the Rectory of 1088 Benedictine Priory. Rebuilt as meeting place of Merchant Guild in 1553. From 1624-1974 used as Magistrates Court and Town Gaol until 1887. Now Mayor's Parlour with historic prints, documents and artefacts. Open Apr-Oct M-F 10-1, 2-5.

Image Bank, Town Mill. Photographic archive of the town. View 1,000s of photographs on a computer database. Heritage exhibition describing the history of Totnes. Open Tu & F 10-1, 2-4. (C7) totnesimagebank.info

Rare Breeds Farm. View the rare breeds, cuddle and fuss the friendly animals, walk and brush the donkeys, see the owls. Refreshments. Open daily East-Oct 10-5. 01803 840387 totnesrarebreeds.co.uk

Totnes Castle. Norman motte and bailey castle probably built about 1100. Open daily Apr-Sept 10-6, Oct daily 10-5, Nov-Mar W/Es 10-4, closed 1-2 in winter. 01803 864406 english-heritage.org.uk

Totnes (Elizabethan House &) Museum, 70 Fore St. Period furniture, toys, exhibition on Charles Babbage and computing. Artisans Kitchen and grocer's shop. Children can dress up in old clothes of bygone days. Open Apr-Oct, M-F 10.30-5. (B7) 01803 863821 totnesmuseum.org

Whitespace Contemporary Art, 72 Fore Street. Exhibits emerging British contemporary artists at affordable prices. Situated just before the Clock Tower. Open Tu-Sa 10-5. (B7) 01803 864088 whitespaceart.com

SPECIAL PLACES TO VISIT...

Berry Pomeroy Castle. Late C15 stone quadrangular fortress and stone Elizabethan mansion. Open daily Apr-Oct 10-6, W/Es in winter from 10-dusk. (D6) 01803 866618 english-heritage.org.uk

Bradley Manor (NT). A small roughcast C15 manor house that is still a home. Great Hall, screens passage, buttery. Perpendicular chapel. Decorated with medieval stencils and paintings. One of the oldest inhabited houses in Devon. Open Apr-Sept Tu-Th 11-5. (E2) 01626 354513.

SPECIAL PLACES OF INTEREST...

Blacksmith South Devon, Brewery Cottages, Old Rd. Spencer Larcombe forges artistic metalwork designs in amazing shapes; chairs, candlelabra and gates. Commissions undertaken. Open M-F 9-5. 07762 198169 spencerfieldlarcombe.com

Coombe Farm Studios, Dittisham. A dynamic oeuvre of creativty that will unlock a burst of magic from within. Tutors and students come back from all over the world. Courses on ceramics, watercolours and oils, drawing in many forms. Accommodation here and nearby. Book on: 01803 722352 (E10) coombefarmstudios.com

Hedgehog Hospital & Prickly Ball Farm, Dentbury Road. Cares for sick and injured hedgehogs, rears baby hoglets. Also, an open farm - lots of "hands on" fun with many animals. Café. Open daily 10-5. (D3) 01626 362319 pricklyballfarm.co.uk

Hill House Nursery & Garden. Construction of over 18,000 sq ft of glass-houses, open to the public with a large range of plants for sale. You are invited to relax in the Garden. Tea Room (Mar-Sept) overlooking water garden. Open daily, all year 11-5. (A4) 01803 762273 hillhousenursery.co.uk

Nkuku Lifestyle Store & Café, Brockhills Barns. An Aladdin's cave of handmade home and lifestyle products

---

LIGHT BITES...

Totnes is spoilt for choice. If you start from the bottom of the **High Street** below William Wills' house is **The Curator Café & Kitchen, The Plains**. An Italian café serving coffee sourced from the supplier - traditional wood (oak) roasted beans. Rustic, Italian food in the evenings. Soon to produce Umbrian Taglio pizzas (delish).
01803 865570 italianfoodheroes.com
Around the corner is **Annies Fruit Shop, Ticklemore Street** for your organic fruit and veg,cheeses and Juice Bar. 01803 867265
anniesfruitshop.co.uk
Next door, a new pasta shop. Turn L up the **High Street** to Amelies, an alternative opposite the pub, **King William IV** who provide pub-grub and B&B. Ascend **Fore Street** through the **East Gate** arch, and on your left is the wine bar, **Rumours**, recently decorated, a convivial and laid back eatery, always popular. A few yards on at **No. 26, Pie Street**, set in a stunning build, English pies made on the premises, and ale the order of the day.
01803 868647 piestreet.co.uk Keep ascending to **No. 50, Ben's Wine and Tapas**, for a glass of chilled Prosecco, or marinated pork skewers or Spanish tortilla, a slice of the **Riverford Farm** empire on 01803 840853. As you reach the bookshop on your left is Totnes' most popular café **The Wild Fig Deli & Café, 53 Fore Street**. Much is gluten free with Vegan options but they also cater for carnivores. It's a pretty hip place to hang out.
01803 864829
thewildfig.co.uk. Across the road their health food shop with tasty sandwiches, fritattas, et al. Keep going, rounding the corner, **Woods Bistro**, getting hungry? And, across on the other side of the road, **Willows Vegetarian Restaurant**. But, if it's an old fashioned tea party you're after, look no further than **Greys Dining Room at 96 High Street.**

1942
HMS Exeter sunk with much loss of life.

1943
Evacuation of the South Hams for invasion exercises.

from artisans throughout the world. Open daily 9-6, for Brunch 9-12, lunch 12-3.30. (B9)01803 866847 nukuk.com

Sharpham Vineyard & Cheese Dairy.
Farm set in 500-acres of vineyard, meadows & wooded slopes. Vineyard & riverside trails. Shop offers full range of wines & cheeses. The Vineyard Café serves fish and crustacea. Opens Mar M-Sa 10-5, Apr-Sept daily 10-5, Oct-Dec M-Sa 10-3. (C8) 01803 732203 sharpham.com

SPECIAL PLACES TO STAY...

Fingals. A complete one-off, in style and attitude. Richard Johnston has created a refuge from our mad, mad world where you can relax, meet old and make new friends in a laid back, comfortable environment. Art is ubiquitous. Fleet of wooden boats moored nearby. B&B accommodation or 5-apartments for self-catering Family rooms, too. (D9) 01803 722398 fingals.co.uk

Kingston House. Rare survivor of C18 architecture. Lovingly restored to former glory with fabrics and furniture true to period. Magnificent 4-poster beds. Candlelit gourmet dinners. Swimming, spa, sauna and steam room for your holistic pampering. Self-catering cottages. A popular wedding venue. (B5) 01803 762235 kingston-estate.co.uk

Dartington Hall Trust. 1,000-acre estate bought in the 1920s by Leonard Elmhirst and his wife, American heiress, Dorothy Whitney as a base to try new methods of farming and forestry, and rural construction. It has developed into an international centre for the generation and application of new ideas in the arts, ecology and social justice. C14 mediaeval courtyard. Music and Literature Festivals. International summer school. Cinema. Small hotel. One of the great independent institutions in Britain that realizes it has had to change its direction. The University School of Drama and Music has moved to Falmouth, and now the Trust is returning

to its roots. I quote: "To seek a new long-term vision for Dartington as a laboratory for living and learning with the purpose of pioneering deep personal and societal change. This is inspired by the Elmhirsts' original Dartington Experiment, their concept of expressing a 'many-sided life' and their ethos of openness, creativity and 'learning by doing'." (B6) 01803 847100 dartington.org

SPECIAL ATTRACTIONS AT DARTINGTON...

Cider Press Centre. A complex of shops and restaurants in a picturesque cluster of C16/C17 stone buildings; bookshop (arts and crafts), Dartington Crystal, jewellery, pottery, farm foods, toys, kitchenware. Open daily M-Sa 9.30-5.30, & Su East-Xmas 10.30-5.30. 01803 847500 dartington.org

High Cross House. A superb Modernist house designed by William Lescaze in 1932. Period furniture, Art exhibited (Ben Nicholson and Christopher Wood) and material derived from The Dartington Hall Trust and its beginnings. Plans are to restore this building for a range of creative and experimental activities. It is closed for the foreseeable future. (B6)

More Café Restaurant. Within the Cider Press Centre, serves breakfast, brunch and lunch, and Devon cream teas. Why not try the Dartington Mushroom burgers? Open M-Sa 9.30-5.30, Su 10.30-5.30. (B6) 01803 847524 dartingtonciderpress.co.uk

White Hart Inn, Dartington Hall. Great value food. Extremely popular with the locals. Relaxed attitude and booking advised. (B6) 01803 847111.

DINING PUBS..AND A BED FOR THE NIGHT...

Hunters Lodge Inn, Cornworthy. A local that has been reborn offering a fine range of ales. Fish and shellfish feature strongly. Children and dogs welcome. (D9) 01803 732204 hunterslodgeinn.com

Maltsters' Arms, Bow Creek. C18 inn accessed via boat, car or foot with many small, bright rooms. Serious selection of ales and wines, cider too. Wholesome food. Child friendly. B&B. A former hostelry of the infamous, mischievous and sadly, late Keith Floyd. 01803 732350. (C9) tuckenhay.com

Sea Trout Inn. A 400-year old inn that has had cosiderable modernisation with the result that it appears a bit fake. Mix of cosy and spacious rooms. Accommodation. 6-rods for fly fishing. (B5) 01803 762274 seatroutinn.co.uk

The Cott Inn, Dartington. Very much your chocolate-boxy and cream tea Devon pub. With thatched roof and interior beams. Always a foodie-pub and fairly expensive to stay in their comfy bedrooms. Live Music Night on W & Su evenings. (B6) 01803 863777 cottinn.co.uk

River Dart

Cattewater
Cattedown
Bridge
Oreston
Summerskill
Brewery
Pomphlett
Turnchapel
Plymstock
ST MARY &
ALL SAINTS
Dunstone
Elburton
ST JOHN
Hooe
Gooseswell
Halwell
West
Sherford
Combe
Spriddlestone
Staddon
Heights
Bovisand Bay
Bovisland
Lodge
Staddiscombe
Raneleigh
Spriddlestone
Ho
Andurn
Point
Down
Thomas
Knighton
Hele
Almshouses
Heybrook
Bay
Wembury
Mill (NT)
Wembury Ho
Renney
Rocks
Wembury
ST WERBURGH
Wembury
Point
Blackstone
Rocks
Season
Point
Warren
Point
Great Mew
Stone
Mouthstone
Point
Gara Point
Worswell
The
Warren
Netton
Blackstone
Point
Hillsea
Point
Netton
Island
Stoke
Pont

East
Sherford
Hareston
Pitten
Popple's
Bridge
Lyneham
Treby
Lotherton
Bridge
Efford
Gorlofen
Worston
Wollaton
Stonycross
Brixton
ST MARY
Yealmpton
ALL SAINTS
Yealmbridge
Winston
Kitley
Kitley Caves &
Country Park
Puslinch
Bridge
Torr
Dun
Ro
Warren
Point
Wrescombe
Creacombe
Lus
Collaton
Brown
River Yealm
Clanicombe
Preston
Battisborou
Cross
Newton
Ferrers
HOLY CROSS
Membland
Pool
Ship Inn
ST PETER
Bridgend
Lambside
St Anchorite's
Rock
Noss
Mayo
Rowden
Beacon
Hill
Blackaterry
Point
Butcher's
Cove
Battisl
Is
Stoke
Ho
Cunnimall

A379
B3186

Coffiete Creek

0   1   2 miles
0   1   2   3 kilometres

200

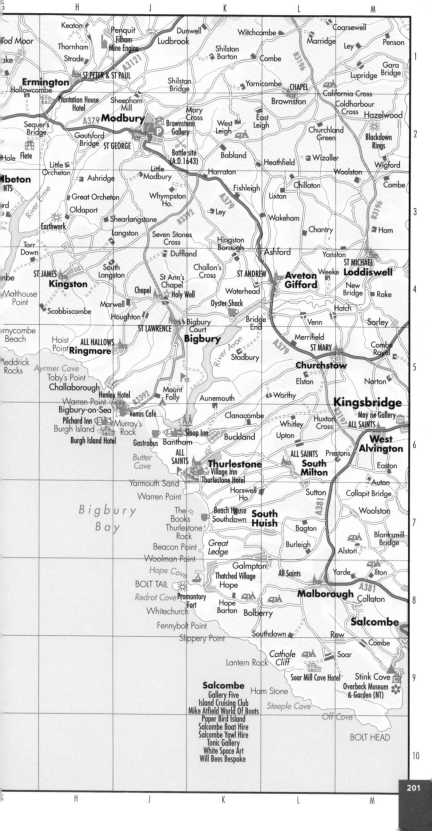

Starehole Bay, Salcombe

MODBURY

A hilltop town set in a deep hollow surrounded by the rolling, undulating hills, of the South Hams. The drive descending the High Street draws you to smart slate-hung houses built in the C18 and C19s. In the Middle Ages the fortunes of the town were derived from wool. The affluent clothiers decorated the C14 church, and built some fine houses burnt down by the Parliamentarians in the Civil War battles of 1642 and 1643. Birthplace of Thomas Savery, business partner to Thomas Newcomen. St George's Fair. Today, there are teashops, art galleries, antique shops and a fine fish deli. (J2)

SPECIAL PLACES TO VISIT...

Brownston Gallery, 36 Church Street. Lively little gallery with an ever-changing venue for new and established artists, sculptures and ceramicists. Open M-Sa 10-5, W 10-1. (J2) 01548 831338 thebrownstongallery.co.uk

Parish Church of St George. Tall, lofty medieval spire is unusual for a C14 church. Tombs of the Crusaders. Prideaux Arms. Carved pulpit. Jacobean chair. (J2)

SALCOMBE

No visitor can come to the South Hams without visiting Salcombe. The setting of the town beside the estuary with the pastoral backdrop of emerald green fields is simply stunning. Its sheltered position, and mild climate, encourages the growth of sub-tropical plants and flowers. The pockets of golden sand on either side of the estuary make for ideal family holidays. It is also a busy and popular location for learning to sail dinghies, and a favourite Port-of-Call for yachtsmen. In July and August the visitors outnumber the locals by 10 to 1. The abundance of second homes is a sore issue for those Salcombe born and bred, who now have to look far and wide for affordable housing. The busy High Street and the narrow streets off it are brimming with mutiples' designer shops (Crew Clothing, Jack Wills, Fat Face, White Stuff, Timberland etc) restaurants and gift shops. To get a real feel of Salcombe you either have to arrive via sail (or coastpath), or failing that, by car. As you descend the steep hill follow the signs to the long term car park on your left. Enter Gould Road into Island Street. This is old-time Salcombe with a bevy of interesting craftspeople

and independent businesses. There is a wide choice of eateries and a number of boat hirers, too. The RNLI Lifeboat is one establishment that has no seasonal shortfall, and for all seafarers, the RNLI Museum is a worthy Port-of-Call. (M8

SPECIAL PLACES TO VISIT...

Gallery FIve, Island Street. This sweet little gallery features original paintings, ceramics, hand-painted furniture and unusual gifts. Open daily 10-5. 01548 288162 gallery5salcombe.co.uk

Island Cruising Club, 10 Island Street. Watersports, sailing centre; courses (residential and non-residential) and daily boat hire. Associated with The Egremont Trust. (M8) 01548 852405. islandcruisingclub.co.uk

Mike Atfield Wooden Boats, **Island Street.** Mike will build you a Salcombe Yawl, the Class (16ft with a 7ft beam) indigenous to Salcombe, and holder of a precious craft that may be lost with time. (M8) 01548 843120.

Overbecks Museum & Gardens (NT). Elegant Edwardian house containing local photos, model boats,

LIGHT BITES...

Fore Street has a fair selection of eateries with a bakery and deli (at 52) to furnish a picnic. On your right is the **Salcombe Coffee Co, 73 Fore St**. A friendly little diner in centre of village. All day breakfast, high teas and supper. Open all year. (M8) 01548 842319 salcombe.co.uk Up the street overlooking the Short Stay car park, **Captain Morgan's** for an all-day breakfast and take-aways. For some rhythm and blues, and funky soul try **Sailor V, 36 Fore Street.** Delish homemade cakes, soups and lunch specials. Lively, funky atmosphere in former HSBC bank.

animals, birds and eggs, moths and butterflies, dolls and toys. Special interest for children. Museum open daily mid-Feb to Oct 11-5. (M9) 01548 842893 nationaltrust.org

Paper Bird Island, Island Street. Just the place to keep your kids busy on a rainy day; painting, decoupage, face-painting and arty workshops. 01548 288723 paperbirdisland. com

Salcombe Art Club, Victoria Quay. Paintings, drawings and ceramics by local artists in large studio overlooking the Estuary. Tuition on painting, woodblock printmaking, Drawing and oil painting. Open East to early Oct M-Sa 10-1, 2-4.30 - also most Su. Victoria Quay. (M8) salcombeartclub.org.uk

Salcombe Boat Hire, 11 Clifton Place. You can hire self-drive 12-16ft fibreglass boats with steering wheels plus life jackets and fishing rods. Great for exploring the estuary and creeks and visiting pubs. 01548 844475 salcombeboathire.co.uk

Salcombe Maritime Museum, Market St. Unique collection of antique paintings. Trading schooners. Shipwrecks, fishing and shipbuilding. Open daily Apr-Oct 10.30-12.30, 2.30-4.30. (M8) 01548 843080 salcombemuseum.org.uk

Salcombe Yawl Hire. Hire a traditional Salcombe Yawl or an 18ft launch. The Yawl is simply rigged and comes with a furling jib, an outboard and rowing tender plus life jackets. Details: 01548 561619.

Tonic Gallery, 30 Island Street. Large canvases of boatyards and "light and memories of Salcombe by Greg Ramsbey 07733 225662 (M8) tonicgallery.co.uk

White Space Art, Coves Quay. One of Salcombe's great attractions not to be missed; a bright and attractive gallery with a wide range of paintings and decorative art in all forms. Open daily Apr-Dec. (M8) 01548 844144 whitespaceart.com

Will Bees Bespoke, Island Street. Handcrafted accessssories made in the finest fabrics and leather: bags, cushions, belts. Open daily. 01548 842119 willbeesbespoke.com

WHERE TO EAT & DRINK...

Crab Shed Seafood Restaurant, Fish Quay. Just beside the long stay car park. Fish and crustacea; hand-dived scallops, crab and lobsters exclusively supplied by local boats. Seasonal vegetables. Open daily. (M8) 01548 844280 crabshed.com

Dick and Wills, 42 Fore Street. Restaurant, bar and brasserie's terrace overlooks the beautiful estuary. Simple, elegant and unfussy describes the style of cuisine, ingredients for one of Devon's finest where you could be forgiven for sitting here all day. (M8) 01548 843408 dickandwills.co.uk

Fortescue Inn, Union Street. This is the best pub in town, popular with the locals. Stripped pine tables, artworks and good, honest pub-grub. Luxurious bedrooms. (M8) 01548 842868 thefortsalcombe.com

SPECIAL PLACES TO VISIT...

Flete. Grade 1 listed building. Originally a Tudor manor house with C18 and C19 additions. Redesigned in late 1800s by Norman Shaw. Private residence with self-contained, private retirement apartments. No longer open. (G2)

Flete Estate. A selection of coastal holiday cottages to rent on this estate designated an Area of Oustanding Natural Beauty and a Site of Special Scientific Interest. All available to you as you walk the coastpath alive with wild flowers and wildlife. (F/G4) 01752 830234 flete.co.uk

SPECIAL PLACES TO STAY...

Burgh Island Hotel. Art Deco meets Agatha Christie who wrote two novels whilst staying here. Indeed, a complete one-off in a sensational position on a private island overlooking Bigbury Bay. Evening Dress is the norm for Dinner in The Ballroom, more casual dining in the Captain's Cabin or in the Ganges Restaurant at lunch. (H6) 01548 810514 burghisland.com

Henley Hotel, Folly Hill. An Edwardian seaside villa with magical views over Bigbury Bay that has been converted into a small, cosy, cluttered, home-like hotel with 6-bedrooms. The Chef, Martyn, takes great care to prepare you feasts. (J5) 01548 810240 thehenleyhotel.co.uk

Plantation House Hotel, Totnes Rd. A highly praised boutique restaurant with rooms a short distance from Plymouth and the south coast. Added, an elegant dining experience to accommodate all foodie afficionados. (H2) 01548 831100. plantationhousehotel.co.uk

Salcombe Harbour Hotel & Spa. If you wish to be pampered, to enjoy some hedonism and to look and linger at a beautiful view, be sure to book a top-floor room with estuary views. Seafood restaurant. 01548 844444 salcombe-harbour-hotel.co.uk

South Sands Boutique Hotel, Salcombe. Bright, blue skies, a golden beach outside your light and airy bedroom, and all furnished in wood created by local craftsmen. Dog friendly. 01548 845900 southsands.com

Thurlestone Hotel. An established family hotel set beside the unspoilt and spectacular South Devon Coast. There are many leisure, sports and spa facilities including a 9-hole golf course and the Dolphin Children's Club. For more informality, the Village Inn, next door. (K6) 01548 560382 thurlestone.co.uk

PUBS SERVING FOOD...

Pilchard Inn, Burgh Island. A glorious watering hole (since 1336) on a sunny day made famous by Tom Crocker whose ghost still haunts it. Fine ales and bar food. Cross via Sea tractor (cut off twice daily). (H6) 01548 810514 burghisland.com

The Ship Inn, Noss Mayo. Light, airy and nautical waterside pub. Fresh fish, Devon lamb and salmon. Log fires and newspapers. What more could you wish for? (C4) 01752 872387 nossmayo.com

The Sloop Inn, Bantham. A former C14 pirates and smugglers' inn now offering fine fresh fish, shell fish and Devon beef and lamb dishes. 6-bedrooms. A good base from which to surf the local beach and walk the coastpath. (J6) 01548 560489. thesloop.co.uk

Village Inn, Thurlestone. C16 Inn belonging to the Grove family for over 100 years. Free house serving real ales and fresh seasonal food, seafood a speciality. Themed nights. Live music. Children and dogs welcome. Open daily from 11.30 for coffee and pastries. (K6) 01548 563525 thurlestone.co.uk

LIGHT BITES...

Beach House, Bigbury Bay. What a great location: add the great food (fish, burgers, bfast butties, crab sarnies) and the chilled ambience and good weather, you have a combo made in...? Open from 11 M-F, 10 at W/Es (K7) 01548 561144 beachhousedevon.com

Oyster Shack, Milburn Orchard Farm. A seafood bistro of great renown and popularity; local oysters and fresh fish al fresco. Masterclass cookery classes on international seafood cooking. Open for breakfast, lunch and dinner. (K4) 01548 810876 oystershack. co.uk

Venus Café, Bigbury On Sea. Environmental award-winning café in stunning beach location. Breakfast, lunch and ice creams. Open daily East-Oct & winter W/Es 10-5. (J6) 01548 810141 venuscompany.co.uk

Wembury Mill (NT). Mill house on beach for breakfasts and cream teas. Open Apr-Oct 10.30-5. (B3) 01752 862314

COASTAL FOOTPATH...

Yealm Estuary to Erme Mouth; 11 miles. From the far side of the ferry the path follows the left bank of the **Yealm** and rounds **Gara Point**, continuing along **Revelstoke Drive**, a scenic C19 carriageway. Up to **Blackstone Point** the coastline is owned by the National Trust. The path

keeps close to the clifftops and there is access to a number of secluded coves. After **Stoke Point** comes the ascent of **Beacon Hill** and a succession of further climbs and descents. Approaching **Mothercombe** the route turns inland and there is a short stretch of road leading to the beach at the mouth of the **Erme**. There is no ferry and the water can only be crossed one hour either side of low tide - otherwise a long detour is necessary.

Erme Mouth to Bigbury; 5 miles. The path continues near the cliff edge with fairly strenuous ups and downs. **Bigbury** is a small resort with modest amenities, from which **Burgh Island** can be visited.

Bigbury to Hope Cove; 7 miles. There is a ferry across the **Avon** on a limited summer schedule, but the river can also be crossed on foot at low tide. From **Bantham** is an easy cliffside walk skirting the golf course to **Thurlestone Sands** and along the shore to **Hope Cove**, an attractive fishing harbour.

Hope Cove to Salcombe; 9 miles. One of the most spectacular sections of the path - the whole stretch is owned by the National Trust. After ascending **Bolt Tail**, the route follows the cliff top all the way, with steep descents to **Soar Mill Cove** and **Starehole Bay.** After ascending **Sharp Tor** the path comes down past **Overbecks Gardens** to join the road to **Salcombe**.

BEACHES & SURFING...

Bovisand. Sand and rocks. R/WC. (A3))

Wembury. Sand and rocks. R. (B4)

Stoke. Pebbly sand and rocks 1/4 mile hike from P. (D5)

Mothecombe. Sand and low cliffs. 1/4 mile hike from P/WC/R. (G4)

Bigbury-on-Sea. Fine sandy beach popular with young families. Rock pools. One of Britain's best locations for windsurfing, canoeing and coastal walks. Beach cleaned daily in summer. Lifeguards May-Sept. Burgh Island and the Pilchard Inn accessible by the unique tractor, or by foot, at low tide. Check tractor times if looking to spend a day on the island. No dogs, May-Sept. Café/gift shops. (H6)

Bantham. Sand and safe bathing. Dogs in restricted areas. Gastrobus for hungry surfers. P/R/WC. (J6)

Thurlestone. Sand and safe bathing. Disabled access. Dogs permitted. Gastrobus. P/R/WC. (K7)

Hope Cove. Sand and safe bathing. Popular with young families. Shop. Inn. P/R/WC. (K8)

Salcombe South Sands. Fine golden sand. Safe bathing. Beach shop. Café and bar. Parking limited but can be accessed by ferry from Salcombe. R/WC. (M9)

Salcombe North Sands. Sand and safe bathing. Limited disabled access. Dogs permitted. P/R/WC. Winking Prawn cafe. (M9)

Burgh Island

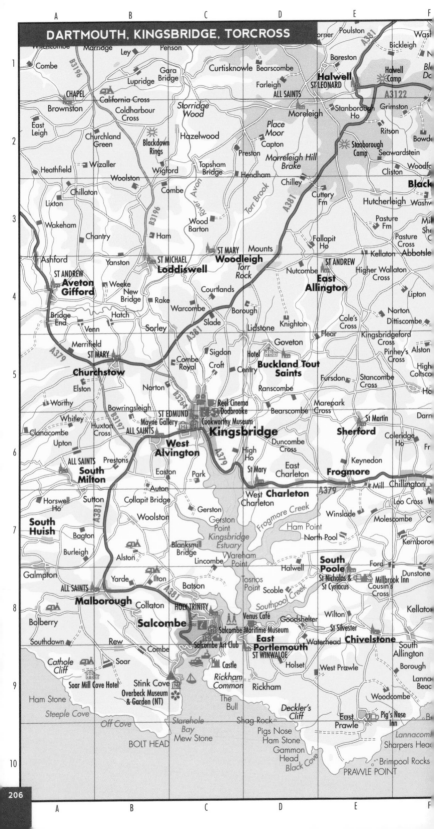

Bayards Cove, Dartmouth

DARTMOUTH

A rare gem. Magnificently situated harbour in deep water, sheltered by steep hillsides and a conduit for trade and pleasure boats sailing up and down the River Dart to Totnes. Few towns in Devon, or England, have had such an influence on the course of England's rich past. In the C12, the assemblage point for the second and third Crusades. The Elizabethan Age encouraged Devon men to explore the globe; to seek the North West Passage, the Straits of Magellan and the piratical waters of the Far East. Their boundless exploits on the High Seas, in the good name of Queen Elizabeth 1, and England, brought maritime supremacy and great bounty to this corner of England. Whether these men; Drake, Raleigh, Hawkins and Davis, be seen as adventurers, privateers or Her Majesty's Most Loyal Subjects, is open to debate. By the time of the Spanish Armada, Dartmouth was to be superseded by Plymouth as Devon's busiest port. The old warships would dock at Warfleet Creek, the smaller craft, largely smugglers, at Bayards Cove, now overlooked by some splendid C18 houses. Notably, the Custom House.

The town has great character and activity. Always a medley of locals and visitors. There is much to see; the finest building, The Butterwalk, enriched with eleven stone pillars. But take the riverside walk to the Castle and St Petrock's church, and look out across the water to smiling Kingswear, a feast of pastel-coloured houses, and junction for the Paignton Steam Railway, a marvellous site when in full steam charging up beside the river.

Behind, dominating the hillside stands the Brittania Royal Naval College, designed by Sir Aston Webb, architect of the V & A Museum. Opened by Edward V11, it is a most impressive building overlooking the Estuary, and the beckoning sea.

Always a popular port-of-call for yachtsmen, the Estuary has two marinas, and many cruisers plying their trade to show you the enchanting River Dart. The town has become something of a food and arts centre. Witness below the many arts and craft galleries, and the bountiful eating out emporia. Regatta time is a rewarding time to visit, the Estuary ablaze with sail and colour, and good times. (K2)

ARTS & CRAFTS...

Ainscough Contemporary Art, 16 Foss Street. London gallery's south-west outpost has ever-changing exhibitions on West Country themes on 3-floors; paintings, pottery and sculpture. Open daily. (K2) 01548 855732 acag.co.uk

Andras Kaldor Gallery, 15 Newcomen Rd. Drawings and paintings of architectural subjects, pots and amphorae. Originals and prints. Open daily. 01803 833874 (K2) kaldor.co.uk

Baxters, 12 Foss St. The enthusiastic owner displays a hive of contemporary art, crafts, jewellery and gifts. Open M-Sa 10-5, Su 11-4 (closed W). (K2) 01803 839000 baxtersgallery.co.uk

Coombe Gallery, 20 Foss St. Exhibits some of the finest artists and craftsmen in the West Country with regular quarterly shows. Associated with Combe Farm Studios of Dittisham. Open daily. (K2) 01803 835820 coombegallery.com

D'Art Gallery, 4 Lower St. Paintings with a broad range of styles. Quarterly exhibitions display 70 + new works over

1960
(Sir) Francis Chichester wins the first Solo Transatlantic Yacht Race.

1961
Tamar Bridge opened to traffic.

2-floors. Open daily 10-4.30 except Tu. (K2) 01803 834923 dart-gallery.com

SPECIAL PLACES TO VISIT...

Britania Museum, Royal Naval College.
The Royal Navy's Officer Training Establishment since 1905. Fine works of naval art. Museum with historic naval artefacts. Fully escorted tours Apr-Nov in term time, M & W; Details and time on: 01803 677565 (K2) britanniaassociation.org.uk/tours

Dartmouth Castle (EH),
Castle Road. Castle dating back to the late C15, stands guard over the Dart Estuary. Features include hands-on exhibitions and displays. Open daily Apr-Sept 10-5, Oct-Mar W/Es 10-4. 01803 833588 (K2)

Dartmouth Museum, The Butterwalk. Housed in a group of C17 merchants' houses with fine panelled rooms. Notable ship models, paintings and rare books. Open all year, Apr-Sept 10-4 (Su & M 1-4), Oct-Mar 1-3. 01803 832923 (K2) dartmouthmuseum.org

Newcomen Engine House, Mayors Avenue. Atmospheric beam engine on the unusual mechanical principle developed by Thomas Newcomen, 1664-1729, a native of the town, in 1725. Now electrically worked. Open Apr-Oct M-Sa 10-5, Su 10-2. Nov-Mar M-F 10-4.30 (W 10-1). (K2) 01803 834224 devonmuseums.net

Parish Church of St Saviour.
In the centre of the town and worth a visit just for seeing its magnificent C15 rood and parclose screen. Multi-coloured Jacobean pulpit in stone. Fine ironwork to South doorway. (K2)

St Petrock's Church. Set within the Castle grounds and the last sacred site sailors would spy as they sailed off to new horizons. Rebuilt in the Gothic style. Fine brasses to wealthy merchants. Pulpit and Royal Arms. Norman font. (K2)

The Flavel Centre, Flavel Place. Multi-purpose arts and entertainment centre housing cinema, theatre and live music. Children's programmes, too. Café and bar with pre-show suppers (01803 832458). (K2) 01803 839530 theflavel.org.uk

BOATING & RIVER INTERESTS...

Dartmouth Boat Hire Centre, North Embankment. Self-drive cabin and open boats. Comprehensive safety brief. Competitive rates include, fuel, life jackets, river charts and info pack. Skippered boat trips available. (K2) 01803 722367 dartmouth-boat-hire.co.uk

River Link, 5 Lower Street.
Cruises on the beautiful River Dart departing from Dartmouth and Totnes. Bar, commentary, toilets. Day time and evening cruises from Apr-Oct, Nov-Mar by arrangement. Daily circular cruises from Dartmouth except M & F. (K2) 01803 834488 riverlink.co.uk

SPECIAL PLACES TO STAY...EAT & DRINK...

Anzac Street Bistro & Guesthouse, 2 Anzac Street.
Bright, wood-panelled bistro/cafe serving locally caught seafood complemented with their home grown herbs and fruit. Contemporary, comfy double bedrooms.
01803 835515 (K2) anzacstreetbistro.co.uk

Browns Hotel, 27-29 Victoria Road.
Classy boutique hotel a short stroll from the harbour. Restaurant specialises in tapas, but this is not the limit of their culinary credentials, for the proprietor organises the local food festival. (K2) 01803 832572 brownshoteldartmouth.co.uk

Dartmouth Castle

LIGHT BITES...

If you arrive on the **Kingswear Ferry** beside **Bayards Cove** pop into the charming C14 **Bayards Cove Inn** for coffee, breakfast, lunch... you may well wish to stay in one of their 7-bedrooms. Open from 8-10pm. 01803 839278 bayardscoveinn. co.uk Continuing in to **Dartmouth**, on your left **Café Alf Resco, Lower Street**. Yes? You could be forgiven for thinking this was an Italian Trattoria, in Italy. A family business, always busy with a lively buzz. All-day breakfasts are a speciality. Coffees. Live music. A great place to meet up. Try their Marmalade flapjacks, just mouthwatering! B&B in Captain's Cabin. Open 7-2pm. (K2) 01803 835880 cafealfresco.co.uk Just past the **Dartmouth Museum/ Butterwalk**, on your left the French boulangerie, patisserie, chocolaterie **Saveurs, 3 Victoria Road**. The pastries and cakes are to die for. 01803 835852 saveurs.co.uk Across the road is **The Deli at Dartmouth**. They will make you up picnic hampers from their local cheeses, sourdough toasties and homemade mackerel pate. Bon Chance!

Dart Marina Hotel & Spa, Sandquay Road. The Wildfire Bar & Restaurant (large) can be a relaxed and informal place to eat and drink with fabulous river views; Try Sushi or grilled fish for lunch, or more formal Dinner. Close to Health Spa (book in advance), Yacht Harbour, hotel and apartments (luxurious boutique-style). (K2) 01803 832580 dartmarina.com

Royal Castle Hotel, The Quay. Former C17 Coaching Inn within the heart of Dartmouth. Bright and colourful bedrooms, some with 4-posters and jacuzzis. Bargain Breaks. Dog friendly. (K2) 01803 833033 royalcastle.co.uk

LUNCH...DINNER...

Spice Bazaar, St Saviours Square. Simple style and relaxed atmosphere offering a fusion of authentic Indian cuisine suited to English tastes. Open 12-2, 6-11.30. (K2) 01803 832285.

Taylor's Restaurant, 8 The Quay. This more traditional restaurant affording spectacular views over the harbour will entice couples for a romantic lunch or dinner. (K2) 01803 832748 taylorsrestaurant.co.uk

KINGSBRIDGE

Old established port at the head of a wide, landlocked estuary, now largely silted up but still active with small craft. The High Street ascends away from the river and is fronted by some attractive C18 and C19 buildings. The Shambles (or Market Arcade) extends over the pavement with Elizabethan piers. Birthplace of William Cookworthy, discoverer of china clay. A centre for the "South Hams" district. St Edmund's church is C13 with C15 additions. Cruises to Salcombe and around the coast. E/C Th. (C6)

LIGHT BITES...

Coasters Coffee Co., Abbots Quay. Since it opened this cafe has been a great hit in South Hams. A full range of eats on offer from sandwiches to panini to delish cakes, and they know their coffee/hot chocs, too and have charm and comfy chairs. 01548 853004

SPECIAL PLACES TO VISIT...

Cookworthy Museum, 108 Fore Street. Toys and dolls, farmhouse kitchen, rural trades, costumes, and local photos. Craft exhibs. "The Story of Kingsbridge". Conservation in farm gallery. Open Apr-Oct M-Sa 10.30-5. (C6) 01548 853235 kingsbridgemuseum.org.uk

Mayne Gallery, 14 Fore St. Sculptures, etchings, watercolours of local and emerging artists. Open M-Sa 9.30-5. (C6) 01548 853848 maynegallery.com

Rivermaid, Rivermaid Boatyard, Embankment Road. Kingsbridge to Salcombe ferry cruises, scenic creeks & coastal excursions, evening cruises. Light refreshments. May-Sept. (C6) 01548 853525/853607 kingsbridgesalcombeferry.co.uk

WHERE TO EAT, DRINK & BE MERRY...

The Reel Cinema, Fore St. For cinema addicts; nightly and matinees with meal/bar deals. (C6) 01548 856636 kingsbridge. merlincinemas.co.uk

SPECIAL PLACES TO VISIT...

Blackpool Gardens. Newly restored C19 sub-tropical garden. Open daily East-Oct. (J4) 01803 771801 blackpoolsands.co.uk

Coleton Fishacre (NT). Sheltered 18-acre garden in stream-fed valley. Uncommon trees and exotic shrubs. New plantings for year-round colour and interest. Set amid spectacular coastal scenery. Associations with D'Oyly Carte family. The house has Art Deco interiors that encapsulate the Jazz Era of the 10920s. Tearoom. Open daily Early Feb to Oct 10.30-5, Nov-Dec W/ERs 11-4. (M3) 01803 842382 nationaltrust.org.uk

Start Point Lighthouse. Set on Devon's most southerly peninsula. Climb the Tower, hear of shipwrecks and lighthouse living. Explore the rugged coastline on each side, and or (if lucky) spy seals and dolphins below. Lighthouse cottages to rent. Open Feb 1/2 term, Apr-July, Sept-Oct, W, Su & BHs 12-5. mid-July to Aug daily 11-5 except Sa, 12-dusk. (H9) 01803 771803 startpointdevon.co.uk

Woodlands Leisure Park. A unique combination; indoor and outdoor attractions and family rides from Watercoasters, Toboggan Run, Arctic Gliders to playzones for all ages. Awesome Avalanche, Polar Pilots, Dizzy Dune Buggies,

1992
University of Plymouth receives charter.

1998
Local government re-organisation. Plymouth and Torbay become unitary authorities.

Falconry centre and Zoo Farm. Huge indoor venture zone, five floors of rides and slides. Big Fun Farm. Award-winning camping site. Open daily mid-Mar to early Nov, winter W/Es & school hols, 9.30-5. (G2) 01803 712598
woodlandspark.com

SPECIAL PLACES TO STAY…

Buckland-Touts-Saints. A magnificent C17 manor house set within romantic gardens that is heavily marketed towards its conference & wedding facilities. Dog friendly. (D5) 01548 853055
tout-saints.co.uk

Soar Mill Cove Hotel. In a quite superb position overlooking one of England's prettiest coves. Unusual in that this family-friendly hotel is on one level with all the necessities to unwind; saunas, indoor and outdoor pools. West Country produce supplies the kitchen's delicous creations. And, Three self-catering properties on hand. (A9) 01548 561566
soarmillcove.co.uk

The White House, Chillington. This is a boutique B&B of high quality, style and comfort. The handmade beds are enormous and you won't wish to leave them, or the cosy bar downstairs for your pre-prandials. Your South Devon home away from home, rather than spending every weekend doing up an old wreck, Better here m'lud! Minimum 2-night stay. Dog friendly. (F6) 01548 580505
whitehousedevon.com

PUBS SERVING FOOD…

Millbrook Inn, South Pool. A touch of Gallic brilliance in the kitchen coupled with a jug or two of English ale, and top-notch bedroom facilities within a boutique apartment. Esprit de Corps lives on! (E8) 01548 531581
millbrookinnsouthpool.co.uk

Pig's Nose Inn, East Prawle. Jolly atmosphere and fine hostelry for walkers and birdwatchers. Children and dogs welcome. Tempting ales. Camping nearby in Stephen's Field and Little Holloway. (E9) 01548 511209
pigsnoseinn.co.uk

Start Bay Inn, Torcross. C14 thatched inn noted for its wealth of seafood; John Dory, bass, skate, cod, sole (Dover and lemon) caught off the beach. Dog and child friendly. (G7) 01548 580553
startbayinn.co.uk

The Cricket Inn, Beesands. One place you could sit for hours, with pint in hand to watch the world come to you, and to watch the sun go down. Old hang out of the youthful Mick Jagger and Keith Richard. 7-bedrooms decorated in the New England style. B&B. (G8) 01548 580215
thecricketinn.com

Tower Inn, Slapton. C14 coaching inn hidden away beside the Chantry Tower. Fresh local produce prepared for lunch and dinner by an anglicized Frenchman. B&B. (G5) 01548 580216
thetowerinn.com

WHERE TO EAT, DRINK & BE MERRY…

Venus Cafe, Blackpool Sands Beach. Alfresco dining; breakfast lunch and ice creams. Organic foods. Open daily from 10am. (J4) 01803 770209
venuscompany.co.uk

The Venus Cafe, Ferry Steps, East Portlemouth. Overlooks Salcombe's best beaches. Specialises in organic and local produce. Open daily East-Oct. (C8) 01548 843558
venuscompany.co.uk

Kingswear Marina

B & BS – A SELECTION...

Blackawton - Woodside Cottage 01803 898164 (F2)
woodsidedartmouth.co.uk

Dartmouth - Hill View House, 76 Victoria Road. 01803 839372 (K2)
hillviewdartmouth.co.uk

East Allington - Lower Norton Farmhouse, Coles Cross. 01548 521246 (E4)

Kingsbridge - Galleons Reach, Embankment Road. 01548 853419 (C6)

High Nature Centre, East Portlemouth. Herewith, eco-tourism that the family will love with 5-yurts in a large field that are cosy and decorated with unusual textiles and furnishings. Solid oak frame beds.
high-nature.co.uk

Kingsbridge - Washbrook Barn, Washbrook Lane. 01548 856901 (C6)
washbrookbarn.co.uk

Kingswear - Nonsuch House, Church Hill. 01803 752829 (K2)
nonsuch-house.co.uk

COASTAL FOOTPATH...

Salcombe to Start Point; 9 miles. There is a frequent ferry service to East Portlemouth throughout the year. The path traverses National Trust land for the first 5 miles and continues along an increasingly rugged coast, with some isolated beaches, and spectacular views around Prawle Point. Walking is moderately strenuous. Start Point has witnessed many wrecks over the years. The lighthouse can be visited and the area is noted for birds and butterflies.

Start Point to Torcross; 5 miles. After the descent to Hallsands the path follows an almost level shore.

Torcross to Dartmouth; 10 miles. For the first 6 miles the path follows the main road alongside Slapton Ley and on to Stoke Fleming. At the NT car park a mile beyond the village the path diverges round the coast and commands some fine views. The road is regained after Dartmouth Castle.

BEACHES...

Mill Bay. Fine golden sands and rock pools. Limited parking. Access is via the ferry from Salcombe, or on foot from East Portlemouth. Considered to be one of the finest sand castle beaches in England. (C8)

East Portlemouth. Fine golden sand and rock pools popular with young families. Dogs permitted. Dinghy sailing centre. (C8)

Venerick's Cove. Access is from the car park at Prawle Point. Walk west along the coast path for a mile, plus, then down a steep path to an isolated silver beach for wild swimming. (E10)

Lannacombe. Small sandy beach accessed via the Coast Path. (F10)

Beesands. Shingle. Safe bathing. Boating pool. Disabled access. Dogs permitted. P/R/WC. (G8)

Torcross. Sand and shingle. Disabled access. Dogs permitted. P/R/WC. (G7)

Blackpool Sands. The most popular family beach on this stretch of coastline. Set in a sheltered cove. The sands (shingle) are cleaned daily in summer. Lifeguards on duty May-Sept. Fine location for water sports; swimming, sailing and scuba diving. Hire of kayaks, paddleboards and surfboards. No dogs permitted. Café serves scallops and chorizo. You could be in the Med. Shop. Parking charge. WC. (J4)

Slapton Sands

2006 December. Sgt (sniper) Steve Ross of the 1st Battalion Grenadier Guards from Barnstaple is awarded the Military Cross at the Battle of Al Amarah, Iraq, June 11.

2007 New Barnstaple Bridge and bypass opens, between Sticklepath and Pottington.

Newton Ferrers

Hope Cove in Winter

Hope Cove in Winter

Devon history starts with the discovery of Early Man in the caves of Torquay (Kent's Cavern) and Brixham. He lived off reindeer and hunted with weapons sharpened from flint. Their successors, the long-headed Iberians settled on Dartmoor living in circular stone huts topped with thatch.

At first they buried their dead in the crouch position. They later burnt them to store their ashes in clay pots. A stone chest was erected around the body or pot and covered with earth. At around 2,500 BC bronze was discovered and Dartmoor streams were washed for tin. In 1,000 BC a Celtic invasion from Ireland subdued the Iberians. With a second Celtic invasion around 500 BC came the knowledge of Iron and a new language with the Brythons. Some words continue in use to this day:- dun – hill, dur – water, combe – hill side valley, pen – head or end, and avon – river. The Celts later gave way to the Romans. But, it is important to understand the countless Neolithic and Bronze Age terms and their original uses.

BURIAL CHAMBERS (Dolmens/Cromlech)

Originally built as family mausoleums made up of several large stones with a capstone, or two across the top. Inside, the unburned body was placed, then filled over with earth. The finest example is "Spinster Rock" at Shilstone Farm, Drewsteignton. You can park beside the road and walk into the field where it remains in fine condition. A more sophisticated development of this design, the chambered tumulus, is to be found at Carnac, Brittany, Belas Knap, Gloucestershire and in Wiltshire. Small burial chambers (Kistvaens) were scattered all over Dartmoor. There is little evidence of these today, all desecrated long ago. You would have seen a heap of stones with ashes placed in a pot. The normal construction would take a surround of stone circles. Examples to be seen at Merrivale Bridge, Postbridge or Lake Head Hill, Hound Tor.

STONE CIRCLES.

These are to be found all over Dartmoor. The stones were set upright in a diameter of between 60-100 feet but often larger. Marked with a small stone (burial chamber) in the centre. A ditch or bank may border the site. The best examples to be seen at Scorhill near Chagford, Greywethers near Fernworthy, and at Langstone Moor near Peter Tavy. Their original purpose is not clear. Some scholars believe they were used for tribal meetings; judicial, religious, sepulchral. Large charcoal remains in the centre suggest great fires or rituals; sacrificial burials, or mass burials following disease or pestilence.

STONE ROWS OR STONE AVENUES (single or double rows).

These have long been associated with funeral rites. At the head of the row, a tumulus or burial chamber and at the end, a blocking stone. Each stone would have represented a household, or family of the tribe, and would have been placed in honour of their chief. Fifty plus such sites have been counted on Dartmoor. The best are to be seen at Drizzlecombe, Down Tor, Merrivale Bridge and Watern Hill.

STANDING STONES (Monoliths/Menhirs)

These are prehistoric memorials, remnants of stone that have survived the elements; wind and rain, and archaeological interference. The Christian Celts sculpted crosses out of the granite blocks, and more recently the Romans and others drew inscriptions. The finest survivors, Caratacus Stone, Winsford Hill and Toreus Stone in Yealmpton churchyard.

ANCIENT VILLAGES (Hut Circles)

There are literally hundreds of these scattered across Dartmoor. The original smallholding, a basic hut with enclosure to protect their animals from preying beasts. Occupied by late Neolithic and Bronze Age Man. The village would be located in a dry, well drained position close to pure water stocked with abundant fish, and on open ground, easily protected against wild beasts and away from the hostile valleys and wild swamps. As time moved on into the Bronze Age, Man learnt to exploit the streams working for tin, later to trade and export to the Continent through the mouths of the rivers Otter, Axe, Dart and Exe. Early trade routes have been traced from Wray Barton in Moretonhampstead, by Berry Road to Merripit, via Postbridge and on to Mis Tor. A Roman route runs south from Okehampton from 100 BC to 100AD.

THE ROMAN PERIOD.

The Romans didn't venture much beyond their garrison at Exeter beside the River Exe although satellite warning forts have been discovered at Countisbury on the North Coast and they would have reached this remote spot via sea, sailing down from Gloucester (Glevum). Evidence of the Roman Occupation has been excavated at Seaton and Uplyme. A Roman road through Honiton and south to Axminster (and Axmouth) connects the Fosse Way.

THE CELTIC PERIOD.

Once the Romans left, Britain was ripe for invasion. In the early C5 the Irish Celts invaded North Devon and Cornwall, and the west became the Kingdom of Dumnovia, to be Christianised by Irish missionaries. They gave firm resistance to the Saxon invaders. Later in the C6 and C7 the mystical King Arthur was born. In the C9 and C10, Kings Egbert and Athelstan pushed to forge a united Kingdom. Thereafter the Saxons settled into the valleys within their enclosures to raise their crops and domestic animals. Peace was interrupted by the invading Danes in the C9 who ravaged the coast. It was not until the Norman Conquest of the C11 that life took on a modicum of stability for the Saxon peasant.

WILLIAM I.

William divided the Saxon lands amongst his favourite Norman knights. The great Lords of Devon became the Earl of Mortain, Earl Hugo, Baldwin the Sherrif, Judhael de Totnes, William de Mohun and Ralph de Pomeroy. Many of the Saxon manors were passed to the churches (Abbeys) in Normandy. Exeter Castle was put to siege and most of the county barring Dartmoor and Exmoor was disafforested and given over to agriculture.

THE TUDOR MONARCHS.

With Henry VII, Henry VIII and Edward VI, life in Devon was

full of strife and difficulty. In 1497, the men of Devon and Cornwall rose up against the burden of taxation, and took to arms under Lord Audley. They were defeated at Blackheath. Later that year the Pretender Perkin Warbeck collected followers from Devon and Cornwall and besieged Exeter to be beaten back by the Earl of Devon. The Dissolution of the Monasteries under Henry V111 kept unrest on the boil. But, things took a turn for the worse under Edward V1 when he introduced changes to the Common Book of Prayer (the following turn of events incomprehensible today). A rebellion started at Sampford Courtenay, and quickly spread. Headed by Sir Thomas Pomeroy, they marched to Exeter, occupied the town and set up fortifications at St Mary Clyst. To be soundly defeated by German mercenaries under the command of Lord Russell. The ringleaders were summarily executed; hung, drawn and quartered. So ended the Devon Rebellion.

ELIZABETH I. Devon men took patriotism (and self-interest) to all corners of the globe. Under a galaxy of famous sea captains; Raleigh, Drake, Gilbert and the Hawkins. Their devotion to England and her cause (or Queen) could not be questioned.

THE CIVIL WAR. The gentry and countryside were Royalist, whilst the towns largely followed the Parliamentarians (Cromwell). The Queen, Henrietta Maria, inspected Prince Rupert's army at Crediton. Plymouth and Dartmouth withstood sieges, and Exeter was garrisoned by the Parliamentarians. Tavistock became a Royalist stronghold in 1643. Tiverton changed hands many times. Torrington was the scene of one of the bloodiest battles when Fairfax defeated the Royalists under Lord Hopton in 1646. The irony was that the Parliamentarian General Monk, a Torrington man, became the main force behind the Restoration (return of Charles 11).

AGRICULTURE. The Devon man was soon to become shaped by his social and economic circumstances. Those living beside, or close to, the sea made a living from it, either as sailors in the Navy, or as fishermen. Devon had long held a tradition of trade well before the Roman Occupation. The development of shipbuilding in the ports of Bideford and Barnstaple, Brixham, Dartmouth and Plymouth, enlivened the entrepreneurial skills of merchants who took to trading on a global scale. The landscape was shaped by the Devon peasant. The small fields, or enclosures were cleared of rock and stones, to shape either drystone walls evident on Dartmoor, or the tall, thick hedges that look soft and inviting as you drive past in the summer but beware they have an underbelly of rock and solid earth. The same earth, mixed with straw and stones, made the mixture known as cob, the vernacular building material to be topped with thatch. The substance of the soil moulded the variations in Agriculture. The rich, red soil of South Hams encouraged cream and cider production, the district of Holsworthy was noted for horses, today it's the Ruby Red Devon cattle. The Tamar Valley took to strawberries. Dartmoor

was overlooked for cereal production but the ruggedness suited sheep farming. The North Devon soil produced clay.

INDUSTRY. The major industry of the time was developed from the metals, tin and copper. The two western counties, Devon and Cornwall were the sole suppliers of tin up until about 1700. Obtained either as stream-tin or mined-tin (from alluvial deposits). The governance of tin came under the auspices of the Courts of Stannary set up under a Charter by Edward 1. The Court was held at Crockern Tor, an isolated location in the middle of Dartmoor Forest, often attended by 300 gentlemen on horseback. They fixed the price and production.

The purchase and distribution of tin was organised through the four Stannary towns; Ashburton, Tavistock, Plympton and Chagford. The manufacture of woollen cloth was an important Devon industry through the Middle Ages and up to the C19. Crediton and later Exeter were the centres, second to only Leeds in the C18. Tiverton and Cullompton were also centres. But by 1825 the trade had declined. Lace production in the towns of Honiton, Bampton, Uffculme, Cullompton, Ottery St Mary compensated for the loss of the woollen industry and the outlying villages were responsible for much of the labour but this was short-lived. The construction of the Grand Western Canal was a hoped-for saviour to connect Topsham with the River Tone at Taunton.

Exeter however continued to grow as a City. The Napoleonic Wars restricted European travel so the gentry were forced to seek out new places to relax. Exmouth became the first watering-place, soon followed by Sidmouth, Budleigh Salterton, Teignmouth and Torquay. So began the great tourist industry. New roads made the sojourn easier, and so the transformation from horse-borne to horse-drawn began along the new road from London to Exeter via Amesbury (A303 today). Later the Golden Age of the Railways brought much needed affluence, and the development of more coastal towns; Ilfracombe, Minehead, Dawlish and Totnes.

The C20 brought prosperity to the county through the increase in tourism. Small companies moved to the region to provide a higher standard of living for their employees, and the ever-present pensioner looked to the South West Coast as a pleasing place to end their days. The great naval dockyard at Devonport flourished in the two World Wars, and continues to this day, maintaining our fleet of nuclear submarines. The fishing fleets of Brixham and Plymouth provide seafood for the many restaurants of the Southwest, and beyond. Shipbuilding has had a similarly precarious time of it. It is difficult to keep up to date with their news.

The results of a recent poll in a national newspaper concluded that Devon would be the first choice county to live in the UK. It is host to the same number of visitors as Cornwall per year.

Sir Francis Drake

SIR JOHN HAWKINS, 1532-1595

Adventurer, Privateer, Slave Trader. Son of Plymouth privateer William Hawkins. He was one of the first to capture slaves in Sierra Leone and to sell them on to the Spanish settlers in the Caribbean. Voyages backed by Elizabeth 1 and the Earls of Leicester and Pembroke. Knighted for his role in defeating the Spanish Armada. Later made Treasurer of the Navy. Foiled plot to assassinate Queen Elizabeth 1.

SIR HUMPHREY GILBERT, 1539-1583

Explorer, MP, Navigator, Soldier. Born at Greenway, lived at Compton Castle. Educated at Eton and Oxford where he studied Navigation and the Art of War. Later called to the Bar at the Inns of Chancery. Half-brother to Sir Walter Raleigh. Military career in Ireland and the Netherlands. Obsessed with the Elizabethan Quest to find the North West Passage. He sailed to America and discovered Newfoundland in 1583, but generally his sea voyages achieved very little and ended disastrously.

SIR FRANCIS DRAKE, 1541-1596

Explorer, Pirate, Privateer, Slave Trader and the Queen's Favourite. Beckoned to the sea aged 13, to learn his trade in the North Sea. Later, aged 23, he made his first voyage to the New World as a slave trader (first started by the Spanish). His dislike of the Spanish endeared him to Queen Elizabeth who encouraged his raiding of Spanish and Portugese shipping. His successful circumnavigation of the world between 1577-1580 on the Golden Hind was his greatest achievement. He was second-in-command during the Armada campaign and Mayor of Plymouth. He died of dysentery off the coast of Panama.

JOHN DAVIS, 1550-1606

Arctic Explorer, Cartographer, Inventor, Scientist. Writer on Seamanship. Born at Sandridge Park near Stoke Gabriel beside the River Dart. He made three unsuccessful voyages in search of the North West Passage. He did, however, map the coastlines of Greenland, Baffin Island and Labrador. The Davis Strait was named after him. He identified the cod fishing banks off Newfoundland, and his famous "Traverse Book" became a model for the ships' log books. Inventor of the navigational device, the backstaff and double quadrant (Davis Quadrant). Commanded the Black Dog against the Spanish Armada. Discovered the Falkland Islands in 1592 aboard the Desire, having earlier failed to pass through the Straits of Magellan. His crew killed 14,000 penguins for homeward bound food, but the meat went foul on reaching the Tropics, and only 14 out of a crew of 76 men survived. Assassinated by Japanese pirates off the coast of Malaysia.

SIR WALTER RALEIGH, 1554-1618

Explorer, Seafarer, Pirate, Poet and Politician (who came to a sticky end – beheaded for Treason on James 1's ruling). Born at Hayes Barton, East Budleigh. His exploits at sea came to the notice of Queen Elizabeth 1 where he became one of her favourites. Posted to the Captain of the Guard, he foiled the "Babington" plot whose purpose was to replace Elizabeth with Mary, Queen of Scots. His trips to the New World, and discovery of tobacco, originally thought of as a cure for coughing, brought him great wealth. He later built Sherborne Castle in Dorset.

Sir Walter Raleigh

Charles Kingsley

JOHN GAY, 1685-1732

Countryman, Dramatist, Journalist, Poet, Satirist, Wit. Born in Barnstaple, and educated at the local Grammar School. Apprenticed to a London silk merchant. He was friend to Pope and Swift, and William Congreve. His patrons were the Duke and Duchess of Queensberry, and the Earl of Burlington. This man loved to party, he loved good food, good company and blue ribbons. He was an early chronicler of country life. His breakthrough came with the play The Beggar's Opera in 1728, a satirical play about highwayman and the corrupt governing class. The two main characters, Captain Macheath and Polly Peacham, have entered the Hall of Fame. The basis for Kurt Weil and Bertolt Brecht's Threepenny Opera. Financially ruined by the South Sea Bubble. He lies in Poets' Corner, Westminster Abbey. On his tombstone, Pope wrote this epitaph: "Life is a jest, and all things show it, I thought so once, and now I know it".

SIR JOSHUA REYNOLDS, 1723-1792

English Painter. Born in Plympton and son of a clergyman. Studied in Rome 1749-52. The most influential of C18 English Painters specialising in portraits and promoting the "Grand Style". First President of the Royal Academy. Friend to Dr Johnson, Oliver Goldsmith, Edmund Burke and David Garrett. In his lifetime, 3,000 portraits commissioned. Buried in St Paul's Cathedral.

SAMUEL TAYLOR COLERIDGE, 1772-1834

Poet, Philosopher and Womaniser. Born in Ottery St Mary and educated at Jesus College, Cambridge. He's considered one of the great Romantic poets (and philosophers). Shakespeare scholar, and friend to the Wordsworths, Southey and Lord Byron. He and Southey married the Fricker sisters of Clevedon. His poem The Rhyme of the Ancient Mariner is listed on many school syllabuses.

THE REVEREND JOHN (JACK) RUSSELL, 1795-1883

Dog Breeder, Huntsman, "The Sporting Parson". Born in Dartmouth. Educated at Blundell's and Oxford where he spotted a terrier bitch called Trump owned by the local milkman. His ambition was to develop a hardy breed of terrier that could flush out the fox. He became a founder member of the Kennel Club, and friend of King Edward VII, who as the Prince of Wales, commissioned a portrait of Trump. Buried in Swimbridge churchyard, opposite the Jack Russell Inn.

CHARLES KINGSLEY, 1819-1875

Chartist, Clergyman, Novelist, Poet, Political Activist, Social Reformer, Wit, Writer. Born at Holne. Educated at Kings College, London and Magdalene College, Cambridge. Brought up around Clovelly. He has the unique legacy of having a town named after his novel, Westward Ho! which in due course inspired the construction of the Appledore-Bideford Railway. Witnessing the Bristol Riots of 1831 formed his social and political outlook. His parish was Eversley in Hampshire.

SIR RICHARD HAWKINS, 1562-1622

Adventurer, Seafarer, Mayor of Plymouth. Son of Sir John Hawkins. Sailed with Drake in 1585 to the Caribbean, to attack Spanish shipping. Later, distinguishing himself commanding The Swallow against the Spanish Armada. Sailed through the Straits of Magellan, attacked Valparaiso (Chile), to be held captive by the Spanish for ten years. Vice Admiral of Devon. Knighted in 1603 by James 1.

JOHN CHURCHILL, 1ST DUKE OF MARLBOROUGH, 1650-1722.

Soldier, Statesman. Born Ashe. The greatest European General of his generation. Served with distinction in Ireland and Flanders, later during The War of the Spanish Succession, 1701-1714 where on the fields of Blenheim (Hochstadt), Ramillies and Oudenarde, his place in history was assured. His wife, Sarah Jennings, was a confidant and friend to Queen Anne whose gift was Blenheim Palace after his victory over Louis XIV at Blenheim halted Louis ambitions to capture Vienna, and dominate Europe.

THOMAS NEWCOMEN, 1663-1729

Inventor. "Father of the Industrial Revolution". Born in Dartmouth. A humble, Ironmonger by profession and Baptist Lay Preacher. He invented the Atmospheric Steam Engine around 1710, and with the help of Thomas Savery, and his patents, one hundred engines were operating in Britain and Europe by the time of his death. His designs were later improved by James Watt who arranged for the steam to be condensed in a separate condenser.

JOHN LETHBRIDGE, 1675-1759

Inventor. Wool Merchant. Based in Newton Abbot, and as a father of seventeen children he sort wealth to feed them. He invented the one-man, enclosed diving suit with glass porthole for viewing and two watertight armholes with sleeves. The suit was made up of reinforced leather over an airtight oak barrel. His salvage work brought him great wealth.

Sir Humphrey Gilbert nt

SIR RICHARD BURTON, 1821-1890

Adventurer, Diplomat, Explorer, Fencer, Linguist, Orientalist, Soldier, Translator. Born in Torquay. He was thrown out of Oxford and continued to undermine authority for much of his life. He had a natural empathy with languages and as a master of disguise managed to enter the Forbidden Cities of Harar, Mecca and Medina. He co-discovered Lake Tanganyika searching for the source of the Nile. He translated the Arabian Nights, and the Kama Sutra, and introduced the words Pyjama and Safari to the English language. Served in India. Diplomat in Equatorial Guinea, and Brazil. Knighted by Queen Victoria. He died in Trieste.

SABINE BARING-GOULD, 1834-1924

Hymn-Writer, Novelist, Scholar, Squire & Parson. Born in Exeter, lived for 40 years at Lewtrenchard Manor where he fathered 15 children with Grace, a Yorkshire mill girl, and his wife for 48 years, who on meeting and then marrying her sent her off to be educated for two years. Wrote Onward Christian Soldiers and 200 published works. His output was immense, not least his enthusiasm for West Country folk songs resulting in the collection "Songs of the West".

CAPTAIN ROBERT FALCON SCOTT, 1868-1912

Antarctic Explorer, Royal Naval Officer and father of Peter Scott; Founder of the Wildfowl and Wetlands Trust, and the World Wide Fund for Nature. Born at Outlands, Stoke Damerel. He led two expeditions backed by the Royal Geographical Society; The Discovery Expedition of 1901-1904 was the first attempt at reaching the South Pole. They turned back 450 miles from their objective. This included Ernest Shackleton in the party. The second, and final attempt, the Terra Nova Expedition of 1910-1913, "The Race to the South Pole" failed. Beaten by the Norwegian, Raold Amundsen, by a month. On their return journey to base camp all four of his party died of exposure and hunger eleven miles from their fuel and food depot.

AGATHA CHRISTIE, 1890-1976

Born and brought up in Torquay, later to live with her archaeologist husband, Max Mallowan, at Greenway on the banks of the River Dart. Known as the Queen of Crime, and inventor of crime's two famous sleuths; Hercule Poirot and Miss Marple. Two billion copies of her books have been sold world-wide.

SIR FRANCIS CHICHESTER, 1901-1972

Aviator, Navigator, Solo Sailor, Map Publisher and Writer. Born in Barnstaple, emigrated to New Zealand aged 18 where he set up a lumber and property business. An interest in flying fostered a passion for navigation. He was to write the official Navigation Manual for the Air Ministry. Best remembered for his epic single-handed circumnavigation of the globe in 1966, from West to East, with one stop in Sydney. Knighted by Queen Elizabeth 11 using Sir Francis Drake's sword.

ROBERT HERRICK, 1591-1674

Cavalier Poet, Country Parson. Born in Cheapside, London. Apprenticed to a Goldsmith. Educated at St John's College, Cambridge. He was a friend of the poets Dryden and Marvel, and one of the "Sons of Ben", the Cavalier Poets who idolized Ben Jonson, meeting regularly in the London tavern, the Devil's Head. In 1629, he was appointed by Charles 1 to be Vicar of Dean Prior. At first, country life bored him. Country people misunderstood him. He was to write his greatest poems in "dull Devonshire". Still hankering for the fleshpots of London. The puritans sent him packing back to London in 1647. In 1648, Hesperides was published, a mighty tome of 1,200 poems. He continued to live well, patronised by the Earls of Buckingham, Pembroke and Westmorland where his poems were read at Court. The Restoration of Charles 11 in 1660 returned him to Devon where he died a bachelor dreaming of fair Julia and Dianeme.

Gather ye rosebuds while ye may,
Old time is still a flying
And this same flower that smiles today
Tomorrow will be dying"
To the Virgins to make Much of Time

CHARLES BABBAGE, 1792-1871

Computer Genius, Inventor, Mathematician. Born in London, moved to Devon, aged 8. Educated in Totnes and at Cambridge where he founded the Analytical Society in 1872 to combat poor learning methods. Designed the first mechanical computer, later the Analytic Engine, a complex machine, and the first mathematical machine to use punch cards (previously used on textile machines).

R. D. BLACKMORE, 1825-1900

Classicist, Horticulturalist, Literary Pioneer, Naturalist, Poet. Born in Oxfordshire, but his roots and ancestry lay in Devon. Educated at Blundell's and Oxford. His early life was spent at Culmstock and Ashford, then later on Exmoor beside Badgworthy Water. The setting for much of his classic novel, Lorna Doone. Called to the Bar in 1852, he was later advised by his Doctor (on account of his epilepsy) to live a calmer life. So he settled for teaching Classics in Teddington, Middlesex. By all accounts a lovely man, reclusive after his adoring wife's death. He started a Market Garden specialising in fruit. Fellow of the RHS.

HENRY WILLIAMSON, 1895-1977

Broadcaster, Farmer, Naturalist, Soldier, Writer. Born in Brockley, South London. He fought on the Western Front during the First World War, at the Battles of the Somme, and Passchendale. Wounded, he returned home to speak out against the horrors of the trenches. Belittled, ignored, he found solace in the writings of Richard Jeffries, WH Hudson, Francis Thompson and the music of Delius, and Richard Wagner. On the publication of his first book, The Beautiful Years, he was thrown out of home, so rode his Norton 500 Motorcycle down to his beloved North Devon, and Skir Cottage, Georgeham. Remembered

for the magnificent Tarka the Otter, Winner of the Hawthornden Prize in 1928, Salar the Salmon, and his tetrology The Flax of Dreams, and his fifteen-book work of Edwardian life, The Chronicle of Ancient Sunlight. He was largely ignored, shunned, ostracised by the British establishment due to his misguided dalliance with Mosleyism in the 1930s. His death coincided, to the day, with David Cobham's filming of Tarka's death scene in the film of the book.

TED HUGHES, 1930-1998

Children's Author, Farmer, Fly Fisherman, Naturalist, OM, Poet Laureate. Born in Mytholmroyd, West Yorkshire and raised on the surrounding farms. He entered Pembroke College, Cambridge to read English but switched to Archaeology and Anthropology. He married the American poet and feminist, Sylvia Plath 1956-63, who committed suicide, aged 30. His second great love, Assia Wevill, gassed herself and their four-year old daughter, Shura six years after Plath's death. He lived at Court Green, North Tawton and fished the River Torridge being a great encourager to fellow children's author, Michael Morpurgo. His last marriage to Carol Orchard, nurse, lasted until his early death from cancer.

MICHAEL MORPURGO, BORN 1943

Children's Author and Laureate, Countryman, Farmer, Fly Fisherman. Born in St Albans, he has lived in Mid Devon for thirty years. Good friend of Ted Hughes, who offered kind encouragement in his early days as a writer. With his wife, he founded the charity, Farms for City Children, in 1976. At the last count, more than 50,000 children have spent at least a week staying in one of their three farms. He has written over 90 books winning countless awards. Now a father and grandfather. He is the current Children's Laureate.

Samuel Taylor Coleridge

CALENDAR OF EVENTS

For specific dates please contact the local Tourist/Visitor
Information Centre (see next page)

MARCH

Easter Egg Hunt, Buckland Abbey
Exeter Vibraphonic Festival
Minehead – West Somerset Railway Diesel Gala

APRIL

Dartmoor Hunt Point to Point, Flete Estate
Dartmouth Gig Regatta
North Devon & Exmoor Walking and Cycling Festival
Stokenham Garden Society Spring Show,

MAY

Appledore Visual Arts Festival
Blackawton Worm Charming Festival
Bluebell Spectacular; Parkham to Buck's Mill walk
Brendon Folk Festival
Brixham Heritage Festival
Combe Martin – Hunting of the Earl of Rone
Cornwood Spring Show, Cadleigh
Dart Music Festival
Devon County Show, Westpoint, Exeter
Exmoor Folk Festival
Exeter - Great West Run
Great Torrington Carnival
Great Torrington May Fair
Ivybridge Horse Show and Family Dog Show
Lord Mayor's Day, Plymouth
Lyme Regis Fossil Festival
Mayor's Sunday Parade, Dartmouth
Minehead & Dunster Hobby Horse Fair
Modbury Fair Week
Modbury Harriers, Point to Point, Flete Estate
Porlock Village Gardens, open
Potwalloping Festival, Westward Ho!
Prawle Fair
Quantock Food Festival
Saltram House Park Fair and Dog Show
Torquy Maritime Festival
Westward Ho! Potwalloping Festival

JUNE

Allerford Spring Fair
Axe Vale Festival
Bigbury Fun Run
Bovey Tracey – Devon Guild Arts Fair
Brixham Trawler Race
Cornish Pilot Gig Regatta, Salcombe
Croyde Ocean Fest
Dartmouth Carnival
Dunster Castle – Grand Western Archery Competition
Ermington Fair
Holesworthy Carnival
Hot Penny Day, East Devon.
Lynton Music Festival
North Devon Festival
Ottery St Mary Pixie Day
Salcombe Festival.
Salcombe Regis Country Fayre.
South Brent Carnival Week.
Vintage Bus Rally, Seaton Tramway
West Country Garden Festival, Westpoint, Exeter
West Somerset Railway – Father's Day Special
Westward Ho! Carnival

JULY

Branscombe Air Day
Braunton Wheels Extravaganza
Budleigh Salterton Flower Show
Dartington International Summer School & Festival of Music
Dartington Literary Festival
Dunsford Show
Exeter Air Day. Teignmouth Regatta.
Exmouth Regatta
Exmouth Summer Fun Time
Filham Fun Day, Filham Park, Ivybridge
Holsworthy Show
Honiton Glove Fair
Honiton Hot Pennies Day
Killerton Open Air Concerts
Kingsbridge Bandstand Concert
Kingsbridge Fair week
Lyme Regis Lifeboat Week
Malborough Fayre
Marldon Apple Pie Fair
Merlin Rocket Week, Salcombe.
Mid Devon Show, Tiverton.
Midsummer Respect Festival, Exeter
Minehead Arts Festival
Porlock Pantomine
Port of Plymouth Regatta
River Yealm Regatta Rowing Finals
Saltram Jazz Picnic
Sidmouth International Folk Festival
Sidmouth Secluded Gardens Week
Sidmouth Society of Artists Annual Exhibition
Tavistock Food Festival
Teignmouth Regatta
Teignmouth Summer Carnival
Torbay Carnival
Totnes & District Agricultural Show
Ugborough Village Day Fair
West Somerset Folk Festival
Wiscombe Hill Climb
World Powerboat Champs British Grand Prix, Plymouth.
Yealmpton Show

AUGUST

Allerford Summer Fair
Beer Regatta
Bideford Folk Festival
Braunton Fair
Brendon Show
Brixham Fish Market Open Day.
Brixham Regatta.
Chagford Craft Fair
Combe Martin Fair
Dartington International Music Festival
Dartington West Country Storytelling Festival
Dartmouth Royal Regatta
Dawlish Carnival
Dawlish Regatta
Dunster Bat Hunt
Dunster Show
Exford Show
Emoor Mountain Bike Marathon
Honiton Show
Ilfracombe Carnival
Ilfracombe Fair
Lustleigh Show
Newton Abbot Antique Fair, The Racecourse
Newton Abbot Cheese & Onion Fayre

North Devon Show, Great Torrington
Okehampton Show
Paignton - Torbay Childrens' Weeks
Paignton Regatta.
Salcombe Regatta
Shaldon Regatta Week
Shaldon Water Festival
Sidmouth Folk Festival
South Devon Railway Fair
South Molton Sheep Fair
South Zeal – Dartmoor Folk Festival
Teignmouth National and World Fireball Sailing
Teignmouth Regatta.
Torbay Fortnight
Torbay Royal Regatta
Torbay Steam Fair
Totnes Carnival.
Woolacombe Creation Festival

SEPTEMBER
Agatha Christie Week
Barnstaple Carnival
Barnstaple Regatta
Bideford Regatta
Colyford Goose Fair
Porlock Festival
Torbay Sea Angling Festival
Wellington Carnival
Widecombe-in-the-Moor Fair

OCTOBER
Beer Rhythm And Blues Festival.
Dartmouth Fishing Festival
Devon Food Festival
Devon Hedge Week
Dulverton Carnival
Exeter Cathedral Trafalgar Day Service
Exeter Off The Wall Comedy Festival
Exmoor Food Festival
Exmouth Illuminated Winter Carnival.
Ivybridge Vintage Club Crank-Up
Tavistock Goosy Fair
Two Moors Festival

NOVEMBER
Ashburton Winter Carnival
Dunster By Candlelight
Dunster Festival Fireworks
Exeter Autumn Festival
Kingsbridge Christmas Extravaganza
Lynton & Lynmouth Festivities
Minehead – Winter Steam Festival
Okehampton Farmers Market
Ottery St Mary – Flaming Tar Barrels
Porlock Fireworks
Shebbear – Turning the Devil's Stone
South Brent Winter Carnival

MAP SYMBOLS EXPLAINED

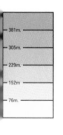

⛪ Abbey/Cathedral	🏺 Pottery	🛶 Inshore Rescue Boat
✕ Battle Site	🍺 Pub/Inn	🏟 Leisure/Sports Centre
🛏 Bed & Breakfast Accommodation	🚂 Railway Interest	⛵ Lifeboat
☕ Café	🍽 Restaurant	🅿 Parking
🏰 Castle	🗿 Standing Stone/Barrow	⛱ Picnic Site
⛪ Church/Chapel of Interest	🎭 Theatre/Concert Hall	⛺ Tents & Caravans
🎬 Cinema	ℹ Tourist Information	⛵ Sailing
🎨 Craft Interest	☼ Tumulus/Tumuli	🏄 Surfing
✚ Cross	ᴽ Viewpoint	ℹ Tourist Information
🚲 Cycleway	🌾 Windmill/Wind Farm	🏄 Windsurfing
🎡 Fun Park/Leisure Park	✈ Airfield	▲ Youth Hostel
⚜ Hill Fort/Ancient Settlement	🐟 Aquarium	🚜 Agricultural Interest
🏛 Historic Building	⚓ Boat Trips	🌳 Arboretum
🏨 Hotel	⛺ Camping Site (Tents)	🐦 Bird Reserve
🏭 Industrial Interest	🚐 Caravan Site	🌸 Garden of Interest
🏎 Karting	👥 Ferry (Pedestrians)	🍇 Vineyard
🔦 Lighthouse	🚗 Ferry (Vehicles)	🚶 Walks/Nature Trails
⛏ Mining Interest/Engine Houses	🎣 Fishing Trips	⋏ Wildlife Park
☆ Miscellaneous/Natural Attraction	⛳ 9/18 Hole Golf Course	🐘 Zoo
🏛 Museum/Art Gallery	⚓ Harbour	🄿 National Trust Car Park

| 381m. |
| 305m. |
| 229m. |
| 152m |
| 76m. |

━━━━━ A Road

━━━━━ B Road

═════ Minor Road

▪▪▪▪▪▪ Other Road or Track
(not necessarily with public
or vehicular access)

●──── Railway

·········· Cycleway

Open Space owned
by the National Trust

Built-up Area

Scale 1:100,000

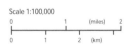

ABOUT THE AUTHOR & PHOTOGRAPHER

William Fricker was born in Somerset and educated at Stonyhurst College, Lancashire, and in various places of learning in Austria and Germany. He has worked in publishing for many years.

William first worked with William Collins in London where he became a Creative Director in their paperback division before taking a sabbatical, to make a 4,000 mile trek across Europe (France-The Alps-Italy, to Greece) along the old mule tracks, footpaths and pilgrim's routes. Inspired by Patrick Leigh Fermor's A Time of Gifts, and Laurie Lee's As I Walked Out One Midsummer Morning. On reaching Greece, his original plan was to then head south and walk up the Nile, but he believes his better judgement prevailed, and returned on a bicycle via North Africa, Spain and France. For the past thirty years he has built up Goldeneye compiling the research, editorial and photography, for more than two hundred UK travel guides and books; on cycling, touring and walking. More recently, he has been re-developing his Guidebooks to The Cotswolds, Cornwall, Devon and the Lake District. He lives with his wife Caroline and their younger children in Penryn, Cornwall.

FURTHER READING
The finest guidebook to have been written about Devon was W G Hoskin's Devon in 1954, published by William Collins. All books written since that date, refer, or nod, in appreciation to this great work. Also published by William Collins, Shirley Toulson's Companion Guide to Devon, is a fine piece of work.

Crossing's Guide to Dartmoor, 1909
Worth's Dartmoor, 1953
Bell's Pocket Guide to Devon, Winbolt & Ward, 1929
Goldeneye's Exmoor and Dartmoor Touring Map & Travel Guides, 2004
Church Pamphlets. These can be bought for a small sum at the back of the church, and rarely credit the author. They are invaluable tools, as they often combine the history of the church with the village and its famous (past) inhabitants.

ACKNOWLEDGMENTS
I would (again) like to thank my wife Caroline for her continued support, encouragement, patience and love in these difficult times of 24-hour care for our youngest daughter. And, to my children, Izy for her editorial skills, Flora and Harry for their design and marketing expertise, and my sister Julia for her erudite proof-reading skills. Not to be forgotten, all my friends who provide me with leads and knowledge about new venues, and existing ones and their ever-changing skills.

Goldeneye would like to thank the following for allowing us to photograph, or of providing us with images of their properties:- Mark Harold & Liz Luck of the National Trust (Devon and Cornwall Regional Office), Lady Arran of Castle Hill, Lady Stucley of Hartland Abbey, Ingrid Oram of Powderham Castle, Rupert Thistlethwayte of Cadhay, Visitor Services at Exeter Cathedral, Trustees of Cothay Manor Gardens, John Rouse of Clovelly Estates, Ilfracombe Museum. And, for this Second Edition: Marwood Hill Gardens, Lympstone Manor, Glazebrook House, Boringdon Hall, The Pig at Combe, North Morte Camping, Arundel Arms Hotel, Culm Valley Inn, Home Farm Cafe, Tomas Carr, Lamb Inn Sandford, Salutation Inn, Noel Corston, Gidleigh Park, Mor shellfish, Broomhill Arts, Poltimore Arms, Red Stag Safaris, St Nectan's, Mortehoe Museum, Hartland Quay Museum, Fisherton Farm, Hotel Endsleigh, Percy's,. Plymouth Aquarium, Bovey Tracey church, Ottery S tMary church, Wiscombe Park hill climbs, Dart Valley Railway, Shoreham Vineyard.
Thank you to all the attractions, places to stay and eat, for showing me around their establishments, and either allowing us to photograph, or for providing an image for use in this book. The bare bones of the Timeline originated from the Devon Regional Library at Exeter. Robert Downes of the Exmoor National Park for checking our mapping details

PHOTOGRAPHERS
We would like to thank the following photographers for providing us with their images; al Andrew Lawson dp Dave Peake bkb/nt
The abbreviation ss (Supplied by Subject) credits an image supplied by the subject and rarely credits the photographer given that the subject may have mislaid this detail. As a photographer I can only apologise for this omission.
William Fricker, May 2017, Penryn

Bayards Cove, Dartmouth >